The Study of
Welfare State Regimes

Comparative Public Policy Analysis Series

Series Editors
Martin Rein, *Massachusetts Institute of Technology*
Lee Rainwater, *Harvard University*

PUBLIC/PRIVATE INTERPLAY IN SOCIAL PROTECTION
Martin Rein and Lee Rainwater, Editors

THE SCANDINAVIAN MODEL: WELFARE STATES AND WELFARE RESEARCH
Robert Erikson, Erik Jørgen Hansen, Stein Ringen, and Hannu Uusitalo, Editors

STAGNATION AND RENEWAL IN SOCIAL POLICY
Martin Rein, Gøsta Esping-Andersen, and Lee Rainwater, Editors

THE STUDY OF WELFARE STATE REGIMES
Jon Eivind Kolberg, Editor

BETWEEN WORK AND SOCIAL CITIZENSHIP
Jon Eivind Kolberg, Editor

THE WELFARE STATE AS EMPLOYER
Jon Eivind Kolberg, Editor

The Study of Welfare State Regimes

EDITED BY
JON EIVIND KOLBERG

M. E. Sharpe, Inc.
Armonk, New York
London, England

The papers in this collection also appeared in Vol. 20, Nos. 3–4 of
International Journal of Sociology.

Library of Congress Cataloging-in-Publication Data

The study of welfare state regimes / by Jon Eivind Kolberg (ed.)
p. cm. — (Comparative public analysis series)
ISBN 0-87332-650-4
1. Social security—Scandinavia.
2. Income distribution—Scandinavia.
3. Labor market—Scandinavia
4. Labor market.
5. Welfare state.
I. Kolberg, Jon Eivind, 1942–
II. Series.
HD7198.S78   1991
330.12′6—dc20
90-32224
CIP

Printed in the United States of America
The paper used in this publication meets the minimum
requirements of American National Standard for
Information Sciences—Permanence of Paper for Printed
Library Materials, ANSI Z39.48-1984.

MV 10 9 8 7 6 5 4 3 2 1

Contents

Figures

Tables

Preface

This volume is the product of a Scandinavian research program initiated by the Nordic Council in 1985. The purpose of this initiative was threefold: to explore the Scandinavian welfare state model; to understand more of the so-called crisis of the welfare state; and to make a contribution to the sociology of the welfare state.

Our exploration of the *Scandinavian model* essentially depends on the questions we raise and the indicators we use: expenditures, outcomes, principles for the creation of the welfare state, and the private-public mix; or, as we suggest, the specific configuration of labor markets and welfare states that exists in Scandinavia.

It is difficult to summarize our contribution to the understanding of the *crisis of the welfare state*. We disagree with the neoliberal contention that the predominant function of the welfare state is the distortion of the market mechanism. We argue the opposite: The welfare state makes the market possible. Today's problems reflect that the welfare state has become the main vehicle of industrial transformation, a task that explodes its format.

Our contribution to the *sociology of the welfare state* is that this part of the discipline should continue to be macro-oriented, historical, and comparative. But we argue against very strict research designs where elements, i.e., the welfare state, are declared as either dependent or independent variables, since the lines of demarcation between the vital institutions of society are becoming increasingly blurred. We call for a research design that highlights instituitional complexes; that is, how welfare states and labor markets, or welfare states and the family institution, are interlocked across nations and over time.

In addition to numerous papers, chapters, and monographs in both

English and other languages, we consider our three volumes in M. E. Sharpe's Comparative Public Policy Analysis Series to be the main outcome of the research program. These books, *The Study of Welfare State Regimes*; *Between Work and Social Citizenship*; and *The Welfare State as Employer*, are interconnected, and our friendly advice is to read them all—they are definitely more than disconnected seminar and conference papers pieced together.

The five-year research program consisted of a coordinating core at the Department of Sociology, University of Bergen, Norway, managed by Jon Eivind Kolberg, and active research teams in Reykjavik, Iceland, led by Stefan Olafsson; Copenhagen, Denmark, directed by Sven Bislev; Umeå, Sweden, chaired by Bengt Furåker; and Helsinki, Finland, conducted by Hannu Uusitalo. The number of research assistants and research fellows who took part in the research program is much larger, and it is difficult indeed to mention them all, let alone give them the credit they deserve. However, as research director and editor of the three volumes I—like all the research participants—know that Paul Farsund and Marita Jakola Skansen, the research assistants at the Department of Sociology, University of Bergen, Norway, were indispensable. Also, Kåre Hagen at the University of Oslo, Norway, did a remarkable job for the project during its entire existence. The whole team worked extremely well together—reflecting Scandinavia at its best—and I thank all who participated.

I also want to express our sincere gratitude to the Nordic Council, which not only initiated this research program, but also funded its Scandinavian core function for three and one-half years, and appointed a board of advisors consisting of top scholars and top ranking civil servants from the participating countries. The board was supportive, patient, and confiding, and most active when it was needed most, namely in the initial stages. I wish to acknowledge in particular the help of its chairman in this vital stage, Ingemar Lindberg, then secretary of state of the Swedish Ministry of Social Affairs.

The research teams of the five different countries, Denmark, Finland, Iceland, Norway, and Sweden, were funded by national sponsors: first and foremost by ministries and research councils, and last, but not least, by the departments and institutes of the project participants. I use this opportunity—on behalf of all of us—to extend our gratitude to all our sponsors.

Since we believe that theoretical progress in sociology must be based on evidence about empirical variation, the three companion volumes rest on a mountain of data. These data are both qualitative (for example changes in legislative content) and quantitative. In part our analyses rest on recalculations of published material; such as population censuses, labor force surveys, data provided by the Organization for Economic Cooperation and Development (OECD), the International Labor Organization (ILO), statistical reports and abstracts, as well as annual reports from both public and private bodies and enterprises. But a considerable piece of the empirical work is based on our own, and far more arduous calculations based on available data files. Most important among these national data files are Labor Force Surveys, Level of Living Surveys, and, in the Norwegian case, a data bank based on a 10 percent sample (panel) from the Population Censuses 1960, 1970, and 1980. We have also utilized data sets from Time Budget Surveys, Health Surveys, Electoral Surveys, and so-called additions to Labor Force Surveys. Our international data sets include The Luxembourg Income Study (LIS), and The International Value Study. Our empirical effort also consists of several special data sets established for our research purposes. Thus, the Finnish part of LIS was established in the context of the present research program. And our study of the rise of disemployment has set up two matched data files connecting population census data at time 1 with data from the National Insurance Institution on pension status at time 2. The research program has developed three data banks with time-series for the period 1960–85 which are as yet not fully operational; such as the Nordic WEEP (Welfare State Exit-Entry) Data Bank, The Nordic Welfare State Regime Data Bank, and a data bank with time series (1948–87) on the structure of welfare state expenditure in the Nordic countries.

Our ambitious program of both recalculation and own calculations (and we wish to stress the distinction) was advanced by helping hands and brains in statistical offices all over Scandinavia, in several research institutions, the most important of which was FAFO (Norwegian Trade Union Center for Social Science and Research in Oslo), and last, but by no means least, in NSD (the Norwegian Social Science Data Archives, University of Bergen), where we want to thank Atle Alvheim and Lars Holm in particular for their assistance, advice, and persistent interest. I also want to extend our appreciation to cand. polit. Henning Hansen at the Institute of Applied Social Research in Copenhagen for his constant altruism, to research director Erik Jørn Hansen at the same institute who kindly opened the gate to the Danish Level of Living surveys 1976 and 1985 for us, and to the Danish Social Science Data Archives (DDA) at the University of Odense.

Furthermore, I want to express our gratitude to the many indispensable librarians who helped us with the retrieval and documentation of publications throughout the project period. It would be impossible to mention all those who deserve it here. Instead, I will nominate Svein Lindblad at the Institute of Social Research in Oslo as their true representative and archetype. In the very final stage, Svein Lindblad meticulously provided outstanding and very generous help in completing the reference lists and in the full specification of the sources.

Our list of acknowledgments must extend outside Scandinavia. First, my thanks go to professor Gøsta Esping-Andersen, at the European University Institute, Florence, Italy, who is a great friend and a true Scandinavian. He, no doubt, was the most influential inspirator for our research effort. He played a major role in the development of the leading concepts and in the creation of the empirical design of the study. Together with professors Lee Rainwater and Martin Rein, he worked with the non-Scandinavian part of what became our joint and informal large project covering not only Scandinavia, but the United States, the United Kingdom, the Federal Republic of Germany, and Italy as well. It goes without saying that this wider scope is essential for the understanding of the Scandinavian model. Through Gøsta Esping-Andersen, we were linked to a network of outstanding scholars in North America, the United Kingdom, Italy, and the Federal Republic of Germany. First and foremost, we met Professor Lee Rainwater of Harvard University and Professor Martin Rein of M.I.T. The many discussions we had—at seminars and elsewhere—during the project, in Berlin, Bergen, Cambridge, Florence, Jerusalem, Luxembourg, and Oslo, provided invaluable input.

In addition to all the institutions and individuals already mentioned, our effort was also "carried" by someone back home—children and adults—who demonstrated in a unique way the importance of generosity and patience for social research. In sum, our thanks go in a wide variety of directions. However, the remaining errors and inadequate explanations and interpretations remain our responsibility alone.

Jon Eivind Kolberg

University of Bergen
January 1991

The Study of
Welfare State Regimes

1

Welfare States and Employment Regimes

JON EIVIND KOLBERG and
GØSTA ESPING-ANDERSEN

Introduction

The underlying research ambition of this volume is threefold: to discuss welfare state models, and the Scandinavian in particular; to make a contribution to the development of the sociology of the welfare state; and to show, by way of empirical analyses, the fascinating variety of approaches to the study of the relationship between the welfare state and the economy.

We intend to transcend the boundary between labor market sociology and the sociology of the welfare state. The overall theme we have in mind is the relationship between welfare states and labor markets, that is, how these two institutions are interlocked and how the interaction between them has changed throughout the last twenty-five years. Despite different interpretations of present problems of the modern welfare state, there seems to be one point of agreement: something is wrong at the interface of the welfare state and the economy. This book sets out to explore how we can think about the relationship between the welfare state and the economy, and starts to specify what characterizes the emergent relations between these institutions in modern Scandinavia.

To clarify our intent, let us spell out what we consider to be the main shortcoming of the present state of the art. We argue that comparative sociological research has, perhaps, been too preoccupied with

---

Note: Throughout this book, Germany refers to the Federal Republic of Germany (West Germany).

the welfare state as a dependent variable. The main interest has been to pinpoint those independent variables that best explain variations in welfare state effort or differences in the institutional setup of welfare states. These approaches are by all means legitimate. But we argue that the welfare state should also be regarded as a very significant institution that has significant repercussions on other societal institutions, such as the labor market, the class structure, the relationship between the sexes, the normative structure, and the systems of distribution and redistribution. In other words, the welfare state should also be conceptualized as a major independent variable. Perhaps even more fundamentally, we argue against very strict designs where variables are declared as either independent or dependent, because what characterizes the relationship between the institutions we explore is covariation, interactions, and multifarious impacts. As a rule, we speak about the welfare state *and* the economy, and the welfare state *and* the labor market, as if these institutions were two different things—distinct and separate institutional categories or areas. Our point is that this way of conceptualization makes less sense, since the line of demarcation between these institutions is becoming increasingly blurred. What we should look at are institutional complexes—how they are patterned, why, and with what effects.

The Scandinavian model

Our contribution also stems from a wish to delineate and understand the Scandinavian welfare state model. The five Nordic countries (Denmark, Finland, Iceland, Norway, and Sweden) are regarded as a class of advanced welfare states, proclaimed to constitute a model in the research literature. This notion raises two problems, one empirical and one conceptual. The first problem is whether the common idea of a Scandinavian model makes sense in empirical terms. What are the differences and similarities within this group of nations? Are these differences and similarities, which make up the postulated model, stable or moving, and if moving, are the trends in the direction of divergence or convergence? But these empirical questions immediately raise other, more fundamental, conceptual issues: What is meant by a welfare state model, and what could—in sociological terms—most fruitfully be included in the concept of a welfare state model? We suggest that the scope of analysis be broadened to incorporate systematically how the welfare state is linked to other societal institutions. The focus of this volume is the relationship between the welfare state and the economy; but this focus requires that we also incorporate other institutions in the analysis, such as the family, the government, and the class structure.

Welfare states and employment regimes

A crucial challenge for comparative research is to begin studying the welfare state as a major complex in modern society that has a profound influence on such social institutions as the labor market, the family, the class structure, the systems of distribution and redistribution, the normative structure, and gender relations.

After the first generation's obsession with variations in aggregate welfare state spending, an emergent second generation of comparative welfare state research has demonstrated growing concern with the institutional characteristics of welfare states, and has attempted to compare rules of entitlements, the strength and scope of rights, patterns of coverage, and the like. Such studies, guided primarily by an interest in explaining international variations in welfare state development, have considerably augmented our capacity to identify salient institutional attributes. Today, however, one of the most pressing analytic tasks is to examine welfare states in their role as independent, causal variables: how do different types of welfare states systematically influence social and economic behavior in advanced capitalism?

Those readers who are familiar with the sociological literature on family, social stratification, or social organization, or those who have studied the literature on labor markets, will easily recognize the glaring absence of the welfare state as a variable to be reckoned with. Yet, be it contemporary Scandinavia, Western Europe, or even North America, the welfare state is not merely some proportion of the national product; it has become deeply embedded in the everyday life of virtually every citizen. Our personal lives are structured by the welfare state, and so is the entire political economy. Given the magnitude and centrality of the welfare state, it is indeed unlikely that we shall understand much of contemporary society unless we incorporate it endogenously in our models. It is this that we propose to do in this book.

Of the many social institutions that are likely to be directly shaped and ordered by the welfare state, the labor market is perhaps the most important. This is so because the core idea of the welfare state has always been to safeguard the population against the exigencies and risks that confront them in their life cycle, especially in the nexus of work and nonwork. The explicit philosophy in the traditional, minimalist welfare state was to establish a safety net, a haven of last resort, for those demonstrably unfit or unable to work. This is clearly no longer the case for the advanced welfare state as it has found expression in Scandinavia.

The advanced welfare state has developed new principles with regard to its proper role in its citizens' life cycles. It aims explicitly to optimize people's capacity to work, their ability to find work, and even their capacity to count on a good job with good pay and a good working environment. It seeks to make it as easy as possible for people to resolve the difficulties of harmonizing working life with familyhood, to square the dilemmas of having children and working, and to combine productive activity with meaningful and rewarding leisure. These are all principles that have shaped recent decades of social policy development; indeed, they underpin the contemporary legitimacy and common understanding of many nations' welfare states.

This is not to say that these principles enjoy undisputed consensus. Some conservative parties, many employers, and most economists invoke the classical fear that welfare rights distort the work incentive. However, our concern is not with incentive effects but with the larger and more complex question of how, in reality, welfare states influence labor market behavior and, more broadly, social stratification.

The objective of this chapter, then, is to undertake a first conceptualization of welfare state–labor market interactions. Our task is organized around three principal cornerstones of the labor market: (1) the conditions under which people exit from the labor market and enter into the status of welfare state client, especially regarding unemployment and retirement; (2) the conditions under which people claim paid absence from a job; and (3) the conditions under which people are allocated to jobs, that is, enter into employment.

Labor market and welfare state regimes

We argue that the labor market is systematically and directly shaped by the welfare state. It follows that we would expect cross-national differences in labor market behavior to be attributable to the nature of welfare state regimes.

This view contradicts prevailing models of labor markets found in standard neoclassical economics. The labor market is typically treated as a rather closed system, autonomous from politics; its actors are discrete and independent, and respond primarily to price signals. The standard assumption is that labor markets will clear and move toward equilibrium by themselves.

When mainstream economists do consider the influence of the modern welfare state, it is generally under two headings: one, its overall "Keynesian" stimulus on demand or, two, its potential for distorting the automatic clearing mechanism by affecting wages, labor supply, or labor costs. The neoclassical model has very little room for the welfare state.

This problem is perhaps less prominent in many of the contemporary "institutionalist" economic models. It is nevertheless rare that the state is examined as an endogenous variable. Be it dual or segmented labor market theory, insider-outsider models, or in efficiency wage contract theories, the principal focus has been on industrial organization and industrial relations arrangements. A theory of what role the welfare state plays for mobility behavior, job tenure, and more generally, for labor market rigidities and stratification, has yet to emerge. In recent years, a few institutional economists have begun to pay closer attention to the importance of the "social wage" for worker behavior and the cost of firing (Shore and Bowles 1984; Bowles and Gintis 1986). This may be regarded as the first stepping-stone toward more systematic analyses.

Economics has obviously not ignored entirely the relationship between labor market behavior and social policy. There is, for example, an abundance of literature on the negative incentive effects of social benefits on labor supply and mobility at the microlevel, and also a few attempts to argue their effects at the macrolevel (Danziger et al. 1981; Lindbeck 1981). But the welfare state in this research is taken for granted or seen as a disturbance in the autonomous clearing process. Most studies are limited to one country and, typically, also to one policy area. Their intent is to estimate to what extent social benefits affect a given worker's labor supply.

For similar reasons, our approach also conflicts with prevailing sociological models of the labor market. Sociology boasts a long tradition of studying the institutional mechanisms of occupation and job attainment. The emphasis here has been on socially inherited labor market chances and/or on the mediating effects of educational systems. The critique of the economists' view is that social forces preclude the possibility that actors in the labor market: (a) act independently and (b) start equally in the competition for jobs and rewards. This literature identifies dividers in the labor market that are sociological, such as the tendency for fathers' class position to affect sons' mobility chances (representative examples of this approach are Blau and Duncan 1967; Featherman and Hauser 1978; Jencks 1982; Colbjørnsen 1986). In the sociology of professions it has also been found that social institutions influence labor market outcomes. It is, for example, typical that entry into, as well as conduct within, professional positions is decided by corporate monopolistic practices. But, job attainment in sociology is rarely, if ever, related to the welfare state.

In recent years, the social sciences have begun to pay closer attention to the role of government in labor market performance. This has perhaps been clearest in recent years' research on the determinants of cross-national differences in full employment performance. For example, Schmidt (1982, 1983), Therborn (1986), and Esping-Andersen (1987) show how nations' capacity to maintain full employment varies with the role of active labor market policies, Keynesian demand management, trade union structure, and their capacity for neocorporatist interest mediation. Recent studies on the comparative growth in service sector employment have demonstrated the centrality of welfare states in accounting for international differences in its structuration (Rein 1985). Scharpf (1985) suggests that taxation levels play a role in explaining welfare states' capacity to expand social service employment. Cusack, Notermans, and Rein (1987) have related this to welfare states' budgetary structure.

From a Marxist perspective, there have also emerged a few attempts to reconceptualize class theory. Van Parijs (1987), for example, suggests that the growing armies of jobless welfare state clients be fully inserted as a social class in class analysis.

The idea that labor markets are autonomous is based on a myth, sustained by ideology and defended by antiquated theory. The idea was also given material life. It has historically been upheld by state power and been given institutionalized existence when social policy and welfare state programs were consciously and deliberately designed so as

not to interfere with the mechanisms of the labor market. The archi-
tects of early welfare policies were adamant about the principle that
social protection was to be limited to those unable to function in the
labor market: the old, infirm, sick, and unemployed. The principle of
prohibiting welfare policy from shaping labor market decisions was
obvious in nineteenth century poor relief, with its ideology of "less
eligibility"; in the early social insurance laws, with their strict ac-
tuarialism and long employment/contribution requirements; and also in
early social assistance schemes, where means tests and low benefits
assured that the marginal utility of working remained substantially
higher than that of depending on welfare.

When we examine the modern "welfare states" that were institutionalized after World War II, we discover the exact same philosophy
of nonintervention. The Beveridge model of the United Kingdom, or
the People's Home model of Scandinavia, was not meant to stimulate
exit from the market; on the contrary, it was designed to encourage
maximum labor market dependence. And, mirroring the intellectual
influence of the social administration tradition, the underlying principle of social reforms was that the welfare state and the labor market
were to remain separated. Thus, when many governments committed
themselves to a "Keynes plus Beveridge" formula after the war, they
never contemplated the idea of integrating social and economic policies. The separation of labor market affairs and social security matters
is also reflected at the administrative level: Most countries kept the
bureaucracies and administration of social protection and labor market
sharply separate.

Governments' attempts to manufacture a sharp separation of policy
domains may, nonetheless, have rested on an artificial logic, as Polanyi
(1957) has argued so powerfully. His point is that an autonomous
market, separated from society and the state, is an artificiality that
could only come about through the application of power. By withdraw-
ing traditional social policies and crushing existing "precapitalist"
institutions and substituting them with a harsh method of "less eligibility," the state allowed the idea of workers as commodities to exist; the
state closed all gates that led out of the market; human survival operated within a market that appeared to be based entirely on freedom of
choice. Yet, the market constitutes, in reality, a prison from which
escape is made impossible.

The case for the sharp, albeit fictitious, separation was premised on classical liberal theory, especially on its assumptions about the equality-efficiency trade-off. Be they hardcore laissez-faire advocates, such as Smiley, or the more tempered and reasoned liberal political economists, such as John Stuart Mill or, later Alfred Marshall, it was universally agreed that governments' attempts to augment equality would impair economic performance.

Still, many of our theoretical forebears recognized that institutions were a necessary (and often desirable) way to achieve positive-sum outcomes in this trade-off. Conservative political economy was adamantly against the idea of workers as commodities. Their answer to the call for efficient allocation and productivity was "*Soldaten der Arbeit*," or loyalty, integration, and hierarchy. Nazi Germany was unwilling to put its faith in a free labor market and preferred instead to assign or conscript people to jobs and to control their mobility with a mandatory workbook. Many reformed liberals, such as Mill, believed that the trade-off was not so hopelessly zero-sum and advocated, to a degree, social policies as a means to uplift economic performance. The reformist socialist tradition took the argument one step further and held that efficiency and optimal productivity presumed not just healthy, well-fed, and educated workers, but that modernization and rapid technological change would occur when workers felt secure and were in command of adequate income guarantees.

Thus, in most of our theoretical heritage, social policy was regarded as integral to labor market behavior. It is therefore astonishing that contemporary scholarship ignores it—all the more so when we take into consideration how a number of creeping revolutions over the past decades have fundamentally altered the nexus of work and welfare.

Silent revolutions

The modern welfare state edifice constructed in the post World War II era based itself upon certain, increasingly outdated, assumptions regarding economic growth and full employment. Economic growth could once be counted on to furnish a large number of new jobs. Today, however, economic growth has declining employment-multiplier effects, and jobless growth may indeed occur. This contradiction implies not merely a greater difficulty for managing full employment with given levels of investment, but also poses serious problems for welfare state finances.

There is more to it than that: a silent but significant revolution has occurred with respect to our conception of full employment. When William Beveridge (and his contemporaries in other countries) launched the notion of a full employment commitment, the reference was only to able-bodied men. One of postwar capitalism's most remarkable silent revolutions lies in the ways this base for full employment has been broadened to encompass all women and, indeed, anyone who wishes to work. This implies a huge increase of the labor base for full employment delivery.

Maximizing labor supply may, of course, have beneficial effects on welfare state finances, since many more will contribute to taxation and social contributions while presumably fewer will demand social protection. But, with a declining employment multiplier and a labor force augmented by, perhaps, an additional 30 percent of the population, it becomes increasingly difficult to fulfill commitments to full employment, meaning paid work for all. It is in the context of this new dilemma that traditional welfare state programs increasingly have come to serve new purposes. Education and retirement programs, for example, help to reduce the economically active part of the working population. Welfare state social services can become a vehicle for the absorption of new, especially female, labor force entrants.

As we discussed, the modern welfare state was designed in such a way that a clear line of demarcation between the labor market and the welfare state should be maintained. Thus, the welfare state should only cater to those absolutely incapable of work; it was not supposed to induce anybody to leave work for welfare. Here a second silent revolution has occurred. Retirement programs have not just been upgraded, but have also been vastly extended. Thus, in Western Europe early retirement has in recent years induced millions of able-bodied workers to leave the labor market and enter the welfare state.

Early retirement may, in some cases, constitute a response to rising unemployment. But, when the welfare state aids a mass exit from working life into retirement, its finances are obviously increasingly strained. In many cases, early retirement has come to serve as an instrument of firm rationalization and restructuration. In this sense, what we observe is that the social collectivity helps both organize and finance improved firm competitiveness. The result is a growing tension between industry level/microlevel rationality and the collective good. The welfare state aids microlevel rationality and efficiency but creates, at the same time, macroeconomic disutilities: underutilization of labor capacity and public budget deficits. If, on the other hand, the welfare state had adhered to the classical dogma of noninterference with the labor market mechanism, it is possible that countries would have been hard pressed to maintain industrial competitiveness.

We can identify a third important silent revolution. Modern welfare states are no longer systems of social provision only. They have, in many nations, become virtual employment machines and have constituted the only significant source of job growth over the past twenty-five to thirty years. Today, the Danish and Swedish welfare states employ about 25 percent of the labor force. Again, this is a remarkable departure from the theory of the labor market as a self-regulatory organism. Thus, the welfare state absorbs labor supply, not only to uphold promises of full employment, but also because the welfare state's own economic logic demands that as many work as possible. For the welfare state it may be more cost-effective to employ excess labor than to subsidize people who do not work.

Taken together, the emerging new patterns of welfare state–labor market relations are characterized by considerable strains. Be it for employment or more general economic objectives, the welfare state's traditional responsibilities have been extended and changed. As a result, social policy and the labor market have become interwoven and mutually interdependent institutions. To an extent, the welfare state has become a major agent of labor market clearing. It eases the exit of women through family programs and of older people through early retirement. It upholds labor demand by employing people in health, education, and welfare occupations. It helps people reconcile their roles as economic producers and members of the social community and family by granting workers paid vacation and temporary absence from work.

We will examine more closely three instances where it is most relevant to anticipate a strong welfare state presence. The three windows into welfare state–labor market interactions are defined around employees' contractual status of work. First, we focus on the conditions for labor supply: what determines whether people remain in or exit from the labor force? Our empirical case here is mainly the behavior of older workers.

The second window examines the conditions that shape behavior within the labor contract. In principle, the work contract stipulates the exchange of labor time for pay. This time is, in principle, "owned" by the employer, and the worker has little authority over the allocation of the worker's time. The relevant question is: To what extent and under what conditions can workers exercise their own choice under the contract? To what degree is their status, then, decommodified? The appropriate empirical case here is paid nonwork, that is, work-absence.

The third relevant window concerns the demand for labor and the conditions under which labor enters into employment. With few exceptions, prevailing theory assumes that labor demand is a function of marginal productivity and price. Much of Keynesian macroeconomic theory assumes, of course, that the welfare state's aggregate demand effect influences labor demand. Economists also recognize wage subsidy effects. But the welfare state's role as a major employer has been vastly underresearched.

In brief, our approach is to understand welfare state–labor market interactions in the areas of exit, absenteeism, and entry.

Exit and labor supply

There is nothing especially new in the recognition that social policy shapes labor supply. Graebner (1980) argues that the principle of retirement is a social invention, inserted as a means to manage unemployment problems and as a mechanism to permit employers to shed its less productive work force. There is also a long tradition in economics of studying retirement/early retirement as a function of leisure-work trade-offs where pension benefits are viewed as a potential source of "negative incentive effects" (Danziger et al. 1981).

These kinds of studies are typically focused at the microlevel, and are therefore unable to see how microlevel choices and macrolevel outcomes interrelate. What may be inefficient at the level of individual choice (leisure via pension benefits) may, simultaneously, constitute efficiency at the firm level (higher productivity financed by taxpayers). At the macrolevel, early retirement may concomitantly lower labor supply, raise aggregate productivity, and siphon resources toward activities that yield zero productive output (retirement).

A second fundamental shortcoming of existing scholarship is its inattention to variations in welfare states. It is to be expected that different types of welfare states will influence the structure of labor supply differently, and this may not be a function solely of pension legislation and the attractiveness of early retirement programs. The demand for early retirement will depend on available alternatives (part-time work, sheltered employment, retraining, and unemployment insurance), on the nature of industrial relations systems (job security), and on the status of the economy; these alternatives owe much of their existence to welfare state activities.

Cross-national variations in the scope of early retirement are astonishingly large, and they have increased over the past decades. The focus is on male workers in the age group fifty-five through sixty-four, since the retirement convention in most nations has normally been around age sixty-five, and since women's traditional role as homemakers makes comparisons of female retirement over time difficult. Table 1.1 below reveals growing cross-national divergence in labor force exit among older males.

Table 1.1 also suggests a systematic relationship between our regime types and labor force exit: The Nordic cluster is characterized by low exit; the continental European by very high exit; and the Anglo-Saxon world by moderate exit. Is this just a function of the quality of pension programs and the availability of early retirement? To an extent it would seem so. Germany, the Netherlands, and France have, since 1970, been front-runners in the development of flexible and early retirement programs, while access to early retirement has remained far less attractive in the United States, the United Kingdom, and Canada. On the other hand, Swedish pension legislation compares very favorably with that of the continental European nations, both with respect to largesse and ease of eligibility. Nonetheless, even if there were a perfect fit between exit and retirement, the question remains: why are there dramatic variations in welfare state intervention in labor force supply?

The task of disentangling the reasons for declining older worker participation is not simple. The trend is similar across all nations, but the variations are too great to be merely accidental. The general trend may, of course, be explained simply by the pervasive upgrading and liberalization of pensions, which have allowed worn-out workers a means of escaping work. Or it may reflect an increasingly difficult labor market situation for older workers. The latter explanation might also help account for some of the dramatic cross-national differences.

Yet, the unemployment hypothesis seems difficult to sustain when we consider the following: (a) in most countries in Europe, at least,

Table 1.1

Labor Force Participation Rates of Males Age 55–64 (approximations)

	1960	1970	1980	Change
Sweden	88	82	76	−12
Norway	92	84	79	−13
Germany	82	78	56	−26
France	79	74	50	−29
Netherlands	88	81	47	−41
United States	84	81	67	−17
Canada	82	80	70	−12
United Kingdom	94	91	68	−26

Sources: ILO 1966; ILO 1975; ILO 1978; OECD 1988; and Nordic WEEP Data Bank (1989).

Notes: The figures for Germany and Canada (1960) are from 1961; and for France (1960) from 1962. The figures for France (1970) are from 1968; the United Kingdom figures (1970) are from 1971. The Canadian figure for 1970 is derived from ILO (1978), and the Norwegian figure for 1985 from the Nordic WEEP Data Bank (1989). Note also that the participation rates pertaining to 1960 and 1970 are based on population census definitions of economic activity, whereas the 1985-figures are based on labor force survey definitions. The former of these definitions is more narrow. Thus, the different definitions of labor force participation tend to underestimate the rate of change between 1970 and 1985.

older workers usually enjoy very strong job rights and are therefore not easy to lay off; and (b) the dramatic reduction in participation in countries such as France and the Netherlands occurred before the onset of mass unemployment in the 1980s. The real explosive movement typically occurred in the 1970s and has, since the early 1980s, actually tapered off.

At present we can offer only rather speculative hypotheses concerning international variations in the exit of older workers. First we must consider the necessary preconditions. These include, obviously, pension system characteristics such as favorable provisions for early retirement and other incentives (such as taxes).

Second, it is likely that there existed a latent pool of partially disabled workers who invaded early retirement programs once they came into existence (in many countries these were enacted in the early 1970s—before there had been any mention of OPEC oil shocks and crisis). But this can explain the general trend, not the international differences.

A third probable explanation has to do with industrial restructuring, very much in response to the post-OPEC crisis. In cases where trade unions are powerful and seniority rules are strict, early retirement provisions certainly come as a godsend to employers searching for strategies to slim their work-force and rid themselves of their older, and frequently less productive, employees. One might formulate a hypothesis based on the interaction effect between the quality of early retirement provisions and industrial rationalization. In many nations, it is clear that labor force supply among older workers is intimately related to the welfare state; the market mechanism appears sidelined.

There is also a fourth, more structural explanation behind the international differences, and that has to do with the relationship between nations' general employment policies and welfare policies. In some countries, especially Germany, the Netherlands, and France, retirement programs have, in tandem with other efforts to reduce labor supply, come to constitute the basic policy of maintaining full employment. One reason has to do with these nations' governments' unwillingness to deflate their economies in response to the crisis. Another has to do with these nations' welfare state bias against social service employment expansion. This explanation receives added credibility when confronted with the Scandinavian experience. These countries, unlike continental Europe, have been considerably more expansionary in their post-1973 economic policies, and they have actively used welfare state employment (and a host of other means) to sustain labor demand. Hence, in Scandinavia the pressures on early retirement as an instrument in full employment management have been weaker.

Our exploration of early retirement in the labor market has been limited to the Nordic countries. Two of these, Norway and Sweden, display internationally very low rates, while two others, Denmark and Finland, show, respectively, medium and rather high rates of early retirement. We have, in part, addressed the relationship between pension program characteristics, general economic conditions, and early retirement. And, in part, we have explored welfare and stratification factors related to early retirement. An adequate understanding of welfare state–labor market interactions has compelled us to examine the extent to which early retirees continue to work, their general activity patterns, and the structure of recruitment into retirement. Their work-welfare nexus provides information about the incentives for retirement, the status of retirees, and recruitment patterns that has helped elucidate some of the forces behind early retirement. We have thus investigated early retirees' previous health status, skills, job histories, and location in the class structure.

Paid work-absence

Aside from unemployment benefits, sickness and related benefits have been a favorite topic for the "negative incentive" literature. The capacity of workers to retain normal earnings and yet not work may reflect nothing more than a humane treatment of those so incapacitated that there is no freedom of choice. In this case, the issue of negative incentives is irrelevant. But if the array of programs offered to workers is such that they can exercise a modicum of discretionary choice about whether to work or pursue alternative activities, their status as commodities is weakened. They enjoy rights within the contract of employment as to the activities they personally prioritize.

The capacity of workers to be absent from work with pay depends on both industrial relations and social policy. Traditionally, collective agreements and policy limited themselves to a narrow field of situations, primarily work injuries and certified illness. In most countries, the field has undergone expansion, embracing vacations, holidays, maternity (and parental) leave, care of sick family members, education, training, and even trade union activities. In most countries, too, the rules of eligibility have been liberalized and benefits raised significantly. These factors alone should clearly have a positive influence on overall rates of paid work-absence and have, indeed, figured heavily in the literature (Salowski 1980, 1983).

Any adequate understanding of absenteeism is, nonetheless, compelled to take into consideration a host of alternative explanations. Where medical certification is required, the role of the doctor becomes crucial; people may command a right to paid absence but may refrain from exercising it due to fear of job loss, employer response, or general economic uncertainty. Working conditions clearly must be considered too. Thus, workers in exceptionally poor job environments may utilize frequent absenteeism as a coping strategy. Paradoxically, employers may "encourage" their workers into absenteeism as a labor hoarding strategy under conditions of slack product demand, especially if benefits are paid out of taxpayers' money. Finally, absenteeism may reflect employees' efforts to equilibrate their roles as workers and as family and community members. That the phenomenon of absenteeism is extraordinarily complex is clear. This is why almost all empirical studies, especially those of the negative incentive variety, provoke controversy and remain largely inconclusive.

It is often thought that sickness absenteeism has increased steadily. This, however, is not the case. Aggregate data show that sickness absence rose sharply from the 1960s to the 1970s. This trend may support a program-based explanation, since it was typically in this period that sickness schemes were liberalized and improved. The lack of change in the United States could be interpreted along these lines, too, since it was the only country where no new legislation occurred. Yet, an increase in sickness absenteeism failed to occur in Germany despite program upgrading in the late 1960s. Table 1.2 reveals, though, that absenteeism does not rise monotonically. Indeed, it has declined in five out of six countries since the mid-1970s. Paid sickness absence varies considerably across nations. According to the Organization for Economic Cooperation and Development (OECD) data on days lost (annually averaged) due to sickness alone, countries cluster with a very high group (twenty days/year), which includes the United Kingdom and Sweden; a middle group (twelve days/year), which includes Germany, France, and the Netherlands; and a low group (less than five days/year), which includes Canada (not included in the table) and the United States.

The main body of literature on sickness absenteeism has been nation-specific and micro-oriented. Very few efforts, if any, have been made to compare data across countries and over time at the macrolevel. The lack of such studies can be ascribed to the difficulties of establishing comparable data sets and to the paucity of significant sociological variables included in administrative statistics.

Most studies have focused solely on sickness absenteeism. But for an understanding of the welfare state in the labor market, this approach is far too narrow. Of equal interest is the array of programs motivated by welfare state ideals of expanding the menu of people's discretionary choice between work, family, and community. Maternity leave, parental leave, and the like are motivated by the desire to allow workers to harmonize family life with work; educational and related work-absence programs, as well as vacation, are designed to allow workers to improve their social status and private lives.

The significance of the entire absenteeism menu for workers' work-

Table 1.2

Sickness Absence from Work; Average Annual Number of Days
(different definitions)

	Sweden	Germany	France	Netherlands	United Kingdom	United States
1960	13.2	13.9	13.2	5.3	13.8	—
1965	15.7	12.6	13.5	6.4	15.1	5.6
1970	19.9	13.1	13.3	7.7	16.7	5.7
1975	21.4	12.0	18.3	8.8	—	5.4
1976	23.2	12.7	17.4	9.3	18.0	5.2
1977	22.8	12.4	16.7	9.3	18.4	5.3
1978	22.8	12.5	16.8	10.0	19.6	5.0
1979	22.0	12.9	15.5	10.0	19.7	5.2
1980	21.0	12.9	14.9	9.4	20.0	5.0
1981	19.6	12.3	14.9	8.5	20.0	5.0
1982	18.5	—	15.1	8.1	—	4.9
1983	—	—	13.9	7.5	—	—

Source: OECD (1985), Table F 5.

family strategies becomes clear when we examine the labor force participation rates and overall absenteeism rates of Swedish mothers over a fifteen- to twenty-five-year period.

Table 1.3 shows that the spectacular rise in female labor force participation in Sweden also applies to mothers with children in all age categories. It also points out a less well-known trend—the simultaneous increase in female temporary absence. In 1985, close to half of all working mothers with children less than two years old were absent from work on any given day.

In this chapter, we will examine work absenteeism from the point of view of elaborating a sociological model, not with the intent to confront and test negative incentive theories. From the perspective of the individual, that is, at the microlevel, we regard temporary work-absence as an effort to bridge the gap between the world of work and the human community: two spheres of life that became sharply divided with the rise of the industrial market economy. In turn, social policy represents, at the macrolevel, an effort to reconcile the two spheres. We can identify four junctures of reintegration: first, personal life problems, such as illness; second, family concerns such as care of children, maternity, and the like; third, community participation and

Table 1.3

Sweden: Labor Force Participation Rates of Mothers and Rate of (Total) Paid Temporary Absence Among Working Mothers on Any Given Day, 1965–85 (in percent)

	All Women with Children Age 0–16	Youngest Child Age 0–2	Youngest Child Age 3–6	Youngest Child Age 0–6
Participation rate				
1965	46.6	—	—	36.8
1970	57.6	43.4	55.9	—
1975	69.0	57.4	63.9	—
1980	80.5	74.6	76.1	—
1985	87.6	82.4	85.7	84.0
Temporary absence				
1965	13.4	—	—	18.0
1970	15.3	26.9	12.0	—
1975	18.8	34.3	15.2	—
1980	24.2	44.1	20.0	—
1985	23.2	47.5	18.0	32.6

Sources: Statistiska Centralbyrån 1972, 1973, 1976, 1981, and 1985.

leisure and; fourth, the capability of influencing one's future life-chances through continued education and training. Thus, we include the following types of temporary absence from paid work: sickness absence, family-related absence, absence for vacations and holidays, and human capital–related absence.

As a rule, the "work-disincentive" literature has concentrated on one program, such as sickness benefits, without simultaneous consideration of other programs. It is, however, highly probable that employees' benefit consumption depends on the program mix that each employee confronts. The relative attraction of one program (for example, sickness insurance) compared to possible alternatives (say, early retirement) must influence choices. In some countries, sickness absence accounts for only a fraction of the total. This is especially the case in Scandinavia where the menu of absenteeism alternatives is especially liberal. In countries where early retirement (and perhaps also unemployment) is very high, we might expect a reciprocally lower absence rate since there are reasons to believe that the disemployed are more likely to have been frequently ill while still working.

When, as in Sweden, approximately 15 percent of the workers on any given day are absent, yet paid to work, it is difficult to sustain the logic of a labor market guided solely by the pure exchange principle. A very large share of what normally is regarded as work time, is in fact ''welfare time.'' The range of alternative choices is such that Swedes are relatively decommodified; they do not just hand over their time to the employer; the employers' control of the purchased labor commodity is heavily circumscribed.

The social policy features that determine such decommodification possibilities are many. The presence of social legislation is a first precondition, and the very low U.S. absenteeism rates may simply reflect the absence of a legislated program. Clearly, waiting days (ranging from zero in Norway and Sweden to fourteen days in Canada) and compulsory medical certification do matter. In Sweden, a medical certificate of illness is not required until the seventh sick day and not until the fourth in Norway. In other countries, it is mandatory on the first day. Compensation levels are obviously decisive: the degree of discretionary choice depends on whether a worker can maintain living standards. Furthermore, it ought to make a decisive difference whether benefits are paid by the employers or whether the costs are socialized. In brief, we should expect systematic variation between welfare state types and absenteeism behavior.

The welfare state as employer

There is nothing especially new about the fact that a share of the labor market is not operating within a genuine market but is under state employment. In this sector, traditional capitalist market principles operate only marginally. The lack of a profit motive (surplus value, if you wish), salaried status, tenured appointments, and the sheer inoperability of the conventional productivity logic mean that orthodox economic models of the labor market hardly apply.

Aside from its age-old role as direct employer, government has traditionally influenced employment entry through a host of instruments. These range from temporary work programs, wage subsidies, and aggregate demand management to industrial subsidies and full-scale active labor market policies. The most direct approach to the study of the welfare state's influence on labor demand and employment allocation is, nonetheless, its role as employer. It is also in this role that it most fundamentally alters the ways in which we must understand labor markets.

What then is the share of employment outside conventional market principles? What is the welfare state's role in shaping the process of employment entry and the structure of labor demand? What concerns us here is not the public sector as such. If we are interested in welfare state–labor market interactions, public industrial enterprises as well as public transport or communications, traditional areas of public administration, and law and order are irrelevant. Our concern is social policy and, therefore, the extent to which collective social welfare criteria dominate the market in the allocation of employment.

To get an idea of cross-national variations, let us examine two indicators: (1) the welfare state's share of total social service employment (health, education, and welfare services) and (2) welfare state social service employment as a share of total employment. The first measures the private-public mix; the second, the overall national bias in favor of welfare state employment. Table 1.4 suggests, once again, that nations cluster rather than distribute themselves linearly.

The Nordic countries form one cluster with their extraordinary large welfare employment, almost exclusively organized by the welfare state. The welfare state proper occupies 20–25 percent of all employment in those nations. A second group of countries is equally homogeneous. These are nations in which social welfare employment as such is vastly underdeveloped and where the public sector's welfare state role is only marginal in overall employment allocation: Austria, Germany, Italy, and Switzerland are the clearest cases. There is a third cluster in which welfare service employment is fairly well developed, but quite dominated by the private sector. This includes Australia, Canada, the Netherlands, and the United States. With few exceptions, these three clusters correspond almost totally to the three welfare state regime types we have developed.

The crystallization of regime clusters

When we combine the evidence from our discussions of exit, absenteeism, and entry (our three windows), there is considerable support for the argument that welfare state structures are systematically related to

Table 1.4

The Welfare State as Employer: The Private-Public Mix in Health, Education, and Welfare Employment, circa 1985 (in percent)

	HEW Employment as Share of Total	Public Share of HEW Total Employment	Public HEW as Share of Total Employment
Denmark	28	90	25
Norway	22	92	20
Sweden	26	93	25
Germany	11	58	7
Austria	10	61	6
Italy	12	85	11
Switzerland	12	58	7
France	15	75	11
United Kingdom	16	77	12
Netherlands	20	38	8
Australia	15	65	10
Canada	15	44	7
United States	17	45	8

Source: WEEP Data Bank. 1990.

labor market outcomes. Our preliminary hypotheses, then, are as follows.

First, some welfare states are strongly biased in favor of maximizing labor supply: their exit behavior is thus comparatively modest. The prime cases here are the Nordic countries. In contrast, there are welfare states that strongly nourish exit and a decline of labor supply. The prime cases here are Germany, the Netherlands, Italy, and France. By and large, the same pattern holds when we examine overall participation rates, especially for women. Internationally, Scandinavia boasts the highest rates of female and total participation; the Netherlands, Germany, and Italy are, on both counts, very low. Welfare state policies may not explain the entire story, but differences in the provision of child care and a host of similar services do affect the supply of female workers, and in general the availability of social service jobs strongly affect women's decision to seek employment. On these counts, too, Scandinavia's welfare states represent one extreme; the continental European countries', the other. The Anglo-Saxon nations are cases where both total and female labor force participation are high, but where the welfare state's direct effect is demonstrably marginal.

Second, some welfare states strongly encourage decommodification at work, while others do not. This is reflected in absence behavior. Again, the Scandinavian countries (except maybe Denmark) are the high-end extreme cases; the continental European countries lie in the middle; and the Anglo-Saxon countries (except the United Kingdom) are very low. Variations in absenteeism are likely to be associated with both entry and exit. On the entry side, the maximization of female participation will naturally also invoke greater absence rates; on the exit side, modest early retirement means the probability of more absenteeism among older workers.

Finally, welfare state dominance of the employment structure is very strong in Scandinavia and very low in both the liberal Anglo-Saxon regimes and in the continental European nations. But the reasons are not identical. In the United States, the private sector has played the role in social service employment that the welfare state did in Scandinavia. Among the continental European countries, neither the welfare state nor the private sector has managed to bring about a similar expansion in social welfare jobs. The paradox is that both the private model of the United States and the no-growth model of continental Europe owe their logic to welfare state–economy interactions.

Conclusions

Our previous discussion indicates that when we combine the cross-national behavioral characteristics within each window of the welfare state–labor market interaction, the result is a high degree of nation clustering. This indicates to us that welfare state regimes and employment regimes tend to coincide. There are, consequently, reasons to uphold our initial hypothesis and regard welfare states as fundamental forces in the organization and stratification of modern economies.

To the extent that this will be borne out in the following empirical analyses, we are left with the formidable theoretical task of recasting prevailing theories of the labor market and social stratification. Such a task cannot be undertaken at this point, yet we can begin to identify some of the major parameters for such a project. First, the lines of demarcation that once created and maintained a firm separation between the welfare state and the labor market no longer operate. The silent revolutions of the welfare state have effectively undermined not only the ideology but also the reality of an autonomous market mechanism. It is not just that social programs increasingly influence people's and firms' choices with respect to labor supply, labor demand, and work-leisure trade-offs within the labor contract. The really fundamental point is that social policy has been systematically transformed so as to deliberately reshape the clearing mechanisms in the labor market.

The transformation that has come about in the wake of the silent revolutions is far from trivial or gradual. If we briefly return to our windows, this becomes clear. Beginning with exit from employment, according to both economic theory and historical practice, the price signal constituted the key mechanism that guided both firm and worker behavior. Today, firms are—at least in many countries—unable to rationalize and shed labor without recourse to the welfare state, be it early retirement, unemployment, or active labor market policies. For the worker, the decision to retire or change jobs is similarly guided by the menu of social policy. Labor force supply decisions of women (who now begin to compose half of the total labor force in some nations) are even more intimately patterned by the welfare state, in terms of its service delivery (child care), transfer system (ability to utilize the option of absenteeism), and labor demand (social welfare jobs).

Turning to employment entry, the story is similar—a mirror image of exit. In some cases, more than a third of the labor market is no market at all in the normal sense, but instead a true politically organized system of collective goods production. Welfare state employment, of course, is also organized around the labor contract, exchanging labor time for wages. Yet, its logic is qualitatively different. The concept of productivity hardly exists, wages are to a degree determined politically, jobs are typically tenured, and employees normally enjoy substantially more autonomy, freedom, and authority over how they allocate their time and make their work-welfare choices. Rather than being a (perhaps odd) partner within the whole economy's labor market, the welfare state may indeed constitute a separate and distinct market, or even a ghetto. Its growth may signal the formation of a new type of dual economy. And, if this be the case, we arrive at a strange paradox: the seminal disintegration of the traditional state-economy boundary brought about by the modern welfare state is replaced with novel lines of demarcation. It may be that these new lines will replace the time-honored axis of industrial class conflict around which our societies are organized, our politics are mobilized, and our theories are forged.

The process of welfare state and labor market fusion explodes our orthodox conception of the equality-efficiency dilemma. This is best seen in the new macro-micro relations. At the microlevel, the firm's efficiency optimization follows the logic of maximum output with minimal input. The welfare state may offer a negative work incentive and induce the worker to retire, but when it does so it also helps underwrite firm productivity. Mass early retirement, then, can restore profits, productivity, and competitiveness among firms. Indirectly, it can also boost exports, improve the trade balance, and strengthen the national currency—all items of vital macroeconomic importance. But, when welfare policy is both micro- and macrolevel efficient in this way, it produces novel inefficiencies. The costs are suboptimal manpower utilization and a heavy financial burden on the collectivity which, in the last analysis, must be borne out of the erstwhile efficiency dividend.

If such conclusions remain within the realm of reason, our normal understanding of the welfare state must be subject to doubt. Its expansion and altered functionality cannot be grasped solely as a working class project for redistribution, equality, and welfare. Neither can the welfare state be regarded simply as a handmaiden to capitalism's (or industrialism's) many exigencies, negative by-products, or externalities. If we continue to view social policies as largely responsive solutions to pressing problems, we will be hard-pressed to dissect the dynamics of advanced capitalist democracies.

The structure of the book

We will study these labor market–welfare state interactions at two levels: at the institutional level (chapters 2 through 7) and in terms of empirical distributions (see the companion volumes entitled: *Between Work and Social Citizenship* and *The Welfare State as Employer*). The institutional level refers to the legislative setup of relevant programs, and how program characteristics have changed over time. The legislative setups, or regime characteristics according to our language convention, tap such elements as eligibility, coverage, duration, compensation levels, and financial structure. A complicating issue is that the private-public mix, and not just public components only, has a potential bearing on people's behavior. Therefore, the private-public mix is one of the elements of welfare state regimes. What we study here, in other words, is how the relationship between welfare states and labor markets has been constructed and changed at the political level; mediated by the class formation and by institutional forces. The next logical question (not dealt with in this volume) is how social policy changes affect empirical distributions, that is, how social policy affects behavior. These areas, especially the latter, are neglected but important parts of comparative research. The empirical distributions refer to actual or evolving exit-entry patterns. These may be influenced by the regime characteristics of programs (social policy effects), but no particular lines of causation are imputed in advance.

Chapters 2 through 7 discuss certain welfare state–economy interactions and the Scandinavian model from different angles. Chapter 2 belongs to a celebrated tradition by emphasizing expenditure; that is, looking at the development of welfare state spending in Scandinavia, and bringing—surprisingly—for the first time ever in comparative sociology, systematic time series about the welfare state effort of these countries (1948–87). The decompositional approach is another definite merit of the analysis. The study alerts us to, and demonstrates many of the pitfalls of the research tradition of welfare state spending. Thus, it shows how different sources (OECD, the International Labor Organization (ILO), The Flora project, and the Nordic Statistical Secretariat (NSS) provide different measures of aggregate spending. It illustrates, secondly, the limits of disaggregation, because spending categories are not uniform over time. It exposes, thirdly, that the question of differences and similarities is partly a question of calculation; that is, before or after tax. Fourthly, the chapter also demonstrates—not surprisingly—that what, exactly, should be included in the concept of welfare state spending is not self-evident. Thus, a trouble with the otherwise relatively high comparability of the Nordic Statistical Series is that negotiated components, in addition to legislated expenditure, were included only after 1974. This means that the composition of legislated and bargained elements at any given point in time is quite crucial.

Any trend toward divergence or convergence, that is, a move in the direction of a unified Scandinavian model, depends upon the method of measurement. The story becomes different if we use welfare state spending as a share of gross domestic product (GDP) or if we calculate the welfare state effort in terms of expenditure per capita at constant prices. Chapter 2 clarifies why such bewildering and contradictory results arise.

As already indicated, the chapter compares the countries in question in terms of disaggregated components and provides a wealth of detailed new knowledge on such different aspects as: old age pensions, disability pensions, sickness insurance, family allowances, unemployment compensation, and social assistance. The explanatory ambition of the chapter is modest, but it contains systematic efforts to use a method developed by the OECD to estimate the relative role that demography and generosity (the demographic versus the transfer ratio respectively) play for the differences in expenditure levels between the countries, in the various functional areas.

Chapter 3 presents another prominent approach in comparative welfare state research: the study of the distributive and redistributive outcomes of the Scandinavian welfare states. The point of departure of this chapter is the remarkable controversy concerning the equalizing impacts of the welfare state: Some authors regard the welfare state as a relatively effective instrument of equalization, others argue that the modern welfare state is mainly beneficial for the middle class, whereas others claim that the welfare state should be seen as a surface phenomenon, unable to modify basic class structures.

The chapter sensitizes us to some of the main methodological problems of this research tradition. The authors demonstrate, first, that there is indeed a long road from the formation of market income to economic welfare, a road twisting through the arenas of politics and the family. They also remind us that there are many distributions of income in a population and that, therefore, the concept of income distributions must be specified, which they do in terms of six different possible directions.

The chapter describes the redistributive impacts of the welfare states of Sweden, Norway and Finland, and compares these impacts with other countries (the United States, the United Kingdom, Canada, and Israel) in the Luxembourg Incomes Study (LIS), which is definitely the most comparable international data set available. The chapter also carefully discusses possible explanations with regard to variations in income inequality between various countries. The study suggests that political factors may be relatively important. One of the proximate political causes of the variation of income inequality is the welfare state, the mere size of which is a significant variable.

Chapter 4 is conceptual and calls for a political economy approach. This means that the crucial concepts of that approach, class, state, market, democracy, and their interaction, should be reintroduced in our intellectual efforts to understand the modern welfare state. It argues that the crucial research questions were formulated 100 years ago: To what extent does the welfare state modify the class structure, and thus radically change capitalist society? and What are the most important determinants of the development of the welfare state? The chapter provides, first, a critical summary of the state of the art in the comparative sociology of the welfare state. Esping-Andersen distinguishes, examines, and criticizes three main theoretical models: a structuralist perspective, an institutional approach, and the class mobilization model. The author then argues that we need a reconceptualization of the welfare state and emphasizes three components: (1) the welfare state as decommodification through the establishment of social rights— which means that people's strategic position vis-à-vis the market changes; (2) the welfare state as a system of social stratification— which implies that welfare states potentially modify the structure of stratification; and (3) the welfare state as an institution at the interface of the state, the labor market, and the family.

Esping-Andersen argues that welfare states are very different with regard to their principles of social rights, stratification, and institutional complexes. He therefore claims that it does not make much sense to rank welfare states according to more or less. It is more appropriate to talk about different clusters or regime types. On the basis of this, the author then goes on to suggest a new mode of inquiry, and locates Scandinavia in terms of principles and processes of a welfare state, that is, in a new and broader conceptual and empirical perspective. Esping-Andersen presents three welfare state regimes, which must be understood as ideal types: the liberal/Anglo-Saxon regime, the conservative/Catholic/Continental regime; and the social democratic/Scandinavian regime. The liberal model identifies a marginal, residual role for welfare state intervention. Its aim is to preserve and cultivate market dependence by means testing and by linking long working records to entitlements. This, in turn, makes for certain likely consequences in terms of social structuration. The stratificational pattern of the market is maintained, and dualisms between the working and nonworking poor are likely to develop. The conservative model, on the other hand, reserves a definite but not necessarily preeminent role for the state. The welfare state was originally meant as an instrument of class politics, whereby the working class was divided into status-distinct program categories. But this welfare state regime type had ambitions beyond this: It was also meant to breed state loyalties and to transform capitalism into an organic society. When compared with the liberal model, this regime type leaves less room for occupational welfare, but is quite explicit about the role of the church and the family. The social democratic conception is based on the People's Home model. The crucial principle is universal rights, where the importance of previous work involvement is less salient than in the conservative regime type. This model is not based on status distinctiveness, but appeals to the working class and the middle class alike through public superannuation and a well-developed system of public social services. Here, then, the social division of welfare differs from the other regime types, since the family and intermediate institution are not regarded as the first line to the same extent. The most prominent characteristic of this regime is, perhaps, its way to link work and welfare. It is committed to full employment, and presupposes full employment, since this construction is more expensive than any other regime type.

The chapter ends with a discussion of how the different regime types can be explained. Esping-Andersen maintains that our standard explanatory models—industrialism, economic growth, capitalism, the strength of the working class—in fact appear to have little to offer. Instead, he suggests three elements: (1) the nature of the mobilization of the working class, (2) class-based coalitions or alliances, and (3) the historical institutionalization of regime characteristics. Thus, he indicates the very different relation of the influential middle class to the welfare state in the three regime types. The residual welfare state persists in the liberal regime because it leaves occupational welfare and private insurance intact. The conservative model retains its middle-class legitimacy through a status-distinct and occupational construction, and in the social democratic model the welfare state appeals to both the working class and the middle class.

Chapters 5 through 7 study the interaction of labor markets and welfare states at the institutional level. Chapter 5 provides a systematic overview of sickness insurance, maternity leave, unemployment insurance, and early retirement programs in Scandinavia, and their development with respect to three dimensions of these various programs throughout the past twenty-five years. These dimensions are eligibility, generosity, and financing. The chapter also surveys the diversification of programs from 1960 to 1985. The author points out that existing research has used the level of compensation as the predominant indicator of the relative attraction of welfare state provision. He reminds us that the difficulties of applying this indicator have often been ignored in the literature; that the questions of who is eligible, and for how long, are obviously important too; and he also advises us to take tax regulations, the family situation, and waiting days into account. The method of financing is another crucial regime component, since there are reasons to believe that, for example, employer periods would induce firms to control absenteeism, recruit healthy workers, or improve working conditions in order to reduce costs. We will not explore the fine details in this introduction. Suffice it to say that the story is one of a remarkable institutional liberalization in all the Scandinavian countries throughout the twenty-five years that are covered by the study. Kåre Hagen argues that there are very strong reasons to assume that the institutional changes of the Scandinavian welfare states during the last twenty-five to thirty years have transformed the parameters of individual labor market behavior. The social wage has reduced the importance of market incomes as a determinant of such behavior. But this does not mean that behavior is a simple function of social programs; behavior is also affected by other circumstances. Thus, one challenge for future research is to assess the relative importance of program components and other factors, over time and across countries and programs.

Chapter 6 studies sickness insurance and traces what is left out in the previous chapter: the private-public mix. The purpose is to analyze the way that public and private resources and institutions interact in the area of sickness insurance, and to find the effects of the private-public mix upon the social structure. The authors make a distinction between four different forms of income protection in case of illness, defined by their sectoral organization and the locus of control of the benefits in question: (1) private individual forms—as a consequence of the individual's general social status as farmer, capitalist, or privileged employee; (2) private collective forms of income protection, consisting of several types, such as benefit societies, occupational and bargained systems of wage continuation, and group insurance where the risks are pooled and shared; (3) public collective forms as publicly organized forms of income protection; and (4) public individual forms of income protection within the public sickness insurance system. The chapter traces in considerable and valuable detail how these four forms of income protection have grown historically in each of the Scandinavian countries—from the experimental stage of the pre–World War II situation, when different models of social policy competed—up to the current situation, where (3) (above) is the dominant type. This part of the chapter ends with a itemized specification of the present systems of sickness insurance in the different countries (coverage, compensation levels, waiting days and duration of benefits, and claimant's contribution).

This chapter looks at sickness insurance not only as a dependent, but also as an independent variable. Thus, in addition, it discusses several possible effects of the systems of income protection during sickness, such as distribution effects, stratification effects, control effects and societal effects. At this point we will only briefly mention what the first two of these effects are about. Regarding the first of these effects, the authors mention the contrafactual argument: that sickness provision has redistributive impacts if we consider a situation with no compensation. They also refer to empirical studies substantiating redistributive effects through proportional contributions, the unification of schemes, benefit ceilings, and higher incidence of sickness among the poorly paid. Bislev and Lindqvist argue that systems of sickness insurance are best understood as social institutions established through struggles where governments, employers, employees, and voluntary benefit societies—all with different goals—take part. The stratificational profile of the systems are the outcome of these struggles. The chapter presents the development of these profiles in the four countries. The authors show, for instance, how the reduction of the compensation level in Denmark recreated the large status differentials between manual and nonmanual workers in the 1980s, and how private supplements have grown very slowly, partly because the trade union federation prefers to work for an improvement of state programs instead of collective-agreement sick-pay arrangements. And they show how agrarian interests account for high coverage and low compensation levels of Finnish public sickness insurance which, in turn, has generated a specific private-public mix in that country, where firm-level benefit funds and collective agreements on sick pay loom large. The cases of Norway (until 1978) and Sweden indicate, according to the authors, that private collective wage continuation can, under certain circumstances, be a route to more equality in income protection during sickness; it does not have to widen income inequalities and nourish privilege as Titmuss (1963) feared. Rational choice theory would expect generous sickness insurance systems to produce high rates of absence. The chapter provides valuable information about the main control aspects of the public sick-pay schemes of the Scandinavian countries. It also refers to empirical studies on the effects of program changes.

Chapter 7 likewise deals with the development of the private-public mix, but here the issue is pension provision. This mix has also been ignored in previous studies of the Scandinavian model. The chapter sets out with several postulates which are substantiated in the following paragraphs: (1) the borderline between private and public is definitely not clear-cut, nor do private pensions constitute a homogeneous universe; (2) there is some justification in applying the concept of a Scandinavian model, but clearly more so in the case of basic pensions, than in terms of other parts of the pension system; (3) the relative size of private pensions has significant consequences for the economic well-being of the elderly as well as the overall inequality among them; and (4) the relative importance of private pensions structures the interests of various major interest groups, and thus has wider implications for public policy initiatives and for the political economy of the welfare state. The chapter unfolds on a continuum from the most public to the most private pension programs. The presentation begins with a discussion of the basic (minimum) pensions, followed by a section on the statutory supplementary (legislated income or work-related) schemes and a section on separate programs for government employees. The relative importance of the collective and individual private programs is then examined by looking primarily at expenditure data, followed by a section in which the benefit structure of the private-public mix is analyzed. The amount of income inequality among the elderly is also related to the relative importance of public pensions. Kangas and Palme include a greater number of countries in the comparative analysis to test hypotheses on the determinants of the private-public mix. The subsequent part of the chapter focuses on the differences in financing and the relative importance of funding in the different programs and countries.

The chapter provides a wealth of useful information on four of the Scandinavian countries (Denmark, Finland, Norway, and Sweden) and represents a remarkable achievement in terms of data which is hard to piece together. It is impossible to do justice to the fine details of this contribution here. Instead, we will call the attention to some of the main components. Kangas and Palme argue, as already mentioned, that Scandinavia constitutes a separate cluster if both the take-up rates and compensation levels of the basic pensions are taken into consideration. But the variation is substantial in terms of the relative importance of private pensions and there is more to it than mere size. Private pensions also differ in terms of coverage, administration, coordination with public schemes, distribution of benefits, and the importance of collective and private arrangements. How, then, can the inter-Scandinavian similarities and differences in the private-public mix be explained? Comparative research has shown that the relative strength of the political left was important for interpreting cross-national differences in minimum pensions. This does not imply, however, that the political right, or the center parties, have been against the basic pension reforms in the Scandinavian countries. Quite the contrary, the major reforms in this area gained unanimous support and in some cases the bourgeois parties were the most eager reformers, not least to get rid of the means testing. The authors try to explain this since these reforms violate the liberal and conservative ideals of a minimalist state.

The history of the statutory supplementary pensions was distinguished by sharper political controversies. The strength of the political left and the strategies chosen by the labor parties came to be of crucial importance for how the occupational pensions were organized. Kangas and Palme show that the strategies chosen by both the left and other actors vary across nations and over time—remarkable shifts took place even during short time periods—depending on the power resources, the need for social security, and the options which appeared to be most advantageous either from the viewpoint of social policy or from more strategic political considerations. They argue that political power constellations alone cannot directly explain the prominence of private pensions. According to this chapter, it may be more fruitful to look at the level and structure of the public pensions. The analysis confirms why. But the level and structure of the legislated pensions are not the only factors affecting the expansion of the private pensions. For one, the chapter also verifies that the formation of the labor market organizations, trade unions, and employers' confederations apparently have conditioned the development of the private schemes. Secondly, the authors emphasize that the relationship between the public and the private institutions is not uni-directional in the sense that only the public pensions affect the extent of private programs. The early occupational arrangements and their integration with the legislated systems are also important for understanding the development of the private-public mix.

References

Blau, P. M., and Duncan, O. D. 1967. *The American Occupational Structure.* New York: Wiley.
Bowles, S., and Gintis, H. 1986. *Democracy and Capitalism.* New York: Basic Books.
Colbjørnsen, T. 1986. *Dividers in the Labor Market.* Oslo: Norwegian University Press.
Cusack, T., Notermans, T., and Rein, M. 1987. *Political Economic Aspects of Public Employment.* Berlin: WZB Working Papers.
Danziger, S., Haveman, R., and Plotnik, R. 1981. "How Income Transfers Affect Work, Savings and Income Distribution." *Journal of Economic Literature,* 19:975–1028.
Esping-Andersen, G. 1987. "Institutional Accommodation to Full Employment." In H. Keman and H. Paloheimo, eds., *Coping with the Crisis.* London: Sage.
Featherman, D. L., and Hauser, R. M. 1978. *Opportunity and Change.* New York: Academic Press.
Graebner, W. 1980. *A History of Retirement.* New Haven: Yale University Press.
International Labor Organization (ILO). 1966. *Labor Statistics 1965.* Geneva: ILO.
International Labor Organization (ILO). 1975. *Labor Statistics 1975.* Geneva: ILO.
International Labor Organization (ILO). 1978. *Labor Statistics 1978.* Geneva: ILO.
Jencks, C., et al. 1982. *Inequality.* New York: Basic Books.
Lindbeck, A. 1981. *Work Disincentives in the Welfare State.* Stockholm: Institute for International Economic Studies, University of Stockholm. Reprint Series No. 176.
Nordic WEEP Data Bank. 1989. Data bank with time series data 1960–85 on employment structure, temporary absence, early retirement, and public employment. With computer application. Bergen: University of Bergen. Department of Sociology. Unpublished.
OECD. 1985. *Measuring Health Care 1960–1983.* Paris: OECD.
OECD. 1988. *Labor Force Statistics 1966–1986.* Paris: OECD.
Polanyi, K. 1957. *The Great Transformation.* Boston: Beacon Press.
Rein, M. 1985. *Women in the Social Welfare Labor Market.* Berlin: WZB Working Papers.
Salowski, H. 1980. *Individuelle Fehlzeiten in Westlichen Industrieländern.* Cologne: DIV.
———. 1983. *Fehlzeiten.* Cologne: DIV.
Schmidt, M. 1982. "The role of Parties in Shaping Macro-economic Policies."

In F. Castles, ed., *The Impact of Parties*. London: Sage.
————. 1983. "The Welfare State and the Economy in Periods of Economic Crisis." *European Journal of Political Research*, 11:1–26.
Scharpf, F. 1985. "Beschäftigungspolitische Strategien in der Krise." *Leviathan. Zeitschrift für Sozialwissenschaft*, 13, no. 1:1–22.
Shore, J., and Bowles, S. 1984. "The Cost of Labor Loss and the Incidence of Strikes." Paper. Cambridge: Department of Economics, Harvard University.
Statistiska Centralbyrån. 1972. *Reviderad bearbetning av arbetskraftsundersökningen. Årsmedeltal 1965. Redovisning enligt 1970 års tabellplan*. Stockholm: Statistiska Centralbyrån. Statistiska tabeller.
Statistiska Centralbyrån. 1973. *Årsmedeltal 1970*. Stockholm: Statistiska Centralbyrån. Utredningsinstitutet.
Statistiska Centralbyrån. 1976. *Arbetskraftsundersökningen. Årsmedeltal. Råtabeller 1975*. Stockholm: Statistiska Centralbyrån. Utredningsinstitutet.
Statistiska Centralbyrån. 1981. *Arbetskraftsundersökningen. Årsmedeltal 1980 exkl. april. Råtabeller*. Stockholm: Statistiska Centralbyrån. Utredningsinstitutet.
Statistiska Centralbyrån. 1985. *AKU. Arbetskraftsundersökningen. Årsmedeltal 1985*. Stockholm: Statistiska Centralbyrån. Utredningsinstitutet.
Therborn, G. 1986. *Why Some Peoples are More Unemployed than Others. The Strange Paradox of Growth and Unemployment*. London: Verso.
Titmuss, R. 1963. *Essays on the Welfare State*. London: Allen and Unwin.
Van Parijs, P. 1987. "A Revolution in Class Theory." *Politics and Society* 15, no. 4:453–82.
WEEP Data Bank. 1990. Data bank with time series data 1960–85 on employment structure, temporary absence, early retirement, and public employment. Florence: European University Institute. Unpublished.

2

Social Expenditure: A Decompositional Approach

MATTI ALESTALO and HANNU UUSITALO

Comparative research on the welfare state in Scandinavia

The aftermath of the economic stagnation of the mid-1970s and the subsequent crisis of the welfare state have witnessed an expansion of comparative research on the welfare state in Scandinavia as well as throughout the advanced market economies. Various approaches have been taken, different methods have been used, and results do not seem to cumulate to a significant degree.

Even the concept of the welfare state is a vague one. One important branch of research operationalizes the welfare state by its cost side and focuses on the variations of public or social expenditure, partly because of the easy access to such data, and correlates welfare expenditure with demographic, economic, and political variables in the sample of advanced industrial countries (see Uusitalo 1984, 403–22; Olsson 1987, 371–78; Pampel and Stryker 1988). This definition of the welfare state has been criticized as too narrow, neglecting the actual contents of social policies and their effects on society (Korpi 1980, 296). Consequently, many comparative studies have typically employed more subtle measures of the welfare state.

For example, in an important comparative study of the development of the Scandinavian welfare states, Gøsta Esping-Andersen and Walter Korpi (1984, 179–208; 1987, 39–74) analyze the welfare state using three key concepts: decommodification (the extent to which needs are satisfied outside the market), stratification (the extent to which status differences generated by the market are replaced in social policy), and scope (the domain of human needs satisfied by social policy). Esping-Andersen and Korpi claim that Denmark, Finland, Norway, and Sweden constitute a distinctive type of the welfare state with strong emphasis on universalism, equality, and solidarity.

Quite similarly, in his analysis of thirteen Western European countries, Peter Flora (1985, 20–22) speaks about the ideal type of "the Nordic Welfare State" (the Scandinavian countries and the United Kingdom) as an important variant of the Western welfare state consisting of universal and egalitarian income maintenance schemes, an extended public health sector, an extended comprehensive school system, and high reliance on general tax revenues in financing.

More historically oriented comparative studies of the Scandinavian countries, like those by Francis Castles (1978), Gøsta Esping-Andersen (1985), and Matti Alestalo and Stein Kuhnle (1987, 3–38), aim to capture the total economic, social, and political configurations behind the development of the Scandinavian welfare states. The research by Lars Mjøset et al. (1986) and Pekka Kosonen (1987) focuses more on economic structures and their interplay with the polity and the welfare state.

Curiously enough, we find very few comparative studies on social expenditure patterns in Scandinavia. The major exception is the study by Lars Nørby Johansen and Jon Eivind Kolberg (1985, 143–76). However, their analysis excludes Finland and Iceland and they compare the developments of the 1970s only. Similarly, Staffan Marklund's recent work (1988) contains analyses on welfare expenditure in the Scandinavian countries but focuses mainly on the crisis period from the mid-1970s onwards.

Thus, in addition to comparative statistical analyses including a larger number of countries (see, e.g., OECD 1985), and some more country-specific presentations (see, e.g., Kuhnle 1983; Alestalo, Flora, and Uusitalo 1985), and the comprehensive case studies of twelve Western European welfare states initiated and coordinated by Peter Flora (1986, 1987) including Denmark, Finland, Norway, and Sweden (Alestalo and Uusitalo 1986; Nørby Johansen 1986; Kuhnle 1986; Olsson 1986), and Olafsson's study about Iceland (1989), the development of social expenditure in the Scandinavian countries in the post–World War II era has not been thoroughly analyzed. The present study is a step in this direction.

Problem and approach

We first describe the development of social expenditure in the Scandinavian countries in a long-term perspective, covering a period of forty years, from the late 1940s to the late 1980s. Has the expansion of the welfare state taken place in a similar fashion, and has the crisis period had the same appearance? Is there a convergence toward a common Scandinavian model or are the Scandinavian countries diverging?

Social expenditure is the outcome of two factors. First, social rights, such as eligibility and benefit levels of social security schemes, and the availability of public services naturally have an impact on social expenditure. Second, social expenditure is a function of demand. When unemployment increases or a population becomes older, the respective expenditures tend to grow.

Our second task is to examine whether the inter-Scandinavian differences in social expenditure emerge from differences in the generosity of their welfare schemes or differences in the size of the target populations. To what extent are the differences between the spending levels explained by the demographic structures of these countries? Third, we hope to shed some light on the question of whether the differences are due to specific social policies or general government policies in the sense that big spenders use more of everything.

Our approach is to compare trends in the five Scandinavian countries. The first step is to compare the growth of total social expenditure, both in relation to gross domestic product (GDP) and in real terms. This allows us to examine the issue of convergence-divergence.

Quantitative research on the determinants of social expenditure has typically assumed that the same causes are effective in all major policy areas: in pension, family, and unemployment expenditures. This, of course, need not be the case (see Castles 1982, 21–96; Myles 1984, 76–99). Therefore, our second step is to disaggregate total social expenditure into its major constituents. This method of disaggregation allows us to specify those policy areas which are mainly responsible for the national variations.

The third step is to examine the proximate causes of the expenditure by applying the method of decomposition developed by the Organization for Economic Cooperation and Development (OECD). When the target populations are defined, as is the case in pension, family, and unemployment policies, this method allows us to study to what extent expenditure differences between the countries and expenditure changes over time are due to differences in the size of target populations and average benefits. Decomposition is useful because it can be applied to remove the effects of the difference in the size of target populations. This is necessary if one aims to take the fourth step of examining processes and backgrounds of policies leading to differences in benefit levels, since social policies typically do not directly focus on expenditure but on benefit levels and eligibility, which jointly determine expenditures. However, we do not proceed very far in that direction. In any case, a strategy outlined here may prove to offer a necessary complement and bridge between purely statistical studies focusing on expenditure and case studies focusing on institutional changes and their structural and political environments.

Social expenditure statistics

There are several comparative statistics for social expenditure, using somewhat different definitions and producing somewhat different results. The major statistics including the Scandinavian countries (Table 2.1) are social expenditure statistics put together by the OECD, the International Labor Organization (ILO), Peter Flora's comparative project (the Flora project), and the Nordic Statistical Secretariat (NSS). The ILO statistics concern only social security expenditure while the definitions used by the OECD and the Flora project give, on the average, somewhat higher social expenditures than the ILO and the Nordic statistics. The differences originate from the inclusion of education expenditures in the OECD definition and from the inclusion of education and housing expenditures in the definition applied in the Flora project. However, the differences do not greatly influence the ranking of the countries: in 1980 the correlations of GDP proportions are 0.92 between the OECD and the ILO, 0.90 between the OECD and the Flora project, and 0.95 between the ILO and the Flora project.

As exemplified by the figures from 1980, the OECD and the Nordic definitions provide very similar pictures about the differences between Denmark, Finland, Norway, and Sweden. Denmark and Sweden are at the same high level and Finland and Norway are at a somewhat lower level. However, the difference between Denmark and Sweden is larger

Table 2.1

Social Expenditure as a Percent of the GDP in Eighteen Advanced Market Economies, 1980 (different definitions)

Country	Definitions				Percent of OECD		
	OECD	ILO	Flora	Nordic	ILO	Flora	Nordic
Denmark	33.3	25.4	32.3	30.1	76.3	97.1	90.4
Finland	25.4	18.5	26.4	21.1	73.1	104.1	83.2
Norway	27.2	20.2	25.9	21.0	74.0	95.2	77.2
Sweden	32.5	31.9	37.4	32.5	98.1	115.3	100.0
Australia	18.6	12.1	—		65.0	—	—
Austria	27.1	22.4	32.6		82.8	120.5	—
Belgium	38.2	26.4	36.5		69.0	95.3	—
Canada	21.0	11.7	—		55.9	—	—
France	28.3	26.7	—		94.5	—	—
Germany	30.8	24.0	31.2		77.9	101.3	—
Ireland	25.6	21.2	29.1		82.7	113.3	—
Italy	26.9	18.1	26.9		67.4	100.2	—
Japan	16.9	10.1	—		59.6	—	—
Netherlands	35.5	28.4	38.4		79.8	107.9	—
New Zealand	19.4	14.4	—		74.1	—	—
Switzerland	20.0	13.9	19.3		69.6	96.3	—
United Kingdom	22.0	15.0	24.5		68.2	111.1	—
United States	20.7	12.7	—		61.2	—	—

Sources: OECD (1985); ILO (1985), 38–55; Flora (1987), 47, 109, 166, 233, 324, 393, 464, 516, 583, 647; NSS (1984).

Notes: Figures for Denmark are from 1979; figures for Australia, Canada, New Zealand, Switzerland, the United Kingdom, and the United States are from 1979–80; the figure for Germany includes wage continuation. The figure for Denmark includes civil servants' pensions.

if the ILO or the Flora definitions are used instead of Nordic or OECD statistics. In the case of Denmark, the difference between the ILO and the Nordic figures comes from a broader inclusion of unemployment schemes in the Nordic Social Security Statistics (see ILO 1985, 4, 100–102; OECD 1985, 75–76; NSS 1984, 116; Flora 1987).

Consistent with earlier research, Table 2.1 points out that the position of Denmark and Sweden as big spenders prevails albeit the definition of social expenditure. Alongside Belgium and the Netherlands, Denmark and Sweden are among the top five regardless of the definition employed. Finland and Norway fall at the middle level among the advanced Western market economies.

Data

This study is based on the "Nordic Social Security Statistics." It covers the period from 1948 to 1987 aiming to include all social security transfer payments and benefits in kind, except benefits received due to voluntary insurance schemes. Only current expenditure is included; investment expenditure is excluded. Social security expenditure has been recorded by net amounts, that is, any charges, refunds, and other income from the running of the social security system are excluded (see NSS 1984).

Due to intensive Scandinavian cooperation, comparability between the countries has improved over time, but it is not yet perfect. Detailed disaggregation leads to increasing problems of comparability. Consequently, comparability is best achieved when using only major disaggregations, as we intend to do here.

The major problem for comparability is that cash benefits are taxed differently in the Scandinavian countries. The trend in all countries has been from flat-rate tax-free benefits to taxable and income-adjusted benefits reflecting a trend from institutionalism to industrial achievement (see Titmuss 1974). The timing of these changes has, however, been different. In Denmark and Sweden, sickness and maternity cash benefits, unemployment benefits, and industrial injury benefits were greatly improved and made taxable in the first part of the 1970s, in Norway in the latter part of the 1970s, and in Finland in the first part of the 1980s. Pensions are taxable in all countries, but the limits on the maximum tax-free pension varies across countries.[1]

A related problem of comparability concerns whether the benefit is given as a transfer or as a tax relief. For example, in Finland, Iceland, and Norway there are tax reliefs for children, whereas in Denmark and Sweden they do not exist. These reliefs are included in social security expenditure.

Despite these problems, the data from the Nordic Social Security Statistics are the best available for the inter-Scandinavian comparisons. However, it is less suitable to reveal changes over time, due to changes in the social security schemes and definitions that have been renewed at various intervals. The most important change took place in the mid-1970s. Until 1974 the statistics only included publicly financed or subsidized schemes as well as types of social insurance that were compulsory under the law. From 1974 onward the statistics have also included schemes that are compulsory for large population groups under collective or other agreements. This change brought in supplementary pensions and wage continuation during sickness. Thus the statistics exaggerate the growth of social expenditure, but the exaggeration is similar in all countries and it does not invalidate comparisons between the countries.

Total social expenditure, 1948–87

There are both change and stability in the post–World War II development of social expenditure in Scandinavia. Social security expenditure has increased tremendously during the post–World War II period in relation to the GDP. It seems that some similarity among Scandinavian countries can be distinguished in this growth. Until the mid-1960s, the intercountry variation was not very large, and the proportion of GDP used for social expenditure grew fairly modestly. It was followed by an expansion period that lasted until the late 1970s. During and after the crisis of the welfare state, the GDP proportion of social expenditure has grown less, and even declined in some years (see Figure 2.1).[2]

During the expansion period, Sweden and Denmark grew apart from Finland and Norway. The crisis of the welfare state has—as far as total social expenditure is concerned—hit Denmark harder than the other countries. Consequently, the five countries currently fall into three groups: Sweden at the top; Denmark, Finland, and Norway in the middle; and Iceland, which has used the smallest proportion of its GDP for social policy throughout the post–World War II period, at the bottom. The differences are large, with Sweden spending more than twice as much as Iceland on social policies.

The growth patterns of real social expenditure are displayed in Figure 2.2. They tell a somewhat different story. Until the mid-1970s, real social expenditure grew almost identically in Denmark, Finland, Norway, and Sweden, but during and after crisis, growth rates have varied. In Denmark, real social expenditure has grown very modestly, while in Finland and in Norway, growth has been considerably higher. Sweden falls in between, yet closer to Finland and Norway.

As regards the real growth of social expenditure, Iceland again proves to be unique. From the late 1950s onwards, and particularly during the crisis, real social expenditure in Ireland has grown very quickly (see Figure 2.2).[3]

Figure 2.1. **Social Expenditure as Percent of GDP, 1948–87**

(S: Sweden; D: Denmark; F: Finland; N: Norway; I: Iceland)

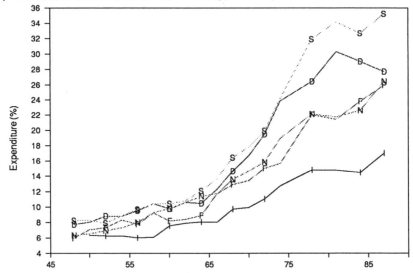

The divergent development of the GDP proportions and real social expenditure is accounted for by the variation in economic growth. In Iceland, economic growth was very fast during the 1970s and early 1980s, and therefore the rapid increase of real social expenditure did not result in a rapid growth of its GDP proportion. The Danish case is the opposite of this: although real social expenditure did not grow very fast during the crisis, the GDP proportion grew quickly, because of deteriorating economic development.

These results indicate a ''catching up'' process. In Finland, Iceland, and Norway, which in the early 1950s and the early 1960s spent a smaller proportion of their GDP on social security than Denmark and Sweden, the real growth of social expenditure has been fast, implying that they have to some extent bridged the gap to Denmark and Sweden. Figure 2.3 allows us to compare the levels of welfare effort per person in a common currency (U.S. dollars) and a common price level (by using purchasing power parities estimated by the OECD (1990). The comparison shows that the rank order of the countries has remained very stable. The only change is that Norway passed Denmark in the late 1980s. The Swedish welfare state makes the greatest effort and can be expected to be the most generous one. It is followed by Norway,

Figure 2.2. **Real Growth of Social Expenditure, 1952–87 (1952 = 1)**

(S: Sweden; D: Denmark; F: Finland; N: Norway; I: Iceland)

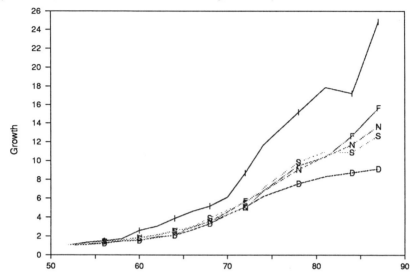

Denmark, Finland, and Iceland. The differences are large: in 1987 social expenditure per person in Sweden was nearly 50 percent greater than in Finland, and over 80 percent greater than in Iceland, (see Figure 2.3).[4]

Is there a convergence toward a common Scandinavian expenditure level, or are the countries more divergent now in their spending levels than forty years ago? A visual inspection of the Figures 2.1 and 2.3 suggests divergence. However, it is more adequate to measure dispersion in relative terms, because on higher levels of social spending, variation is almost automatically larger. Relative dispersion can be measured by the coefficient of variation (standard deviation/mean), and its change over time is shown in Figure 2.4. As regards the GDP proportions of social expenditure, we observe a process of divergence, although not a linear one. In the 1980s, the trend turned to convergence again.

The picture is partly different if we look at real social expenditure per capita. Contrary to the GDP proportion, its variation decreased in the 1970s and similar to the GDP proportion, continued to decline in the 1980s. During the last two decades the Scandinavian countries have converged toward a similar real level of social expenditure. Finland,

Figure 2.3. **Real Social Expenditure Per Capita, 1970–87**

(PPP-adjusted U.S.$, thousands, 1980 prices.
S: Sweden; D: Denmark; F: Finland; N: Norway; I: Iceland.)

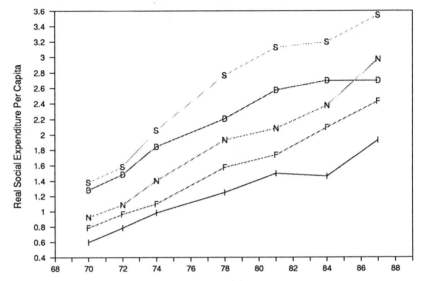

Note: The PPP-adjustment implies that the data have been converted to United States dollars using purchasing power parities. PPP's are the rates of currency conversion that equalize the purchasing power of different currencies. This means that a given sum of money, when converted into different currencies at the PPP rates, will buy the same basket of goods and services in all countries. Thus, PPP's are the rates of currency conversion which eliminate differences in price levels between countries (OECD 1990, 143).

Iceland, and Norway have, to some extent, eliminated the advantage of Denmark and Sweden, whose welfare states started to develop somewhat earlier. In general, our findings are consistent with the hypothesis that in the takeoff of the welfare state development, expenditure patterns diverge, because forerunners expand, while in the consolidation, expenditure patterns converge, because latecomers catch up.

How are the differences between the Scandinavian countries explained? As outlined above, we approach this question first, by disaggregating social expenditure into its major constituents—for old age and invalidity, sickness, family, unemployment, and social assistance and, within these functional areas, in terms of cash and kind—and second, by decomposing the expenditures, when possible. In this way we hope to shed some light on the proximate causes of the Scandinavian variations.

Figure 2.4. **Variation of Social Expenditure among Scandinavian Countries**

(□ GDP proportion; ■ real expenditure)

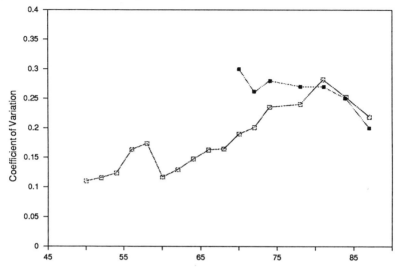

Analysis of disaggregated expenditure patterns, 1962–87

Old-age and invalidity expenditure

Old-age and invalidity expenditure covers old-age and disability pensions and includes the costs of services for these groups. For brevity, however, we use the term pension expenditure as a synonym for all old-age and invalidity expenditure. Pension expenditure is a crucial factor in understanding the development of social expenditure over time and its variations among countries. It is currently the largest social expenditure, except in Iceland, where health expenditure is larger. Pension expenditure has grown more rapidly than total social expenditure.

Because of its significance in relation to total social expenditure, pension expenditure's variations among the countries are much the same as those for total social expenditure. Of all the Nordic countries, Sweden has always used the largest share of its GDP on pensions, except in the early 1960s, when Denmark used more. Despite slower real growth, Denmark still takes second place, and is followed by Finland, Norway, and Iceland.

Table 2.2

Social Expenditure for Old Age and Invalidity; Five Nordic Countries, 1962–87

	1962	1966	1970	1974	1978	1981	1984	1987
Fixed prices (1962 = 100)								
Denmark	100	146	270	386	438	510	536	527
Finland	100	157	315	524	667	742	907	1,086
Iceland	100	143	150	333	439	492	470	710
Norway	100	143	237	409	502	534	602	719
Sweden	100	153	226	382	574	687	717	683
Percent of GDP								
Denmark	4.4	5.4	7.4	10.4	10.6	12.8	12.8	12.7
Finland	2.9	4.0	6.0	7.6	9.9	9.5	10.4	11.1
Iceland	2.6	2.7	2.7	3.8	4.4	4.3	4.0	4.8
Norway	3.8	4.5	6.3	8.9	9.6	8.7	9.1	10.7
Sweden	4.0	5.1	6.3	9.5	13.2	15.3	14.8	14.1
Demographic ratio								
Denmark	11.0	11.5	12.3	13.1	14.1	14.5	15.0	15.4
Finland	7.5	8.2	9.1	10.3	11.5	12.1	12.4	12.9
Iceland	8.3	8.5	8.9	9.1	9.7	9.9	10.1	10.4
Norway	11.4	12.2	12.9	13.5	14.4	14.9	15.6	16.1
Sweden	12.1	12.9	13.7	14.8	15.9	16.5	17.1	17.7
Transfer ratio								
Denmark	.40	.48	.50	.79	.75	.88	.85	.82
Finland	.39	.49	.66	.74	.86	.79	.84	.86
Iceland	.30	.31	.30	.41	.41	.42	.40	.46
Norway	.32	.35	.47	.66	.67	.58	.58	.66
Sweden	.32	.38	.39	.64	.82	.93	.87	.80
Coefficient of variation for								
Total social expenditure	.13	.16	.19	.24	.24	.28	.25	.22
Old age expenditure	.19	.22	.28	.29	.30	.37	.36	.30
Transfer ratio	.10	.16	.25	.20	.20	.26	.27	.20

Sources: OECD (1989; 1990); NSS (1965–1989). (For full references, see Reference list, Nordisk Statistisk Skriftserie.)

Notes: In 1974 compulsory additional pensions due to negotiated agreements were included in pension expenditure. The Finnish expenditure figures before 1974 include some pension types which were included in the other countries only after 1974; demographic ratio: percent of population over sixty-five years of age; transfer ratio: pension expenditure per population over sixty-five years of age to GDP per capita.

The variation of the GDP proportion of pension expenditure among the Scandinavian countries is larger than the variation of total social expenditure. To what extent is this accounted by the fairly large differences in the demographic structures? For example, in 1987, 17.7 percent of the population in Sweden was over sixty-five years of age, while in Iceland the respective proportion was 10.4 (see Table 2.2).

The impact of demographic differences and pension levels can be distinguished by decomposing pension expenditure into two components: a demographic component—representing the proportion of people in need for these transfers and services—and a transfer component—representing the average level of transfers and services consumed by those in need (OECD 1976, 1977; Flora 1986).[5] In the application utilized here, the demographic ratio is the proportion of the population over sixty-five years of age, and the transfer ratio is the proportion of pension expenditure per older citizens to GDP per capita.[6]

Transfer ratios help remove the differences in demography both between countries and over time. They can be interpreted to represent pension expenditure in the standard population. A transfer ratio of 1.00 means that social expenditure for the old is the same as the GDP per capita, and a transfer ratio below 1.00 implies that older citizens get less than the GDP per capita (assuming that all their income comes from public transfers).

The coefficient of variation for transfer ratios is much smaller than for pension expenditure, demonstrating that the differences in demographic structures between the Scandinavian countries explain a part of the variation in pension expenditure. This means that if the Scandinavian countries had the same proportion of elderly citizens, pension expenditure would vary no more than social expenditure in general.

The rest of the variation in total expenditure is explained by differences in transfer ratios, or to put it more boldly, by generosity differences. Transfer ratios improved rapidly throughout Scandinavia during the expansion period, except in Iceland. During and after the crisis, the upward trend has turned to yearly fluctuations. Denmark, Finland, and Sweden are more generous than Norway, which again is ahead of Iceland.

Further disaggregation into various types of pension expenditure would be necessary in order to understand the causes of the differences in transfer ratios between the countries (cf. chapter 7 in this volume).

Table 2.3

**Decomposition of GDP Proportions of Pension Expenditure;
Five Nordic Countries, 1962–87**

	Denmark	Finland	Iceland	Norway	Sweden
1962–70					
Expenditure change	3.0	3.1	0.1	2.5	2.3
Due to demographic change	0.5	0.6	0.2	0.5	0.5
Due to transfer change	2.2	2.0	−0.1	1.8	1.6
Interaction	0.3	0.4	−0.0	0.2	0.2
1974–87					
Expenditure change	2.3	3.5	1.0	1.8	4.6
Due to demographic change	1.8	1.9	0.5	1.7	1.9
Due to transfer change	0.4	1.3	0.4	0.1	2.3
Interaction	0.1	0.3	0.1	0.0	0.4

Sources: OECD (1989; 1990); NSS (1965–89). (For full references, see Reference list, Nordisk Statistisk Skriftserie.)

Anyway, it is interesting to note that fairly similar transfer ratios can come out of fairly different welfare regimes toward the elderly. Denmark has high expenditure due to national pensions and services for the old and disabled. In fact, services for the elderly people account for more than one-fourth of all old-age and invalidity expenditure in Denmark, while in the other countries their share is only about one-tenth. In Finland and Sweden supplementary pensions have the major role. Norway lies in between. The Danish peculiarity comes from the fact that its supplementary pension scheme is flat-rated, while in Finland, Norway, and Sweden it is income-graduated (Alestalo and Uusitalo 1986, 209–11; Nørby Johansen 1986, 310–12; Kuhnle 1986, 130–31; Olsson 1986, 18–20). Iceland has clearly the lowest transfer ratio. It seems that this is not due to a lower replacement level of old-age pensions, but rather to the small proportion of disability pensions and to the less developed services for the elderly (Olafsson 1989).

The significance of demographic and transfer ratios for the development of pension expenditure over time also varies across countries. Table 2.3 includes a decomposition of pension expenditure for the expansion period of the welfare state, and for the crisis and its aftermath. In general, during the expansion period transfer change was more important, while during the crisis the demographic change had a greater impact on expenditure. There are exceptions, however. In Iceland, the change in the demographic ratio was important for the increase of pension expenditure in both periods. The other exception is Sweden, where the improvement of the transfer ratio had a greater impact in the crisis period. The figures for the other three countries fall in between: in Denmark, Finland, and Norway the transfer ratio grew quite rapidly during the 1960s and early 1970s, but after 1974, the demographic ratio has been a more important determinant for pension expenditure.

Three conclusions need to be emphasized. First, pensions tend to increase the variation of social expenditure between the Scandinavian countries. This is, however, due to demography. If the countries had the same proportion of elderly population, pension expenditure would vary less than total social expenditure. Second, the distinction of the expansion period and the crisis period is more clear, if transfer ratios are considered instead of total pension expenditure, for the obvious reason that the average benefit level is liable to political adjustment, while demography—at least in the short run—is not. Third, the crisis has affected the countries differently; Denmark more than the others.

Sickness and health expenditure

In Finland and Iceland sickness and health expenditure has grown very rapidly since the early 1960s. Their spending in this category has thus approached that of the other countries. Denmark, on the other hand, has increased its health expenditure only modestly. As a consequence, the rank order of the countries has changed since the early 1960s. As in the case of pensions, Sweden has been at the top all the time, but Denmark, which until the mid-1970s held second place, has been passed by all the other countries. Currently Norway uses the second largest share of GDP for health, followed by Iceland and Finland.

This development decreased the intercountry differences in sickness and health expenditure until 1984, as shown by the coefficients of variation in Table 2.4. In recent years the development has been towards divergence, because the leading nations, Sweden and Norway,

Table 2.4

Social Expenditure for Sickness and Health; Five Nordic Countries, 1962–87

	1962	1966	1970	1974	1978	1981	1984	1987
Fixed prices (1962 = 100)								
Denmark	100	151	246	369	411	369	327	308
Finland	100	176	285	524	588	643	832	1,000
Iceland	100	157	240	602	793	919	945	1,370
Norway	100	129	207	373	518	581	625	763
Sweden	100	157	268	380	499	499	478	599
Percent of GDP								
Denmark	3.8	4.8	5.7	7.8	7.8	7.3	6.2	5.9
Finland	2.0	3.0	3.7	5.1	5.9	5.7	6.6	7.1
Iceland	2.4	2.7	4.0	6.4	6.8	7.3	7.5	8.6
Norway	3.5	3.7	5.1	7.5	9.1	8.8	8.8	10.5
Sweden	4.1	5.3	7.5	9.6	11.6	11.3	10.0	12.6
Cash benefits (percent of GDP)								
Denmark	0.2	0.2	0.6	1.7	2.1	1.8	1.1	1.2
Finland	0.1	0.7	1.1	—	1.2	1.1	1.3	1.6
Iceland	0.1	0.1	0.1	1.6	1.5	1.6	1.5	1.7
Norway	0.5	0.4	1.6	1.6	2.3	2.5	2.7	3.1
Sweden	0.8	1.0	1.6	3.9	4.7	4.1	3.3	2.3
Services (percent of GDP)								
Denmark	2.3	3.2	3.7	—	5.8	5.6	5.1	4.6
Finland	1.9	2.4	2.7	3.1	4.8	4.6	4.4	5.5
Iceland	1.1	1.3	0.5	4.7	5.3	5.8	6.0	7.0
Norway	1.3	1.4	3.4	—	6.9	6.3	6.1	7.4
Sweden	2.6	3.6	4.9	5.7	7.0	7.2	6.7	10.3
Coefficients of variation								
Total	.13	.16	.19	.24	.24	.28	.25	.22
Sickness	.26	.26	.26	.21	.24	.23	.18	.27
Total sickness	.09	.16	.20	.29	.30	.37	.36	.29

Sources: OECD (1990); NSS (1965–89). (For full references, see Reference list, Nordisk Statistisk Skriftserie.)

Notes: Figures for Finland (1984) are from 1983 except total health expenditure, which is for 1984; in 1974 wage continuation during sickness was included in statistics.

have increased their expenditure, while in Denmark the GDP proportion has continued to decline.

In terms of sickness and health expenditure, the distinction between expansion and crisis periods is as clear as in the case of pensions. Even here it seems that Denmark has reacted most forcefully to the changed economic situation. In 1982 sickness benefits were frozen and one waiting day was reintroduced in sickness insurance (see Nørby Johansen 1986, 361–66). In Sweden, a similar attempt was made in 1982 but in the same year, after the Social Democratic comeback, the law was abolished (see Olsson 1986, 84–89; Marklund 1988, 41–43).

In all Nordic countries, health services cost more than cash transfers. As regards Finland, it has been estimated that the most important factors behind the growth of health care expenditure have been the increase in the availability of services (i.e., increases in the number of hospital beds and doctors) and the changes in care practices (i.e., changes in hospital technology). Factors like population change (increase of population and its aging), growth of real wages, and social security payments have been of minor importance (Marjanen and Vinni 1986). Partly as an effort to lower costs, the shift from in-patient to out-patient health care has taken place in most countries (NCM 1988, 323).

The variations in sickness and health expenditure among Scandinavian countries diminish the differences among these countries in total social expenditure (except in the 1960s). This is because Iceland, which in general is a low spender, is generous with its health expenditures, and because Denmark, which in general spends a great deal on social policies, does not spend particularly much on health.

Family expenditure

A common feature of all Scandinavian countries today is that family policy is much less costly than pension and health policies (cf. Flora 1985, 20–22). However, the development of family expenditure reveals interesting differences. In Finland and Iceland, the expansion period of the welfare state witnessed a decline of the GDP proportion of family expenditure, whereas during and after the crisis, considerable increase has taken place. In Norway and Sweden, a more or less

Table 2.5

Social Expenditure for Families; Five Nordic Countries, 1962–87

	1962	1966	1970	1974	1978	1981	1984	1987
Fixed prices (1962 = 100)								
Denmark	100	122	249	292	288	311	303	333
Finland	100	109	123	153	229	263	379	519
Iceland	100	102	110	158	294	318	300	466
Norway	100	123	358	328	421	624	639	900
Sweden	100	146	193	291	344	352	372	410
Percent of GDP								
Denmark	2.0	2.0	3.0	3.2	2.8	3.2	3.0	3.3
Finland	2.0	1.9	1.6	1.5	2.4	2.4	3.1	3.8
Iceland	2.2	1.6	1.7	1.5	2.3	2.3	2.1	2.7
Norway	0.9	0.9	2.2	1.6	1.8	2.3	2.2	3.1
Sweden	2.0	2.4	2.7	3.6	3.9	3.9	3.9	4.2
Demographic ratio								
Denmark	24.2	23.8	23.3	22.7	21.8	20.3	18.8	17.7
Finland	29.1	26.7	24.6	22.4	21.0	20.0	19.5	19.3
Iceland	35.0	34.3	32.6	30.7	28.4	27.2	26.5	25.5
Norway	25.3	24.7	24.5	24.0	22.9	21.8	20.4	19.3
Sweden	21.5	20.9	20.9	20.7	20.3	19.2	18.3	17.9
Transfer ratio								
Denmark	.08	.08	.13	.14	.13	.16	.16	.19
Finland	.07	.07	.07	.07	.11	.12	.16	.20
Iceland	.06	.05	.05	.05	.08	.08	.08	.11
Norway	.04	.04	.09	.07	.08	.11	.11	.16
Sweden	.09	.11	.13	.17	.19	.20	.21	.23
Coefficient of variation for								
Total social expenditure	.13	.16	.19	.24	.24	.28	.25	.22
Family expenditure	.26	.28	.24	.41	.27	.23	.23	.15
Transfer ratio	.29	.39	.34	.49	.35	.31	.32	.24

Sources: OECD (1989; 1990); NSS (1965–89). (For full references, see Reference list, Nordisk Statistisk Skriftserie.)
Notes: Demographic ratio: percent of population under fifteen years of age; transfer ratio: family expenditure per population under fifteen to GDP per capita.

continuous upward trend can be observed. The Danish figures show growth during the 1960s, and stability after that (see Table 2.5).

There is no clear trend toward convergence or divergence in family expenditure among Scandinavian countries. It seems that a process of divergence took place from 1962 to 1974, after which the countries have become more similar. The variation in family expenditure has been greater than that of the total social expenditure until the late 1970s, but in the 1980s the Scandinavian countries were more similar. During the expansion period, family expenditure tended to increase intra-Scandinavian differences in total social spending, whereas the opposite was true after the late 1970s.

To what extent are these differences accounted for by demographic differences? In 1987 the proportion of the population under fifteen years of age—which is used here as the basis for the need of family support—was 25.5 percent in Iceland but only 17.9 percent in Sweden. Because Sweden spends more on family policy than does Iceland, the differences between the countries are larger if demographic differences are controlled for. In family policy, demographic differences decrease the differences between the countries.

Transfer ratios allow us to compare the welfare effort per child. In all countries the trend has been upwards, in both the expansion and the crisis periods. Sweden has been most generous toward children all the time, while Finland and Denmark shared second place during the 1980s. Norway is next, followed by Iceland, which spends less than half of what Sweden spends.

The differences between the countries are partly explained by the different mix of cash and kind benefits. Like in pension policy, Denmark proves to be a welfare service state (see Kohl 1981, 314). During the 1980s, the level of its cash benefits was lower than in the other countries, whereas its family service expenditure was as high as Sweden's. Iceland and Norway lean heavily on cash transfers, the level of which is higher than in Finland. However, they spend much less on services than Finland, and consequently their total family expenditure remains lower (see Table 2.6).

The decreasing proportion of children in all countries has naturally lowered family expenditure. More interestingly, changes in the transfer ratios have generally had a greater impact on expenditure growth during the crisis of the welfare state than during the expansion period. Remember that in pension policy it was the opposite. The ups and downs of benefit levels of different policies do not follow a common pattern. Thus, instead of a general crisis, the question concerns a more subtle pattern of policy choices.

Table 2.6

Decomposition of Changes in GDP Proportions of Family Expenditure; Five Nordic Countries, 1962–70 and 1974–84

	Denmark	Finland	Iceland	Norway	Sweden
1962–70					
Expenditure change	1.0	−0.4	−0.5	1.3	0.7
Due to demographic change	−0.1	−0.3	−0.1	−0.0	−0.1
Due to transfer change	1.1	−0.1	−0.4	1.4	0.8
Interaction	−0.0	0.0	0.0	−0.0	−0.0
1974–87					
Expenditure change	0.1	2.3	1.2	1.5	0.6
Due to demographic change	−0.7	−0.2	−0.3	−0.3	−0.5
Due to transfer change	1.0	2.9	1.8	2.3	1.3
Interaction	−0.2	−0.4	−0.3	−0.4	−0.2

Sources: OECD (1989; 1990); NSS (1965–89). (For full references, see Reference list, Nordisk Statistisk Skriftserie.)

Unemployment expenditure

Unemployment expenditure is the result of measures to diminish unemployment through vocational training, relief work, and employment service, and covers unemployment insurance as well. It reflects the overall employment situation, the level of unemployment compensation, and the quality of services for the unemployed.

The common pattern is a considerable increase in unemployment expenditure in the late 1970s and early 1980s, reflecting, at least partially, increasing unemployment. Especially in Denmark, unemployment expenditure has increased significantly (Esping-Andersen 1985, 213–14, 240–43; Esping-Andersen and Korpi 1987, 62). It is the only country that spends more on unemployment than on the family. While the Danish welfare state has deteriorated during the last two decades as compared to those of the other Nordic countries, its deterioration does not affect its unemployment expenditure. Iceland is another exception:

Table 2.7

Social Expenditure for Unemployment; Five Nordic Countries, 1962–87

	1962	1966	1970	1974	1978	1981	1984	1987
Fixed prices (1962 = 100)								
Denmark	100	82	207	631	1,408	1,939	2,066	1,462
Finland	100	1,214	922	1,260	3,124	2,725	2,957	4,183
Iceland	100	186	1,172	717	968	993	2,874	2,035
Norway	100	108	131	114	297	417	814	598
Sweden	100	166	354	442	950	917	1,942	956
Percent of GDP								
Denmark	0.5	0.3	0.6	1.7	3.5	5.0	5.0	3.6
Finland	0.1	1.2	0.7	0.7	1.8	1.4	1.3	1.7
Iceland	0.0	0.0	0.2	0.1	0.1	0.1	0.2	0.1
Norway	0.3	0.3	0.3	0.2	0.5	0.6	1.1	0.8
Sweden	0.4	0.5	0.9	1.1	2.1	2.0	2.1	1.9
Unemployment ratio								
Denmark	—	—	0.34	1.74	4.17	5.39	4.52	3.04
Finland	0.62	0.72	0.89	0.83	3.62	2.65	3.24	2.64
Iceland	—	0.05	0.54	0.19	0.18	0.17	0.63	0.24
Norway	0.41	0.32	0.31	0.63	0.84	0.98	1.47	1.07
Sweden	—	0.76	0.73	0.98	1.14	1.30	1.63	1.00
Transfer ratio								
Denmark	—	—	1.76	0.98	0.84	0.93	1.11	1.18
Finland	0.16	1.67	0.79	0.84	0.50	0.53	0.40	0.64
Iceland	—	0.00	0.37	0.53	0.56	0.59	0.32	0.42
Norway	0.73	0.94	0.97	0.32	0.60	0.61	0.75	0.75
Sweden	—	0.66	1.23	1.12	1.84	1.54	1.29	1.90
Coefficient of variation for								
Total social expenditure	.13	.16	.19	.24	.24	.28	.25	.22
Unemployment expenditure	.71	.88	.48	.78	.76	.94	.85	.73
Transfer ratio	—	.92	.45	.39	.58	.45	.49	.54

Sources: OECD (1989; 1990); NSS (1965–89). (For full references, see Reference list, Nordisk Statistisk Skriftserie.)

Notes: Unemployment ratio: percent of population unemployed; transfer ratio: unemployment expenditure per unemployed to GDP per capita; unemployment ratio for Sweden in 1987 is not comparable with previous years.

Table 2.8

Decomposition of Changes in GDP Proportions of Unemployment Expenditure; Five Nordic Countries, 1962–70 and 1974–87

	Denmark	Finland	Iceland	Norway	Sweden
1962–70					
Expenditure change	0.1	0.6	0.2	0.0	0.5
Due to unemployment change	—	0.0	—	−0.1	—
Due to transfer change	—	0.4	—	0.1	—
Interaction	—	0.2	—	−0.0	—
1974—87					
Expenditure change	1.9	1.0	0.0	0.6	0.8
Due to unemployment change	1.3	1.5	0.0	0.1	0.0
Due to transfer change	0.4	−0.2	0.0	0.3	0.8
Interaction	0.3	−0.4	0.0	0.2	0.0

Sources: OECD (1989; 1990); NSS (1965–89). (For full references, see Reference list, Nordisk Statistisk Skriftserie.)

Both the level of unemployment and its costs have remained at a very low level at all times.

The differences between the countries are great. The coefficient of variation of the GDP proportion of unemployment expenditure between the countries is much larger than for any other item of social expenditure. As stated above, this is to some extent explained by differences in unemployment. Table 2.7 shows that from the mid-1970s on, the coefficient of variation for transfer ratios has been much lower than for unemployment expenditure.

The difference between Denmark and Sweden is fully explained by their unemployment situations. Expenditure per unemployed is higher in Sweden than in Denmark. Similarly, even if Finland spends more on unemployment policies than does Norway, the welfare effort per unemployed is clearly higher in Norway, although the difference declined in the 1980s. The differences in the transfer ratios are large: In 1984, Sweden spent three times more per unemployed than Finland and four times more than Iceland (see Olafsson 1989).[7]

The fluctuation of the transfer ratios from year to year is considerable, and is largely accounted for by changes in the rates of unemployment. It is obvious that the growth of unemployment expenditure is not significantly determined by the improvement of transfer ratios. Rather, the worsening of the employment situation is the major explanation, at least after the economic recession (see Table 2.8).

The differences in unemployment policies among the countries are even larger than Table 2.7 indicates. Contrary to its pension and family policies, Denmark is clearly a cash welfare state as far as unemployment expenditure is concerned. In 1987 unemployment insurance accounted for about 75 percent of all unemployment expenditure and the other 25 percent was spent on employment services, training, and relief work. At the other pole is Sweden, where more than 60 percent of the expenditure is used for services for the unemployed (see Nørby Johansen and Kolberg 1985, 158–66; Marklund 1988, 90–92).

Social assistance

Social assistance is the last resort in the safety net of the Scandinavian welfare states to provide maintenance. It could be tempting to use the GDP proportion of social assistance as an indicator of the adequacy of the welfare state: in the highly developed welfare state it can be expected to have a minor role, whereas in less developed welfare states it can be expected to form an important source of expenditure. However, it is not as simple as that. It is true that Denmark and Sweden used very little for social assistance in the 1960s, but so did Iceland. More problematic is the development during the period of the welfare state crisis: social assistance expenditure grew very quickly especially in Denmark and Sweden, but much less in the less developed welfare states of Finland, Norway, and Iceland (see Table 2.9).

Explanation is found elsewhere. In most respects, the Scandinavian countries have similar legal statutes and practical procedures. A study comparing social assistance laws, practices, and utilization in Denmark, Finland, Norway, and Sweden suggests that Denmark has a more generous system and a more liberal definition of need, while Finland has lower levels of benefits (Tanninen and Julkunen 1988). The major proximate cause of the expenditure growth is the increase in the clientele of social assistance. For example, the proportion of families receiving social assistance grew from about 5 percent to 12 percent

Table 2.9

Social Expenditure for General Assistance; Five Nordic Countries, 1962–87

	1962	1966	1970	1974	1978	1981	1984	1987
Fixed prices (1962 = 100)								
Denmark	100	125	297	527	1,169	1,432	1,505	1,862
Finland	100	139	169	136	87	83	96	282
Iceland	100	109	222	190	172	215	300	611
Norway	100	146	179	191	269	286	394	865
Sweden	100	103	178	198	399	—	—	—
Percent of GDP								
Denmark	0.1	0.1	0.2	0.4	0.8	1.0	0.9	1.1
Finland	0.3	0.4	0.3	0.2	0.1	0.1	0.1	0.3
Iceland	0.1	0.1	0.2	0.1	0.1	0.1	0.1	0.2
Norway	0.2	0.2	0.2	0.2	0.2	0.2	0.2	0.5
Sweden	0.2	0.2	0.2	0.2	0.5	—	—	—

Sources: OECD (1990); NSS (1965–89). (For full references, see Reference list, Nordisk Statistisk Skriftserie.)

in Denmark between 1974 and 1982. Also, in Norway the proportion of families who received social assistance grew during the crisis of the welfare state period, but much less than in Denmark. In Sweden and Finland the proportion declined up through the early 1980s, but has increased somewhat after that (Marklund 1988, 52–54). Unemployment, dissolution of families, and inadequate social insurance are perhaps the major causes of these trends.

Stability and change in the Scandinavian welfare states

Our survey of social expenditure in Scandinavia shows both the stability of the differences and the similarities of the changes. The rank order of the countries according to total social expenditure has not changed considerably during the post–World War II period. Sweden has been the leading welfare state spender for most of the time, and only occasionally has Denmark reached the same level. The major change is due to Denmark, which during and after the crisis of the welfare state, has somewhat lost its position and declined to the level of Norway and Finland. In Iceland social expenditure has been the lowest when compared to the GDP. In real terms the rank order of the countries has remained otherwise stable but Norway has passed Denmark.

The distinction between the development of social expenditure in relation to the GDP and in real terms needs to be emphasized. One is easily impressed by the rapid growth of the GDP proportion of social expenditure in Denmark and Sweden especially from the early 1970s onwards. However, in real terms social expenditure has grown the most slowly in Denmark. Iceland is the opposite: the GDP proportion of social expenditure has increased most modestly, but the real expenditure growth has been largest. To look at GDP proportions only, as has been done in much of the research, can be misleading, and should be supplemented by a comparison of real expenditure.

Even if the rank order of the countries has not altered dramatically since World War II, the degree of change has varied between the countries. Is there a convergence toward the Scandinavian model, or is the question rather of a process toward divergence? Our findings suggest growing differences in the GDP proportions from the early 1950s to the late 1970s, after which the countries have become more similar. If one looks at the real social expenditure, a converging process started even earlier. Because the expansion of the welfare state started somewhat earlier in Denmark and Sweden than in Finland, Iceland, and Norway, a diverging process is a natural outcome. Once latecomers caught up, a more unified Scandinavian model emerged.

However, the degree of convergence varies in different policy areas. In unemployment policy, the common Scandinavian model is not a reality. The countries differ greatly, and there is no clear trend. Denmark, which has had the highest unemployment levels after the economic recession, uses much more than the other countries for cash benefits, while in Sweden services for the unemployed are emphasized. In pension expenditure, the countries have also differed, even though this trend turned between 1984 and 1987. Since the early 1970s, a slow process of convergence has taken place in sickness and health expenditure as well as in family policy.

The disaggregation of expenditures by function and into cash and kind reveals that the differences between the countries have a important global element, that is, they cannot be traced back to single policies. Sweden, the leading welfare state, uses more resources on nearly all major programs, and Iceland, whose welfare state is smallest, uses less than other countries for nearly all programs.

Also, the impact of various policies on convergence varies. Pension expenditure has an increasing impact on the variation of total social expenditure. However, health and family expenditures have had a differing impact in different periods. Health expenditure increased the variation of total social expenditure in the 1960s and family expenditure up to the late 1970s, but after that both have had an equalizing impact on total expenditure.

The importance of demographic factors for social expenditure can be studied by decomposing pension, family, and unemployment expenditures. Demographic differences between the countries increase the variation of pension and unemployment expenditure, but decrease the variation of family expenditure. Even if the effects of demographic variation to some extent balance each other out, their overall effect is to increase the total social expenditure differences.

Decomposition is also useful when examining the expenditure growth in the expansion and crisis periods of the welfare state. During the expansion period, the growth of pension expenditure is largely explained by the improvement of average benefits, while during the crisis, the increase of the proportion of elderly people is more important. As regards unemployment expenditure, its growth after the mid-1970s is in most countries mainly accounted for by increased unemployment. However, in the area of family policy the pattern is different. During the crisis of the welfare state, the average welfare effort per child improved more than during the expansion phase.

What kind of country profiles emerge from this survey? During the first post–World War II decade, the differences between the countries were not very significant. In the early 1960s, Denmark and Sweden became the pioneers of welfare state development. However, Denmark has gradually lost this position, and is currently at the same level as Norway and Finland. Its economic growth has been slower than that of the other countries, and it has been hit most by the crisis of the welfare state. Marklund's study, based on an analysis of the development of social rights, also suggests that this has been the case (1988, 30–43). Unemployment and social assistance expenditures, especially, have increased much more than in the other countries. Denmark also has an interesting mix of cash and services. In old age and family policy, its service sector is well developed, whereas in unemployment policy it leans heavily on cash benefits.

In Finland and Norway social expenditure has grown fairly similarly. Currently, together with Denmark, these two countries form the middle category of the Scandinavian welfare states. Finland has higher transfer ratios in old-age and family policies; Norway in unemployment policies. Expenditure figures and transfer ratios indicate that both welfare states survived fairly well during the crisis.

Iceland deviates most from the Scandinavian model. It continues to have the smallest welfare state, although in real terms expenditure growth has been very impressive. Also, its profile is different from the other countries. Iceland uses nearly twice as much for sickness and health as for old age and invalidity.

Not unexpectedly, Sweden proves to be the leading welfare state. For decades its social expenditure has been higher than in the other countries, and it uses more resources on nearly all major programs. Even the real expenditure growth from the early 1960s has been fairly close to that of Finland and Norway, although its initial level was higher and its economic growth has been fairly modest. In general, its benefit levels are above the other countries'. Despite being a top spender in the world, Sweden has not been severely affected by the crisis of the welfare state.

Notes

1. The Nordic Committee on Social Security Statistics has commissioned a special study about the effects of taxation on benefits and expenditure (Søndergard and Sørensen 1984). The study was made for the year 1980. It estimated net benefit levels for the major cash programs and the GDP proportions of social expenditure when the net principle was applied. When the different tax regulations of social security benefits are taken into account, the differences between the countries become smaller: Sweden and Denmark are not as far ahead of Norway and Finland as the Nordic Social Security Statistics indicates. This implies that our comparisons exaggerate the differences between the countries. Obviously, this exaggeration was at its largest in the mid-1970s, whereas it has declined in the 1980s.

2. Sources: Flora 1987, 55, 119, 177, 241; Central Statistical Office of Finland 1968, 19; OECD 1990; Sosiaali- ja terveysministeriö 1988, 15, 27; Statistiska Centralbyrån 1952, 412; United Nations (no year), 2, United Nations 1979; and Nordic Council of Ministers 1988, 316.

3. Ibid.

4. Ibid.

5. The OECD method also allows us to examine the impact of eligibility, but our applications are based on the assumption that all persons belonging to target groups are covered by the scheme in question.

6. This decomposition is only a first approximation. Pensions are not limited to those over sixty-five years of age. Even the general old-age pension age varies: it is sixty-seven in Denmark, Iceland, and Norway, but sixty-five in Finland and Sweden. Furthermore, old-age and invalidity expenditure also includes other pension schemes, like disability and family pensions, plus services typically but not only consumed by the elderly. Therefore, the transfer ratio is only a proxy measure of the effort of the welfare state toward the old and disabled.

7. It should be observed, however, that transfer ratios in this case are inexact because employment expenditure may be used to employ or retrain people and thus withdraw them from the ranks of the unemployed. Therefore, the target population of unemployment expenditure is considerably larger than the unemployed.

References

Alestalo, M., Flora, P., and Uusitalo, H. 1985. "Structure and Politics in the Making of the Welfare State: Finland in Comparative Perspective." In R. Alapuro et al., eds., *Small States in Comparative Perspective. Essays for Erik Allardt.* Oslo: Norwegian University Press, 188–210.

Alestalo, M., and Kuhnle, S. 1987. "The Scandinavian Route: Economic, Social, and Political Developments in Denmark, Finland, Norway, and Sweden." In R. Erikson et al., eds., *The Scandinavian Model. Welfare States and Welfare Research.* Armonk, NY and London: M. E. Sharpe, 3–38.

Alestalo, M., and Uusitalo, H. 1986. "Finland." In P. Flora, ed., *Growth to Limits. The Western European Welfare States Since World War II.* Berlin and New York: de Gruyter, 200–92.

Castles, F. G. 1978. *The Social Democratic Image of Society. A Study of the Achievements and Origins of Scandinavian Social Democracy in Comparative Perspective.* London: Routledge and Kegan Paul.

———. 1982. "The Impact of Parties on Public Expenditure." In F. G. Castles, ed., *The Impact of Parties. Politics and Policies in Democratic Capitalist States.* London: Sage, 21–96.

Central Statistical Office of Finland. 1968. *National Accounting in Finland in 1948–64.* Helsinki: Central Statistical Office of Finland.

Esping-Andersen, G. 1985. *Politics Against Markets. The Social Democratic Road to Power.* Princeton: Princeton University Press.

Esping-Andersen, G., and Korpi, W. 1984. "Social Policy as Class Politics in Post-War Capitalism: Scandinavia, Austria, and Germany." In J. H. Goldthorpe, ed., *Order and Conflict in Contemporary Capitalism.* Oxford: Clarendon Press, 179–208.

———. 1987. "From Poor Relief to Institutional Welfare States: The Development of Scandinavian Social Policy." In R. Erikson et al., eds., *The Scandinavian Model. Welfare States and Welfare Research.* Armonk, NY and London: M. E. Sharpe, 39–74.

Flora, P. 1985. "On the History and Current Problems of the Welfare State." In S. N. Eisenstadt and O. Ahimeir, eds., *The Welfare State and its Aftermath*. London and Sydney: Croom Helm, 11–30.

Flora, P., ed., 1986 and 1987. *Growth to Limits. The Western European Welfare States Since World War II*. Vol. 1 (1986), *Sweden, Norway, Finland, Denmark*. Vol. 4 (1987), *Appendix (Synopses, Bibliographies, Tables)*. Berlin and New York: de Gruyter.

International Labor Organization (ILO). 1985. *The Cost of Social Security. Eleventh International Inquiry, 1978–1980*. Geneva: ILO.

Kohl, J. 1981. "Trends and Problems in Postwar Public Expenditure Development in Western Europe and North America." In P. Flora and A. J. Heidenheimer, eds., *The Development of Welfare States in Europe and America*. New Brunswick and London: Transaction Books, 307–44.

Korpi, W. 1980. "Social Policy and Distributional Conflict in the Capitalist Democracies. A Preliminary Comparative Framework." In A. J. Heidenheimer, ed., *West European Politics* 3 (October 1980):296–316.

Kosonen, P. 1987. *Hyvinvointivaltion haasteet ja pohjoismaiset mallit*. Tampere: Vastapaino.

Kuhnle, S. 1983. *Velferdsstatens utvikling: Norge i komparativt perspektiv*. Bergen: Universitetsforlaget.

Kuhnle, S. 1986. "Norway." In P. Flora, ed., *Growth to Limits. The Western European Welfare States Since World War II*. Berlin and New York: de Gruyter, 117–96.

Marjanen, T., and Vinni, K. 1986. "Terveydenhuoltomenojen kasvun syistä Suomessa vuosina 1963–1983"(On the factors affecting the growth of health care expenditure in Finland in 1963–1983). *Official Statistics of Finland. Special Social Studies* 32, no. 118. Helsinki: Research Department, Ministry of Social Affairs and Health.

Marklund, S. 1988. *Paradise Lost? The Nordic Welfare States and the Recession 1975–1985*. Lund: Arkiv förlag.

Mjøset, L., ed., 1986. *Norden dagen derpå. De nordiske økonomisk-politiske modellene og deres problemer på 70- og 80-tallet*. Oslo: Universitetsforlaget.

Myles, J. 1984. *Old Age in the Welfare State. The Political Economy of Public Pensions*. Boston: Little, Brown and Co.

Nørby Johansen, L. 1986. "Denmark." In P. Flora, ed., *Growth to Limits. The Western European Welfare States Since World War II*. Berlin and New York: de Gruyter, 293–391.

Nørby Johansen, L., and Kolberg, J. E. 1985. "Welfare State Regression in Scandinavia? The Development of the Scandinavian Welfare States from 1970 to 1980." In S. N. Eisenstadt and O. Ahimeir, eds., *The Welfare State and its Aftermath*. London and Sydney: Croom Helm, 143–76.

Nordic Council (NC). 1967. *Yearbook of Nordic Statistics 1966*. Stockholm: Nordic Council. Vol. 5.

Nordic Council (NC). 1968. *Yearbook of Nordic Statistics 1967*. Stockholm: Nordic Council. Vol. 6.

Nordic Council (NC). 1969. *Yearbook of Nordic Statistics 1968*. Stockholm: Nordic Council. Vol. 7.

Nordic Council (NC). 1970. *Yearbook of Nordic Statistics 1969*. Stockholm: Nordic Council. Vol. 8.

Nordic Council (NC). 1971. *Yearbook of Nordic Statistics 1970*. Stockholm: Nordic Council. Vol. 9.

Nordic Council (NC). 1972. *Yearbook of Nordic Statistics 1971*. Stockholm: Nordic Council. Vol. 10.

Nordic Council of Ministers (NCM). 1973. *Yearbook of Nordic Statistics 1972*. Copenhagen: Nordic Council of Ministers and the Nordic Statistical Secretariat. Vol. 11.

Nordic Council of Ministers (NCM). 1974. *Yearbook of Nordic Statistics 1973*. Copenhagen: Nordic Council of Ministers and the Nordic Statistical Secretariat. Vol. 12.

Nordic Council of Ministers (NCM). 1975. *Yearbook of Nordic Statistics 1974*. Copenhagen: Nordic Council of Ministers and the Nordic Statistical Secretariat. Vol. 13.

Nordic Council of Ministers (NCM). 1976. *Yearbook of Nordic Statistics 1975*. Copenhagen: Nordic Council of Ministers and the Nordic Statistical Secretariat. Vol. 14.

Nordic Council of Ministers (NCM). 1977. *Yearbook of Nordic Statistics 1976*. Copenhagen: Nordic Council of Ministers, and the Nordic Statistical Secretariat. Vol. 15.

Nordic Council of Ministers (NCM). 1978. *Yearbook of Nordic Statistics 1977*. Copenhagen: Nordic Council of Ministers and the Nordic Statistical Secretariat. Vol. 16.

Nordic Council of Ministers (NCM). 1979. *Yearbook of Nordic Statistics 1978*. Copenhagen: Nordic Council of Ministers and the Nordic Statistical Secretariat. Vol. 17.

Nordic Council of Ministers (NCM). 1980. *Yearbook of Nordic Statistics 1979*. Copenhagen: Nordic Council of Ministers and the Nordic Statistical Secretariat. Vol. 18. NU A 1979:26.

Nordic Council of Ministers (NCM). 1981. *Yearbook of Nordic Statistics 1980*. Copenhagen: Nordic Council of Ministers and the Nordic Statistical Secretariat. Vol. 19.

Nordic Council of Ministers (NCM). 1982. *Yearbook of Nordic Statistics 1981*. Copenhagen: Nordic Council of Ministers and the Nordic Statistical Secretariat. Vol. 20. NU 1981:15.

Nordic Council of Ministers (NCM). 1983. *Yearbook of Nordic Statistics 1982*. Copenhagen: Nordic Council of Ministers and the Nordic Statistical Secretariat. Vol. 21. NU 1982:17.

Nordic Council of Ministers (NCM). 1984. *Yearbook of Nordic Statistics 1983*. Copenhagen: Nordic Council of Ministers and the Nordic Statistical Secretariat. Vol. 23. NU 1983:18.

Nordic Council of Ministers (NCM). 1985. *Yearbook of Nordic Statistics 1984*. Copenhagen: Nordic Council of Ministers and the Nordic Statistical Secretariat. Vol. 23. NU 1984:16.

Nordic Council of Ministers (NCM). 1986. *Yearbook of Nordic Statistics 1985*. Copenhagen: Nordic Council of Ministers and the Nordic Statistical Secretariat. Vol. 24. NU 1985:12.

Nordic Council of Ministers (NCM). 1988. *Yearbook of Nordic Statistics 1987*. Copenhagen: Nordic Council of Ministers and the Nordic Statistical Secretariat.

Nordisk Statistisk Skriftserie (NSS). 1955. *Samordning af de nordiske landes statistik vedrørende den sosiale lovgivning.* Copenhagen: Nordisk Statistisk Sekretariat, no. 2.

Nordisk Statistisk Skriftserie (NSS). 1959. *Statistikk vedrørende den sosiale lovgivning i de nordiske land 1956 (1956/57).* Oslo: Nordisk Statistisk Sekretariat, no. 6.

Nordisk Statistisk Skriftserie (NSS). 1961. *Samordnad nordisk statistik rörande sociallagstiftningen 1958 (1958/59).* Stockholm: Nordisk Statistisk Sekretariat, no. 8.

Nordisk Statistisk Skriftserie (NSS). 1965. *Sosial Trygghet i de nordiske land. Utgifter til og omfanget av visse sosiale tiltak 1962 (1962/63).* Oslo: Nordisk Statistisk Sekretariat, no. 11.

Nordisk Statistisk Skriftserie (NSS). 1971. *Sosial Trygghet i de nordiske land. Utgifter til og omfanget av visse sosiale tiltak 1968 (1968/69).* Oslo: Nordisk Statistisk Sekretariat, no. 22.

Nordisk Statistisk Skriftserie (NSS). 1973. *Social Trygghet i de nordiska Inderna. Utgifter och verksamhetens omfattning 1970 (1970/71).* Stockholm: Nordisk Statistisk Sekretariat, no. 24.

Nordisk Statistisk Skriftserie (NSS). 1978. *Sosial Trygghet i de nordiske land. Utgifter og virksomhetens omfang 1974 (1974/75).* Bergen: Nordisk Statistisk Sekretariat, no. 34.

Nordisk Statistisk Skriftserie (NSS). 1980. *Social Trygghet i de nordiska länderna. Verksamhetens omfattning, utgifter och finansiering 1978.* Stockholm: Nordisk Statistisk Sekretariat, no. 37.

Nordisk Statistisk Skriftserie (NSS). 1984. *Social Trygghet i de nordiska länderna. Omfattning, utgifter och finansiering 1981.* Helsingfors: Nordisk Statistisk Sekretariat, no. 43.

Nordisk Statistisk Skriftserie (NSS). 1986. *Social Tryghed i de nordiske lande. Omfang, udgifter og finansiering 1984.* Copenhagen: Nordisk Statistisk Sekretariat, no. 47.

Nordisk Statistisk Skriftserie (NSS). 1989. *Social Tryghed i de nordiske lande. Omfang, udgifter og finansiering 1987.* Copenhagen: Nordisk Statistisk Sekretariat, no. 50.

Olafsson, S. 1989. *The Making of the Icelandic Welfare State. A Scandinavian Comparison.* Reprint Series no. 12. Reykjavik: Social Science Research Institute.

Olsson, S. 1986. "Sweden." In P. Flora, ed., *Growth to Limits. The Western European Welfare States Since World War II.* Berlin and New York: de Gruyter, 1–116.

———. 1987. "Welfare State Research Inc.—The Growth of a Crisis Industry." *Acta Sociologica* 30, nos. 3 and 4, 371–78.

Organization for Economic Cooperation and Development (OECD). 1976. *Public Expenditure on Income Maintenance Programmes.* Paris: OECD.

———. 1977. *Public Expenditure Trends.* Paris: OECD.

———. 1985. *Social Expenditure 1960–1980. Problems of Growth and Control.* Paris: OECD.

———. 1989. *Labor Force Statistics 1962–1987.* Paris: OECD.

———. 1990. *National Accounts 1960–1988. Main Aggregates.* Vol 1. Paris: OECD.

Pampel, F. C., and Stryker, R. 1988. *State Context and Welfare Development in Advanced Industrial Democracies 1950–1980*. Working Paper Series. Iowa City: Department of Sociology, the University of Iowa.

Søndergard, J., and Sørensen, H. 1984. "Sammenligning af udgifter til sociale kontantydelser i Norden" (Comparisons of expenditure in social security cash benefits in the Nordic Countries). *Tekniske rapporter* 33. Copenhagen: Nordisk statistisk sekretariat.

Sosiaali- ja terveysministeriö. 1988. *Social Security Expenditure*. Helsinki: Sosiaali- ja terveysministeriö. Suunitteluosasto. Julkasuja 2:1988.

Statistiska Centralbyrån. 1953. *Statistical Abstract of Sweden 1952*. Stockholm: Statistiska Centralbyrån.

Tanninen, T. and Julkunen, I. 1988. "Utkomststödet i Norden." Helsinki: Sosiaalihallituksen Julkaisuja: 8.

Titmuss, R. M. 1974. *Social Policy*. London: Allen and Unwin.

United Nations. 1979. *Demographic Yearbook: Historical Supplement*. New York: United Nations.

United Nations. No year. *Statistics of National Income and Expenditure*. Statistical Papers, Series H, no. 8. New York: United Nations.

Uusitalo, H. 1984. "Comparative Research on the Determinants of the Welfare State: the State of the Art." *European Journal of Political Research* 12:403–22.

3

Income Distribution and Redistribution in the Nordic Welfare States

STEIN RINGEN and HANNU UUSITALO

Markets, politics, and families

Classical theorists sought the causes of inequality primarily in the economy: the market place, the structure of ownership, and wage dependency. In modern political economy, inequalities are commonly seen as the outcome of interacting processes in several arenas: The most important ones, in addition to the economy, are politics and family. One of the major issues in contemporary theoretical controversy is the relative importance of these arenas in explaining economic and social results. The markets versus politics issue, in particular, has attracted much attention. "Markets and politics, the invisible hand and the visible hand, can be seen as institutionalized, partly alternative, strategies or arenas for mobilization of resources, distribution of rewards and the steering of society" (Korpi 1987).

The welfare state can be seen as a set of transfer and tax policies aimed, in part, at equalizing the distribution of economic welfare in a population. As such it has been characterized as an experiment in politics and has been an attractive object of study for social scientists who want to approach the markets versus politics issue. There are diverging positions as to the success of the welfare state in this respect. Some writers interpret the welfare state as a relatively effective instrument of equalization (Ringen 1987), others as beneficial mainly for the middle class (Le Grand 1982), and others again as a surface phenomenon unable to modify basic class structures (Westergaard and Resler 1975).

While the economic and political arenas are now firmly integrated into the analysis of inequality, the incorporation of factors such as family formation, demographic structure, and labor force participation—and hence the expansion of the problem to one of markets versus politics versus families—is still tentative. Figure 3.1 suggests a frame of reference for such an analysis. Here, political factors are seen to influence, first, the distribution of income from work and capital between individuals; and second, the transformation of factor income to disposable income through transfers and taxes. The influence of family structures on the distribution of income occurs, first, in the way individual incomes add up to family income; and second, in what well-being individual family members derive from the use of aggregate family income. This is, of course, a simplified illustration—feedbacks and interactions (e.g., the effects of progressive taxation on labor supply) are not considered—but it does illustrate that there is, metaphorically speaking, a long road from the formation of market income to economic welfare, a road twisting through the arenas of politics and family.

This chapter compares income distributions in Finland, Norway, and Sweden (comparable data for the other Nordic countries, Denmark and Iceland, were not available), and compares these distributions to those of some other industrial nations. The intention is mainly descriptive but we do approach, tentatively, some questions of causality. The chapter is intended as a contribution to the markets versus politics debate, while the systematic empirical analysis of markets versus politics versus families issue is still pending.

In particular, we focus on the following questions. Have the changes in income distribution in the Nordic countries been similar or different during the last twenty years or so? Are there differences in income inequality between these countries? Where do the Nordic countries fall when using broader comparisons of income inequality? To what extent are differences in income inequality explainable by differences in the welfare state? How well do the comparisons in this sample of nations fit the expectations of major theories of income inequality? In particular, does politics matter?

The specification of income distribution

There are many distributions of income in a population. A first question for the student of income distribution is: The distribution of what

Figure 3.1. **The Impacts of Economy, Politics, and Family on the Distribution of Income**

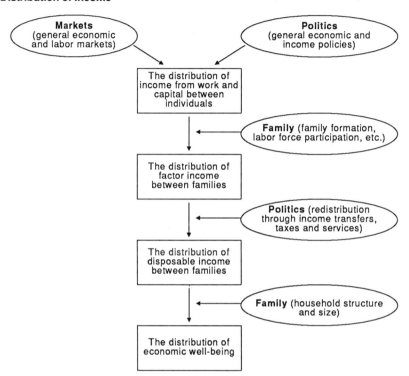

income? If we are interested in economic welfare, the most relevant concept is usually disposable income (the sum of income from all sources minus taxes), or "final income" if noncash incomes are included (see Table 3.1). The second question is: Whose disposable income? Since family members largely pool their incomes so that those who earn little or no income of their own are "subsidized" by other family members, we should mainly look at family income. In so doing, we need to take into account differences in family size and composition and economies of scale in larger families. A final question is: Between what units should we study the distribution of income? There are at least six differently specified distributions of family income, as outlined in Table 3.1.

Specification A gives the distribution of family income per family between families. This is probably the most common specification, but

Table 3.1

Alternative Specifications of Income Distribution

	Unit of Analysis	
Method of Income Accounting	Family	Individual
Per family	A	D
Per person	B	E
Per consumer unit	C	F

it is not ideal since differences in family size and composition are disregarded. Specification B corrects for differences in family size, but neglects family composition as well as economies of scale. While specification A overestimates the economic welfare of large families, specification B overestimates the economic welfare of small families. These objections apply to specifications D and E as well. In specifications C and F, consumer unit scales are used. These specifications lie between the extremes of the per-family and per-person solutions. The use of reasonable consumer unit scales is recommended.

In specifications A, B, and C, economic inequalities between families are analyzed, but the number of people affected by these inequalities is not considered. This is not reasonable. In the welfare equation of the society, which includes income distribution, each individual should hold equal weight regardless of the size of the family to which he or she happens to belong. Ideally, we should therefore take the individual, and not the family, as the unit of analysis. The economic welfare of an individual depends on the total income of the family to which he or she belongs, but only individuals are ultimately the consumers of welfare. The specification of type F is recommended, as is now widely accepted in the methodological literature (van Ginneken 1979, 368; Cowell 1984, 359; Uusitalo 1985, 163–76; O'Higgins et al. 1985; Kakwani 1986), and as was first used empirically by Gustafsson (1984).

The analysis of income redistribution

The standard method for the empirical analysis of the redistributive impact of transfers and taxes is the so-called fiscal incidence method in

Table 3.2

The Process of Income Formation in Standard Method Redistribution Analysis

	wages and salaries
+	income from self-employment
+	income from property

=	factor income
+	cash transfers

=	gross income
−	taxes

=	disposable income
−	indirect taxes
+	benefits in kind

=	final income

which the distributions of the various income concepts referring to the process of income formation are compared (see Table 3.2). The difference between the distributions before and after some policy intervention is taken as a measure of the redistributive impact of that particular intervention. For example, the redistributive impact of cash transfers is found by comparing the distribution of gross income to that of factor income, and the redistributive impact of taxes is found by comparing the distributions of disposable and gross income.

The major limitation of this approach is that it catches only direct effects; indirect effects are ignored. Implicitly, the standard method assumes that the factor income distribution is the distribution of income before the welfare state. This is, of course, a considerable simplification. Taxation, for example, may have incentive effects that could influence the distribution of factor income; social security benefits may encourage some people to work less than they would have done in the absence of the benefit, and thereby influence the distribution of factor income. By restricting the study to direct effects, the degree of redistribution is generally exaggerated. On the other hand, the estimated redistribution is real in the sense that it reflects existing flows of income and services, and the resulting income distributions.

Earlier comparisons

On the basis of the comparative Scandinavian welfare study, carried out in 1972 with identical survey questionnaires in Denmark, Finland, Norway, and Sweden, Uusitalo (1975) compared income distributions in the four participating countries. The survey was a representative study of the population between fifteen and sixty-five years of age. The sample size was relatively small, about one thousand people in each country, and the concept of gross income relied on the respondent's definition. The results showed the distribution of gross income between families (specifications A and B in Table 3.1) to be more egalitarian in Sweden and Norway than in Denmark and Finland.

Since the late 1960s, household budget surveys have greatly improved our knowledge of the distribution of income. In many countries, these studies follow UN recommendations, but with variations. With the use of such data, Sawyer (1976, 1982) compared income distributions in twelve countries (using specification A). The author makes a number of reservations as to comparability, but the results suggest that in the early 1970s, the Nordic countries included in the comparison, Finland, Norway, and Sweden (along with Australia, Japan, and the United Kingdom), were on the egalitarian side as compared to, for example, France, West Germany, Italy, and the United States.

In recent years, researchers have started to work directly with micro–data sets for several countries in order to apply common standards and definitions to these data sets and thereby increase comparability. In the Nordic area, Sandström (1980 and 1982) and Nygård (1984) have compared Finland and Sweden by using household budget data for the early 1970s and specification A. Their studies demonstrate the importance of a careful coordination of the data. When the distributions of disposable income as defined in the national data sets were compared, Sweden was shown to have a more egalitarian distribution than Finland. When differences in the estimates of imputed income from home owner occupancy were removed, the difference disappeared or changed so that Finland was shown to have a more egalitarian distribution. When the differences in family definitions were removed, Sweden was again shown to be more egalitarian.

Ringen (1986) has compared income distributions in Norway and Sweden in 1982 by using coordinated income survey data and specification C. This comparison shows the distribution of disposable income in Sweden to be more egalitarian than in Norway. This difference is attributed mainly to differences between the two countries in transfer and tax policy. The distribution of factor income is almost identical in both countries, but transfers and taxes redistribute more income in Sweden than in Norway and thereby cause the nations to become different in the distribution of disposable income.

The Luxembourg Income Study (LIS) is an international research project in which a data bank of coordinated income data for a number of industrial countries is established. Through this project, data of good comparability are now available for more than pairs of countries (cf. Smeeding, Schmauss, and Allegreza 1985). At present, the data refer to the years 1979–81. From the Nordic countries, only Norwegian and Swedish data have been included. In our study we added Finnish data to this data set by adjusting the Finnish household budget survey of 1981 to LIS definitions as closely as possible. This matching is perhaps not as good as it might have been if the Finnish data had been incorporated into the original LIS data bank, but the resulting comparability is satisfactory (Uusitalo 1989).

The results presented below are based on specifications A and F. It should be observed that the use of consumer unit scales brings some arbitrariness into the analysis since there is no single universally accepted consumer unit scale. In this study we use a scale that is in the middle of per-family and per-capita scales. The first adult is counted as one, while all additional household members have half of this weight.

Trends in income distribution in the Nordic countries

In Denmark, the long-term trend in the distribution of income has been in the direction of greater equality. This development was strong from about 1940 to 1950, moderate from about 1950 to 1970, and again strong from 1970 to 1978. This trend applies to the distribution of gross income, both between households and individuals. Around 1978, the trend in the distribution of gross income shifted moderately in the direction of greater inequality. This has persisted at least until 1982. Data on the distribution of disposable income from 1976 to 1982, in part between persons and in part between households (specifications A and C), show stability or a moderate decline of inequality (Hansen 1984; Egemose et al. 1985; Hansen 1985).

In Finland, the distribution of income has been studied by using household budget data (Suominen 1979; Allén 1986). A recent study by Uusitalo (1989) uses the same data and covers the period from 1966 to 1985. It shows that the distribution of income (specifications A and F) became more egalitarian until 1981, after which the A-distribution changed toward greater inequality, while the F-distribution has continued to change toward greater equality. This difference in trends is due to the rapid increase in the proportion of one-person households. As measured by the gini-coefficient, a measure fairly insensitive to changes, income inequalities have decreased by one-third during this period (F-distributions). The development has not been even, however. While income inequality decreased rapidly from the mid-1960s to the mid-1970s, the change during the last ten years has been only modest, although still in the direction of increased equality. Three factors account for this trend toward a more egalitarian distribution of economic welfare in Denmark and Finland: first and foremost, the development of the welfare state. This study shows that the fingerprints of both the expansion of the welfare state from the early 1960s to the mid-1970s and the slower development from the mid-1970s to 1985 are visible in income distribution trends. Second, some proportion of the change in income inequality is explained by structural changes in Finnish society. While the increasing numbers of pensioners and the growth of the middle class have intensified the tendency toward inequality, the decline in the number of farmers, especially small holders, has had an equalizing impact. Third, egalitarian income policies have reduced income inequality, especially from 1968 to the mid-1970s, by causing factor income inequalities among wage and salary earners to decrease more than among other groups.

In Norway, several studies have shown the distribution of income to have been virtually unchanged since 1970. In a study of the distribution of household pretax income, using specification A, from 1970 to 1979, Andersen and Aaberge (1983) found only very modest changes that did not add up to a consistent and significant trend. Bojer (1987) found the distribution of pretax income between income earners to have remained unchanged from 1970 to 1984 and the distribution of disposable income between households (specification A) to have been stable from 1973 to 1984. Estimates by Ringen (1991) have modified the previous conclusions of stability. Analyzing longer time series than previously, and achieving better comparability over time, Ringen has found F-specification distributions to have changed toward more inequality from 1970 to 1976 and toward more equality from 1976 to 1986. Since these trends more or less balance each other out, the degree of inequality in 1986 is about the same as in 1970.

In Sweden, trends in the distribution of income have been studied by Spånt (1979), Åberg, Selen, and Tham (1987), and Gustafsson (1987). These studies are somewhat different in approach and methodology and use various types of data. Taken together, they suggest that the development from 1950 to 1985 can be divided into the following three periods: the 1950s in which the degree of income inequality was stable; from 1960 to about 1980 when there was a considerable equalization in the distribution of income, in large measure as a result of a steady improvement of the relative income position of the elderly and other transfer recipients; whereafter income inequalities widened slightly, especially in 1984 and 1985.

Until recently, reliable comparisons of income inequality trends in the Nordic countries have not been available. Comparable estimates for Finland, Norway, and Sweden have, however, recently become available for a fairly long time period. These estimates are not fully comparable as measures of the level of income inequality, since specifications of income concepts differ slightly, and different equivalence scales are used, but the comparison of trends should be reliable. Gini-coefficients of income inequality (specification F) are shown in Figure 3.2.

The graph shows that Norway is distinctly different from Finland and Sweden. First, there is apparently a higher level of inequality in Norway, although caution is warranted in the comparison of gini-levels. Second, the degree of inequality has changed less in Norway than in the two other countries. Third, the trends are in some respects different. During the 1970s, the trend in Finland and Sweden was toward equality, while in Norway it was toward inequality. After about 1980, the trends in Finland and Norway are toward equality and in Sweden toward inequality.

Income packaging

There are considerable differences in the composition of income among industrial countries (see Table 3.3). The impact of transfers and taxes on households is largest in Sweden, where both taxes and trans-

Figure 3.2. **Trends in Income Inequality in Finland, Norway, and Sweden**

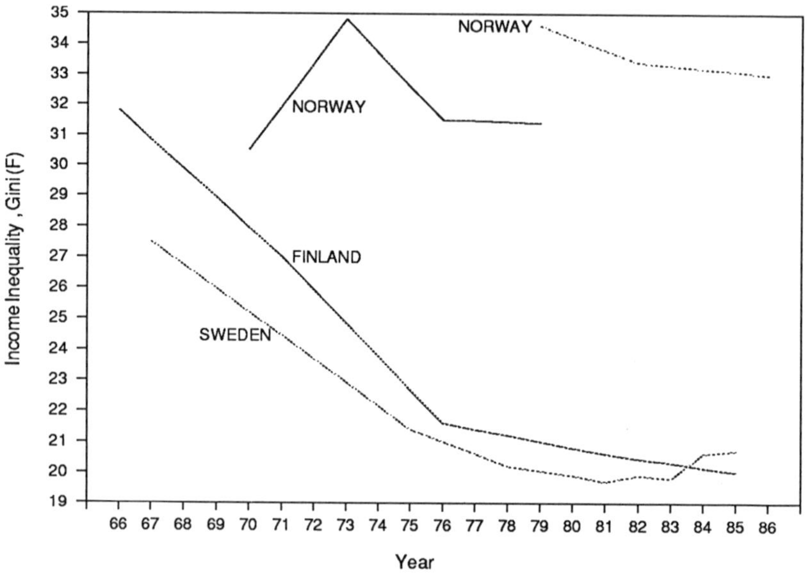

Sources: Finland and Sweden: Gustafsson and Uusitalo (1990); Norway: Ringen (1991).
Note: There is an interruption in the Norwegian time series in 1979.

fers are higher relative to gross income than in any other nation included in the comparison. The two other Nordic countries, Finland and Norway, show the same pattern, but to a more modest degree. The United Kingdom has roughly the same transfer ratio, but its tax ratio is lower. Israel is a special case: the tax ratio is almost on the Swedish level but transfers are on the same level as in the United States. In both the North American countries, the impact of the public sector of the economy on the average household is relatively modest, although the tax level is surprisingly high in the United States.

Income distribution

Pre-LIS comparisons of income inequality across countries have tended to emphasize similarity. This was in part because the margins of uncertainty were so wide in these comparisons that one could not necessarily accept observed differences as real. The improved quality and comparability of income distribution data has, however, shown

Table 3.3

Income Packaging in Three Scandinavian Countries and in Other LIS Countries circa 1980 (percent of gross income)

	Factor Income	Income Transfers	Gross Income	Direct Taxes	Disposable Income
Finland	82.2	17.6	100	24.5	75.5
Norway	83.7	14.1	100	25.3	74.7
Sweden	70.8	29.2	100	29.7	70.2
Canada	88.3	9.1	100	15.2	84.8
Israel	87.7	8.3	100	28.7	71.3
United Kingdom	79.3	17.2	100	16.9	83.1
United States	88.3	8.0	100	21.0	79.0

Sources: O'Higgins et al. (1985) and Uusitalo (1989).

Note: Income transfers include only transfers paid by the public sector. Therefore the sum of factor income and income transfers is not 100 in all countries.

that there are, in fact, considerable differences among industrial nations in the distribution of income. Table 3.4 includes the comparison of income inequality among LIS countries and Finland.

This comparison shows that in 1980 the three Nordic countries had relatively egalitarian income distributions. The United Kingdom came close to Norway and Finland, whereas the other countries have wider income inequalities. The differences between countries are large. For example, the quintile of persons with the lowest level of income has about 6 percent of disposable income in the United States, as compared to over 10 percent in Sweden. The rank order of the countries is similar in all distributions. Within the Nordic countries, the distribution of disposable income among individuals (F-specification) is more egalitarian in Sweden than in Finland and Norway, and is more egalitarian in Finland than in Norway. There is some discrepancy for the Nordic countries between the LIS estimates and those reported in Figure 3.2. The ranking of the countries is the same. For Finland and Sweden, the LIS estimates of inequality are higher than estimates in Figure 3.2, but the difference is relatively small. For Norway, the LIS estimates are lower and the difference is considerable. These results are consistent in showing that Norway is the most inegalitarian of these Nordic countries, but they are not consistent in showing how much more inegalitar-

Figure 3.3a. **Disposable Income Inequality (F) by the Age of the Head of the Family (Finland, Norway, and Sweden)**

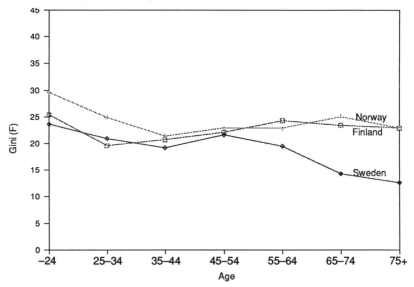

Figure 3.3b. **Disposable Income Inequality (F) by the Age of the Head of the Family (Canada, Israel, United Kingdom, and United States)**

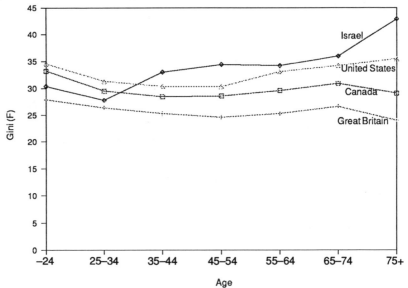

Sources: Hedström and Ringen (1987). Figures for Finland have been calculated for this study based on a data set from the Household Budget Survey in 1981 (for documentation, see Central Statistical Office of Finland 1986).

Table 3.4

Income Distribution and Poverty in Three Scandinavian Countries and in Other LIS Countries circa 1980

	I	II	III	IV	V	Gini coeffi-cient
Gross income (A)						
Finland	5.4	11.7	17.9	25.3	39.6	34.9
Norway	4.9	11.4	18.4	25.5	39.8	35.6
Sweden	6.6	12.3	17.2	25.0	38.9	32.9
Canada	4.6	11.0	17.7	25.3	41.4	37.4
Israel	4.5	10.5	16.5	24.9	43.6	39.5
United Kingdom	4.9	10.9	18.2	25.3	40.8	36.5
United States	3.8	9.8	16.6	25.3	44.5	41.2
Disposable income (A)						
Finland	6.5	12.6	18.7	25.4	36.8	31.2
Norway	6.3	12.8	18.9	25.3	36.7	31.1
Sweden	8.0	13.2	17.4	24.5	36.9	29.2
Canada	5.3	11.8	18.1	24.6	39.7	34.8
Israel	6.0	12.1	17.9	24.5	39.5	33.8
United Kingdom	5.8	11.5	18.2	25.0	39.5	34.3
United States	4.5	11.2	17.7	25.6	41.0	37.0
Gross income (F)						
Finland	8.5	14.0	18.6	23.6	35.3	27.0
Norway	8.1	13.6	17.9	23.4	37.0	28.9
Sweden	9.4	14.6	18.5	23.3	34.2	24.9
Canada	6.7	12.6	17.5	24.0	39.2	32.7
Israel	6.1	10.3	15.9	23.7	44.0	38.2
United Kingdom	7.9	13.0	17.9	23.7	37.5	29.7
United States	5.1	11.4	17.1	24.2	42.1	37.1

	I	II	III	IV	V	Gini coeffi-cient	Poverty
Disposable income (F)							
Finland	9.9	15.3	19.1	23.4	32.2	22.5	7.0
Norway	9.9	14.8	18.4	22.9	34.1	24.3	4.8
Sweden	10.6	16.1	19.1	23.1	31.1	20.5	5.0
Canada	7.6	13.3	17.9	23.8	37.4	29.9	12.1
Israel	7.5	11.7	16.8	23.7	40.3	33.3	14.5
United Kingdom	9.0	13.5	18.0	23.4	36.1	27.3	8.8
United States	6.1	12.8	18.1	24.4	38.6	32.6	16.9

Sources: O'Higgins et al. (1985), 17; Hedström and Ringen (1987), 236; Uusitalo (1989).
Notes: Poverty: percent of persons belonging to families with a disposable income per consumer unit less than half of the median for all persons. The Gini coefficient is described in Kakwani (1986). Poverty rates for Finland have been estimated for this study.

ian Norway is. As seen in Figure 3.2, after around 1980, the degree of income inequality has diminished in Finland and Norway, and increased in Sweden.

Table 3.4 also shows the extent of relative poverty. The comparison shows that the Scandinavian countries have lower poverty rates than the other countries, the Finnish figure being perhaps somewhat higher than the Norwegian and Swedish rates. The United Kingdom comes close to the Nordic countries, while the poverty rates for Canada, Israel, and the United States are much higher. Because the measure focuses on relative poverty, the differences between the countries are similar to those found in the distribution of income.

Figure 3.3 shows the degree of income inequality among age groups (according to the age of the head of the household). The common pattern for all countries is that income inequality is higher in the youngest age group than in the next age group, or even higher than in any other age group, as in the Nordic countries. This is perhaps explained by the diversity of this age group: it includes on the one hand, young adults who have just entered the labor force, and on the other hand, students.

The difference between the countries is greater for older than younger age groups. Deviating countries are, on the one hand, Sweden, and on the other hand, Israel and the United States. In Sweden, income inequality diminishes after age fifty-four, whereas in Israel and in the United States it increases. The other countries are found in between, having much the same age-inequality profiles but on different levels of inequality. Up to the forty-five to fifty-four-year-old group, Finland is close to Sweden, but in the older age groups, inequalities are wider in Finland. Norway and Finland are close to each other except for the two youngest age groups, in which Finland shows less inequality. The difference in inequality between Sweden and the two other Nordic countries is in large measure, although not completely, due to much less inequality in Sweden among the elderly. Compared to the non-Nordic nations, it is clear that the fairly egalitarian income distribution in the Nordic countries cannot be attributed to an egalitarian distribution in any specific age groups, but is a more global aspect of these societies.

Redistribution

Estimates of the redistributive impact of transfers and taxes (see Table 3.2) are reported in Table 3.5. With regard to transfers, the countries

Table 3.5

**Income Redistribution in Three Scandinavian Countries
and in Other LIS Countries circa 1980**

	Redistributive Effect of		
	Transfers	Taxes	Both
Finland	28.9	16.7	40.8
Norway	27.8	15.9	39.2
Sweden	(37.8)	17.7	(48.8)
Canada	17.8	8.6	24.9
Israel	16.7	12.8	27.4
United Kingdom	28.3	8.1	34.0
United States	15.7	12.1	25.9

Sources: Ringen (1986), 13; Uusitalo (1989); Kakwani (1986), 83–84.
Notes: Redistributive effect of transfers: 100 x (gini of factor incomes – gini of gross incomes)/gini of factor incomes. Redistributive effect of taxes: 100 x (gini of gross incomes – gini of disposable incomes)/gini of gross incomes. Redistributive effect of transfers and taxes: 100 x (gini of factor incomes – gini of disposable incomes)/gini of factor incomes (Kakwani 1986, 83–84); the Swedish figures in parentheses are estimated by assuming the same distribution of factor income in Sweden as in Norway (cf. Ringen 1986).

fall into three categories. Sweden is by itself in the first category. Finland, Norway, and the United Kingdom form the second group. Canada, the United States, and Israel form the third category in which transfers are less redistributive. The redistributive impact of direct taxes is strongest in the Scandinavian countries and weakest in Canada and the United Kingdom.

Regarding the combined effect of transfers and taxes on income redistribution, the Nordic welfare states are the most redistributive ones—Sweden leads Finland and Norway. The United Kingdom is in the middle. In Israel, Canada, and the United States, redistribution of income by the state is less significant.

Toward an explanation

We have seen that there are considerable differences among the nations that we compared in the degree of income inequality. What are the mechanisms that produce such variations? This is, of course, an

Figure 3.4. **Redistributive Effect of Transfers by Size of Welfare State**

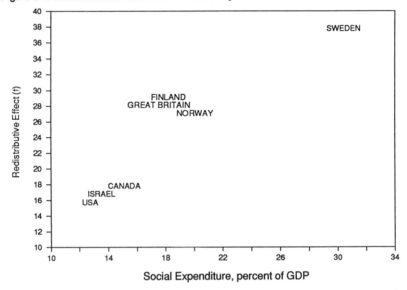

Social Expenditure, percent of GDP

Figure 3.5. **Redistributive Effect of Taxes by Size of Tax State**

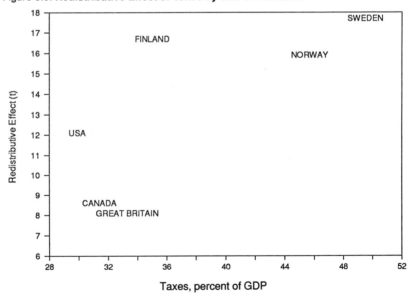

Taxes, percent of GDP

Figure 3.6. **Income Inequality by Size of Welfare State**

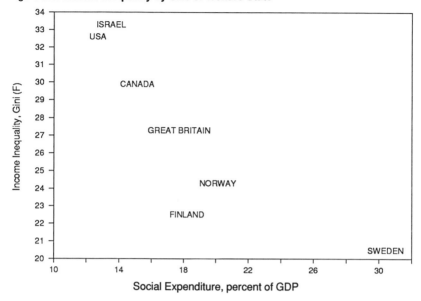

Social Expenditure, percent of GDP

enormous question to raise and we can do no more than offer some tentative suggestions as to where to look for answers. Several theories have been suggested. One important distinction between these theories is their relative emphasis on economic versus political determinants, that is, the markets versus politics issue. Simon Kuznets's (1955) well-known suggestion of a curvilinear relationship between economic development and inequality is an example of a theory that emphasizes economic factors (see Branco and Williams 1988). Other theories point to political factors such as democracy, the political strength of social democratic parties, and the unionization of the labor force, but the adequacy of such theories remains contested (for the debate, see, for example, Hewitt 1977, 450–64; Korpi 1980, 296–316; Hollingsworth and Hanneman 1982, 61–80; Weede 1982, 151–65; and Bollen and Jackman 1985, 438–57). Cross-national research can shed some light on issues such as these although what can be learned is limited by methodological constraints.

One of the weaknesses of previous cross-national research has been the low comparability of income distribution data. The advantage of LIS studies, such as the present one, is that the data are comparable; the disadvantage is that the number of nations is too small for proper

Figure 3.7. **Income Inequality by GDP per Capita** (PPP-adjusted)

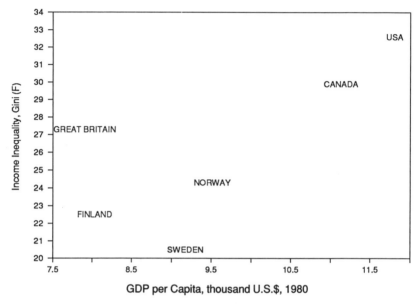

Note: The PPP-adjustment implies that the data have been converted to United States dollars using purchasing power parities. PPP's are the rates of currency conversion that equalize the purchasing power of different currencies. This means that a given sum of money, when converted into different currencies at the PPP rates, will buy the same basket of goods and services in all countries. Thus, PPP's are the rates of currency conversion which eliminate differences in price levels between countries (OECD 1990, 143).

causal analysis. We approach the problem by presenting simple pair-wise scatterplots between income inequality and the redistributive effect of transfers and taxes, on the one hand, and between income inequality and some potential explanatory variables, which have been suggested in the literature, on the other. We ignore methodological problems such as control for other variables, the direction of causality, period effects, and the like. Some would no doubt say that with only seven observations we have stretched the data further than they go. Our goal is modest: scatterplots are merely a way of organizing data in order to show what kinds of hypotheses are supported or are not supported in this simple comparison. The scatterplots are presented in Figures 3.4 through 3.9.

Figures 3.4 and 3.5 show that the redistributive effects of transfers and taxes correlate positively with the relative expenditure levels of

Figure 3.8. **Income Inequality by Unemployment Rate**

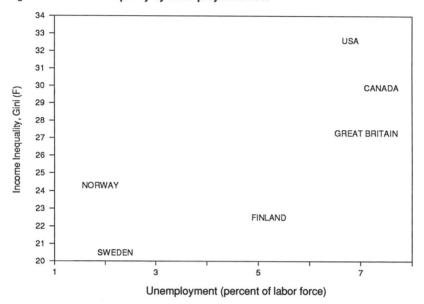

these policies. This suggests that in relatively advanced welfare states the redistribution that can be achieved with the use of transfers and taxes depends on what transfers and taxes are implemented, that is, that the potential effect of additional policies is not necessarily absorbed by circularity in the transfer/tax system, and generally that transfer and tax policies are redistributively effective.

If this is true, the next question is whether these redistributions really have a significant effect on disposable income inequality, or whether this is determined by totally different factors, for example economic ones, so as a result, politically induced redistributions have no real effect. In Figure 3.6, disposable income inequality (specification F) is correlated with a measure of the size of the welfare state (social expenditure in percent of GDP). Again, there is a clear relationship: the larger the welfare state, the more egalitarian the income distribution.

Figures 3.7 and 3.8 show the relationship between income inequality and two economic measures—economic level (GDP per capita)— and the efficiency of the economic system (unemployment). With some goodwill one might identify some covariation in these figures (although not necessarily the expected ones: Figure 3.7 appears to

Figure 3.9. **Income Inequality by Left Power**

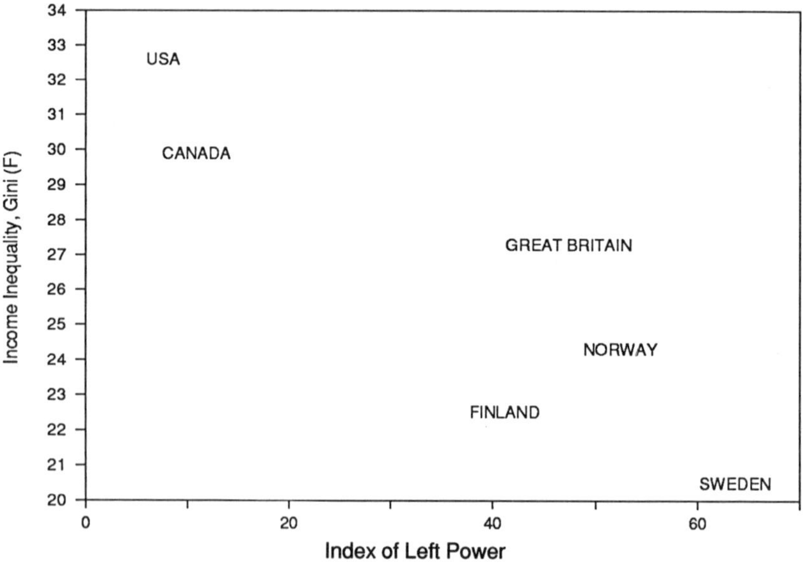

Note: The Index of Left Power is the average of the sum of (a) percentage of left seats in Parliament 1960–1980 (period average); (b) percentage of left seats in cabinet 1960–1980 (period average); and (c) percentage of unionization of labor force 1960–1980 (period average).

suggest that there is more inequality the higher the economic level), but the correlations are weak and unclear. If we take the association between income inequality and potential causal factors in simple bivariate correlations as a suggestion of the importance of these factors in explaining income inequality, we suggest that economic factors are of relatively modest direct importance, at least among the developed industrial nations, which other research seems to suggest (Branco and Williams 1988).

Figure 3.9 correlates an index of leftist power in the polity with inequality. The index incorporates the number of leftist seats in parliament and government, and the level of unionization during the period 1960–80. The correlation here suggests that more inequality tends to be found in polities where leftist influence is weak. This suggests that the degree of inequality may be influenced by ideological constellations and power relations in the polity, and again is in support of theories of income inequality that emphasize political factors.

Conclusion

This chapter shows that Finland, Norway, and Sweden, when compared with some other industrial countries around 1980, have fairly egalitarian income distributions and relatively low poverty rates. This is partly explained by the size of their welfare states and the subsequent redistributive impact of welfare state policies. The notion of the Scandinavian model is not wholly fiction. However, among the Nordic countries, Sweden was the most egalitarian one until the mid-1980s when Finland achieved the same degree of equality. There is more income inequality in Norway than in Finland and Sweden, although it is not clear just how much more. This difference is largely due to the fact that income inequalities decreased considerably in Finland and Sweden during the 1970s, whereas they remained fairly stable in Norway. As for the markets versus politics debate, the degree of inequality in a mixed economy obviously depends on both economic and political factors. This study suggests that political factors may be relatively important and that both structures and actions within the polity should be included in a model for explaining differences in income inequality between nations. One of the proximate political causes of the variation of income inequality is the welfare state, the mere size of which is a important variable.

References

Åberg, R., Selen, J., and Tham, H. "Economic Resources." 1987. In R. Erikson and R. Åberg, eds.; *Welfare in Transition. A Survey of Living Conditions in Sweden 1968–1981*. Oxford: Clarendon Press, 117–52.

Allén, T. 1986. *Tulonjako ja tulojen uudelleenjako Suomessa vuosina 1976–1981*. Helsinki: Labour Institute for Economic Research. Research reports No. 38, 1986.

Andersen, A. S., and Aaberge, R. 1983. *Analyse av ulikhet i fordelingen av levekår*. Rapport 83/21. Oslo: Central Bureau of Statistics.

Bojer, H. 1987. *Personlig inntektsfordeling i Norge 1970–1984*. Oslo: Tidskrift for samfunnsforskning, 247–58.

Bollen, K. A., and Jackman, R. W. 1985. "Political Democracy and the Size Distribution of Income." *American Sociological Review* 50:438–57.

Bornstedt, G. W., and Knoke, D. 1988. *Statistics for Data Analysis*. Itasca, Illinois: F. E. Peacock Publishers Inc.

Branco, K. J., and Williams, J. B. 1988. "Economic Development and Income Distribution—A Cross-National Analysis." *American Journal of Economics and Sociology* 47 (3): 277–97.

Central Statistical Office of Finland. 1986. *Household Budget Survey 1981 III.* Helsinki: Central Statistical Office of Finland. Statistical Surveys no. 71.

Cowell, F. A. 1984. "The Structure of American Income Inequality." *The Review of Income and Wealth* 30:351–75.

Egemose, S., et al. 1985. *Uligheten, politikerne og befolkningen.* Report no. 139. Copenhagen: Danish National Institute of Social Research.

van Ginneken, W. 1979. "Generating Internationally Comparable Income Distribution Data: Evidence from the Federal Republic of Germany (1974), Mexico (1968) and the United Kingdom (1979)." *The Review of Income and Wealth* 28:365–79.

Le Grand, J. 1982. *The Strategy of Equality. Redistribution and the Social Services.* London: Allen and Unwin.

Gustafsson, B. 1984. *Transfereringar och inkomstskatt samt hushållens materiella standard.* Stockholm: Rapport till expertgruppen för studier i offentlig ekonomi, Finansdepartementet. Ds Fi 1984:17.

———. 1987. *Ett decennium av stagnerande realinkomster.* Living Conditions Report no. 54. Stockholm: Statistics Sweden.

Gustafsson, B., and Uusitalo, H. 1990. "Income Distribution and Redistribution during Two Decades—Experiences from Finland and Sweden." In I. Persson-Tanimura (ed.), *Generating Equality—The Swedish Experiment.* Oslo: Norwegian University Press. Forthcoming.

Hansen, F. K. 1984. "Udviklingstendenser for indkomstfordelningen." In J. Goul Andersen, F. K. Hansen, and O. Borre, eds., *Konflikt og tilpassning.* Copenhagen: Aschehoug Dansk Forlag.

———. 1985. Fordelingspolitikken og dens virkninger. Report no. 137. Copenhagen: Danish National Institute of Social Research.

Hedström, P., and Ringen, S. 1987. "Age and Income in Contemporary Society: A Research Note." *Journal of Social Policy* 16:227–39.

Hewitt, C. 1977. "The Effect of Political Democracy and Social Democracy on Equality in Industrial Societies: A Cross-National Comparison." *American Sociological Review* 42:450–64.

Hollingsworth, J. R., and Hanneman, R. A. 1982. "Working-Class Power and the Political Economy of Western Capitalist Societies." *Comparative Social Research* 5:61–80.

International Labor Organization (ILO) 1985. *Social Security Expenditure 1978–80.* Geneva: ILO.

Kakwani, N. 1986. *Analyzing Redistribution Policies. A Study Using Australian Data.* Cambridge, Cambridge University Press.

Korpi, W. 1980. "Social Policy and Distributional Conflict in the Capitalist Democracies. A Preliminary Comparative Framework." *West European Politics* 3:296–316.

———. 1987. "Power Resources, State Autonomy, and the Politics of Social Policy: Sickness Insurance in 18 OECD-countries, 1930–1980." Paper presented at the 14th Nordic Conference on Sociology, Tampere, August 21–23.

Kuznets, S. 1955. "Economic Growth and Income Inequality." *American Economic Review* 45:1–28.

Nygård, F. 1984. Inkomstbildningen och inkomstfördelningen i Finland och Sverige under 1970-talet. In Statistisk analys av inkomstfördelningar. Åbo:

Meddelanden från Ekonomisk-statsvetenskapliga fakulteten vid Åbo Akademi, Statistiska institutionen, Serie A:197, 1–11.

O'Higgins, M., Schmauss, G., and Stephenson, G. 1985. *Income Distribution and Redistribution*. Working Paper. Luxembourg: Luxembourg Income Study.

Organization for Economic Cooperation and Development. (OECD). 1984. *Tax/Benefit Position of Production Workers*. Paris: OECD.

———. 1987. *Economic Outlook 41, June 1987*. Paris: OECD.

———. 1991. *National Accounts 1960–1989. Main Aggregates*. Vol. 1. Paris: OECD.

Ringen, S. 1986. *Difference and Similarity. Two Studies in Comparative Income Distribution*. Stockholm: Institutet för Social Forskning, Meddelande 2.

———. 1987. *The Possibility of Politics. A Study in the Political Economy of the Welfare State*. Oxford: Clarendon Press.

———. 1991. "Households, Standard of Living, and Inequality." *Review of Income and Wealth*. Forthcoming. March.

Sandström, A. 1980. "On the Effect of Changing Definitions on Income Components. A Comparison of Finnish and Swedish Data." *Statistisk tidskrift* 6:487–500.

———. 1982. "Various Income Sources and Inequality of Total Income in Sweden in 1972 and 1976." *Statistisk tidskrift* 4:288–99.

Sawyer, M. 1976. "Income Distribution in the OECD Countries." *OECD Economic Outlook, Occasional Studies*, 3–36.

———. 1982. "Income Distribution and the Welfare State. In A. Boltho, ed., *The European Economy*. New York: Oxford University Press.

Smeeding, T., Schmauss, G., and Allegreza, S. 1985. *An Introduction to LIS*. Luxembourg: Working Paper. Luxembourg Income Study.

Spånt, R. 1979. *Den svenska inkomstfördelningens utveckling 1920–1976*. Stockholm: Liber.

Suominen, R. 1979. *Tulonjako Suomessa vuonna 1976*. Helsinki: Official Statistics of Finland, Special Social Studies, OSF XXXII:58.

Uusitalo, H. 1975. *Income and Welfare. A Study of Income as a Component of Welfare in the Scandinavian Countries in 1970s*. Research Report No. 8. Helsinki: Research Group for Comparative Sociology, University of Helsinki.

———. 1985. "Redistribution and Equality in the Welfare State: An Effort to Interpret the Major Findings of Research on the Redistributive Effects of the Welfare State." *European Sociological Review* 1: no. 2, 163–76.

———. 1989. *On Income Distribution in Finland 1966–1985. The Effects of the Welfare State and the Structural Changes in Society*. Helsinki: Central Statistical Office of Finland. Studies No. 148.

Weede, E. 1982. "The Effects of Democracy and Socialist Strength on the Size Distribution of Income." *International Journal of Comparative Sociology* 23:151–65.

Westergaard, J., and Resler, H. 1975. *Class in a Capitalist Society*. London: Heinemann.

4

The Three Political Economies of the Welfare State

GØSTA ESPING-ANDERSEN

Introduction

The protracted debate on the welfare state has failed to produce con-
clusive answers as to either the nature or the causes of welfare state
development. This chapter has three aims: (1) to reintegrate the debate
into the intellectual tradition of political economy thus putting into
sharper focus the principal theoretical questions involved; (2) to specify the salient characteristics of welfare states since the conventional
ways of measuring welfare states in terms of their expenditures will no
longer suffice; and (3) to "sociologize" the study of welfare states.
Most studies have assumed a world of linearity: more or less power,
industrialization, or spending. This chapter insists that we understand
welfare states as clusters of regime types, and that their development
must be explained interactively.

The legacy of classical political economy

Contemporary welfare state debates have been guided by two questions. First, does social citizenship diminish the salience of class? Or,
in other words, can the welfare state fundamentally transform capitalist
society? Second, what are the causal forces behind welfare state development? These questions are not recent. Indeed, they were formulated
by the nineteenth-century political economists one hundred years before any welfare state can rightfully be said to have come into exis-

tence. The classical political economists—whether of liberal, conservative, or Marxist persuasion—were preoccupied with the relationship between capitalism and welfare. Their answers obviously diverged, but their analyses were unequivocally directed to the relationship between market (and property) and the state (democracy). The question they asked was largely normative: What is the optimal division of responsibility between market and state?

Contemporary neoliberalism echoes the contributions of classical liberal political economy. To Adam Smith, the market was the superior means for the abolition of class, inequality, and privilege. Aside from a necessary minimum, state intervention would likely stifle the equalizing process of competitive exchange and create monopolies, protectionism, and inefficiency: in short the state upholds class; the market can potentially undo class society (Smith 1961, vol. 2 especially 232–36).[1]

Liberal political economists were not necessarily of one mind when it came to policy advocacy. Nassau Senior and later Manchester liberals emphasized the laissez-faire element of Smith, rejecting any form of social protection outside the cash nexus. John Stuart Mill and the "reformed liberals," in turn, were willing to let markets be regulated by a modicum of political regulation. Yet, they all agreed that the road to equality and prosperity should be paved with a maximum of free markets and a minimum of state interference.

This enthusiastic embrace of market capitalism may now appear unjustified. But, we must take into account that the state, which confronted these early political economists, was tinged with legacies of absolutist privileges, mercantilist protectionisms, and pervasive corruption. They were attacking systems of governance that repressed the ideals of both freedom and enterprise. Hence, theirs was revolutionary theory, and from this vantage point, we can understand why Adam Smith sometimes reads like Karl Marx.[2]

Democracy was an Achilles' heel to many liberals. Their ideals of freedom and democratic participation were grounded in a world of small property owners, not of growing propertyless masses who held in their sheer numbers the possibility of seizing state power. The liberals feared the principle of universal suffrage, for it would likely politicize the distributional struggle, pervert the market, and fuel inefficiencies. Many liberals discovered that democracy would contradict the market.

Both conservative and Marxist political economists understood this contradiction, but proposed, of course, opposite solutions. The most coherent conservative critique of laissez-faire came from the German historical school; in particular from Friedrich List, Adolph Wagner, and Gustav Schmoller. They refused to believe that capitalist efficiency was best assured by the pure commodity status of workers in the raw cash nexus of the market. Instead, conservative political economists believed that patriarchal neoabsolutism could provide the kind of legal, political, and social framework that would assure capitalism without class struggle.

One prominent conservative school promoted a "Monarchical Welfare State" that would, at once, provide for social welfare, class harmony, loyalty, and productivity. It was discipline, not competition, that would guarantee efficiency. The state (or church) was the institution best equipped to harmonize conflicting interests.[3]

Conservative political economy emerged in reaction to the French Revolution and the Paris Commune. It was avowedly nationalist, anti-revolutionary, and sought to arrest the democratic impulse. It feared social leveling and favored a society that retained both hierarchy and class. It held that class conflicts were not natural; that democratic mass participation and the dissolution of recognized rank and status boundaries were threats to social harmony.

The key to Marxian political economy, of course, was its rejection of the liberal claim that markets guarantee equality. Capitalist accumulation, as Dobb (1946) put it, disowns people of property with the end result being ever deeper class divisions. Here, the state's role is not neutrally benevolent, nor is it a fountain of emancipation; the state exists to defend property rights and the authority of capital. According to Marxism, this capitalist state is the foundation of class dominance.

The central question, not only for Marxism but for the entire contemporary debate on the welfare state, is whether and under what conditions the class divisions and social inequalities produced by capitalism can be undone by parliamentary democracy.

The liberals feared that democracy would produce socialism and they were consequently not especially eager to extend it. The socialists, in contrast, suspected that parliamentarism would be little more than an empty shell or, as Lenin suggested, a mere "talking shop" (Jessop 1982). This line of analysis, echoed in much of contemporary Marxism, leads to the conclusion that social reforms emerge in response to the exigencies of capitalist reproduction, not the emancipatory desires of the working classes.[4]

Among socialists, a more positive analysis of parliamentarism came to prevail after the extension of full political citizenship. The theoretically most sophisticated contributions came from Austro-Marxists such as Adler and Bauer, and from German social democrats, especially Eduard Heimann. Heimann's (1929) starting point was that even conservative reforms may have been motivated by desires to repress labor mobilization, but that their very presence nonetheless alters the balance of class power: the social wage lessens the worker's dependence on the market and employers. The social wage is thus also a potential power resource that defines the frontier between capitalism and socialism. It introduces an alien element into the capitalist political economy. This intellectual position has enjoyed quite a renaissance in recent Marxism (Offe 1985; Bowles and Gintis 1986).

The social democratic model, as outlined above, did not necessarily abandon the orthodox assumption that fundamental equality requires economic socialization. Yet, historical experience soon demonstrated that socialization was a goal that could not be pursued realistically through parliamentarism.[5]

Social democracy's embrace of parliamentary reformism as its dominant strategy for equality and socialism was premised on two arguments. The first was that workers require social resources, health, and education to participate effectively in a democratized economy. The second argument was that social policy is not only emancipatory, but it is also economically efficient (Myrdal and Myrdal 1936). Following Marx on this point, the strategy therefore promotes the onward march of capitalist productive forces. The beauty of the strategy was that social policy would also assure social democratic power mobilization. By eradicating poverty, unemployment, and complete wage dependency, the welfare state increases political capacities and diminishes the social divisions that are barriers to political unity among workers.

The social democratic model, then, puts forward one of the leading hypotheses of contemporary welfare state debate: the argument that parliamentary class mobilization is a means for the realization of socialist ideals of equality, justice, freedom, and solidarity.

The political economy of the welfare state

Our political economy forebears defined the analytic basis of much recent scholarship. They isolated the key variables of class, state, market, and democracy, and they formulated the basic propositions about citizenship and class, efficiency and equality, and capitalism and socialism. Contemporary social science distinguishes itself from classical political economy on two scientifically vital fronts. First, it defines itself as a positive science and shies away from normative prescription (Robbins 1976). Second, classical political economists had little interest in historical variability; they saw their efforts as leading toward a system of universal laws. Although contemporary political economy sometimes still clings to the belief in absolute truths, the comparative and historical method that, today, underpins almost all good political economy is one that reveals variation and permeability.

Despite these differences, most recent scholarship has as its focal point the state-economy relationship defined by nineteenth-century political economists. And, given its enormous growth, it is understandable that the welfare state has become a major test case for contending theories of political economy.

Next, we shall review the contributions of comparative research on the development of welfare states in advanced capitalist countries. We will argue that most scholarship has been misdirected, mainly because it became detached from its theoretical foundations. We must therefore recast both the methodology and concepts of political economy in order to adequately study the welfare state. This will constitute the focus of the final section of this chapter.

Two types of approaches have dominated in the explanation of welfare states: one, a systemic (or structuralist) theory; the other, an institutional or actor-oriented explanation.

The systemic/structuralist approach

The first approach, system—or structuralist—theory, seeks to capture the logic of development holistically. It focuses on the functional requisites for the reproduction of society and economy; it tends to emphasize cross-national similarities rather than differences.

One variant of structuralist theory begins with a theory of the industrial society, and argues that industrialization makes social policy both necessary and possible. It makes welfare states necessary because preindustrial modes of social reproduction, such as the family, the church, noblesse oblige, and guild solidarity, are destroyed by the forces attached to modernization—social mobility, urbanization, individualism, and market dependence. The crux of the matter is that the market is no adequate substitute because it caters only to those who are able to perform in it. Hence, the "welfare function" is appropriated by the nation state. The welfare state is also made possible by the rise of modern bureaucracy as a rational, universalist, and efficient form of organization. It is a means for managing collective goods, but also a center of power in its own right, and will thus be inclined to promote its own growth.

This kind of reasoning has formed the so-called logic of industrialism perspective, according to which the welfare state will emerge as the modern industrial economy destroys traditional forms of social security (Flora and Alber 1981; Pryor 1969). But, the thesis has difficulties explaining why government social policy only emerged fifty or even one hundred years after traditional community was effectively destroyed. The basic response draws on Wagner's Law (1962) and on Marshall (1920), namely that a certain level of economic development, and thus surplus, is needed in order to permit the diversion of scarce resources from productive use (investments) to welfare (Wilensky and Lebeaux 1958). In this sense, the perspective follows in the footsteps of the old liberals. Social redistribution endangers efficiency, and only at a certain economic level will a negative-sum trade-off be avoidable (Okun 1975).

The new structural Marxism offers a surprisingly parallel analysis. It breaks with its classical forebears' strongly action-centered theory. Like the industrialism thesis, its analytical starting point is not the problems of markets, but the logic of a mode of production. Capital accumulation creates contradictions that social reform can alleviate (O'Connor 1973). This tradition of Marxism or "logic of capitalism" much like its "logic of industrialism" counterpart, fails to see much relevance of actors in the promotion of welfare states. The point is that the state, as an actor, is positioned in such a way that it will serve the collective needs of capital. The theory is thus premised on two crucial assumptions: first, that power is structural and, second, that the state is "relatively" autonomous from class directives (Poulantzas 1973; Block 1977; for a recent critical assessment of this literature, see Therborn 1986; and Skocpol and Amenta 1986).

The logic of capitalism perspective invites difficult questions. If, as Przeworski (1980) has argued, working class consent is assured on the basis of material hegemony, that is, self-willed subordination to the system, it is difficult to see why up to 40 percent of the gross national product must be allocated to the legitimation activities of a welfare state. A second problem is to derive state activities from a "mode of production" analysis. Eastern Europe may perhaps not qualify as socialist, but neither is it capitalist. Yet, there we find "welfare states," too. Perhaps accumulation has functional requirements in whichever way it proceeds (Skocpol and Amenta 1986; Bell 1978).

The institutional approach

The classical political economists made it clear why democratic institutions should influence welfare state development. The liberals feared that full democracy might jeopardize markets and inaugurate socialism. Freedom, in their view, necessitated a defence of markets against political intrusion. In practice, this is what the laissez-faire state sought to accomplish. But it was this divorce of politics and economy that fueled much of the institutionalist analyses—the second approach used to explain the welfare state. Best represented by Polanyi (1944), but also by a number of antidemocratic exponents of the historical school, the institutional approach insists that any effort to isolate the economy from social and political institutions will destroy human society. The economy must be embedded in social communities in order for it to survive. Thus, Polanyi sees social policy as a necessary precondition for the reintegration of the social economy.

An interesting recent variant of institutional alignment theory is the argument that welfare states emerge more readily in small, open economies, which are particularly vulnerable to international markets. As Katzenstein (1985) and Cameron (1978) show, there is a greater inclination to regulate class distributional conflicts through government and interest concertation when both business and labor are captives to forces beyond domestic control.

The impact of democracy on welfare states has been argued ever since the days of J. S. Mill and Alexis de Tocqueville. The argument is typically phrased without reference to any particular social agent or class. It is, in this sense, institutional. In its classical formulation, the thesis was simply that majority groups will favor social distribution to compensate for market weakness or market risks. If wage earners are likely to demand a social wage, so are capitalists (or farmers) apt to demand protection in the form of tariffs, monopolies, or subsidies.

Democracy is an institution that cannot resist majoritarian demands.

In its modern formulations, the democratic-institutionalist thesis has many variants. One identifies stages of nation-building in which full citizenship incorporation requires social rights (Marshall 1950; Bendix 1964; Rokkan 1970). A second variant, developed by both pluralist and public choice theory, argues that democracy will nurture intense party competition around the median voter that will, in turn, fuel rising public expenditures. Tufte (1978), for example, argues that major extensions of public intervention will occur around elections as a means of voter mobilization.

The democratic-institutionalist approach faces considerable empirical problems (Skocpol and Amenta 1986). According to the thesis, a democratic polity is the basic precondition for welfare state emergence, and welfare states are more likely to develop the more democratic rights are extended. Yet, the thesis confronts not only the historical oddity that the first major welfare state initiatives occurred prior to democracy, but also that they were often motivated by desires to arrest its realization. This was certainly the case in France under Napoleon II, in Germany under Bismarck, and in Austria under von Taaffe. Conversely, welfare state development was most retarded where democracy arrived early, such as in the United States, Australia, and Switzerland. This apparent contradiction can be explained, but only with reference to social classes and social structure: nations in which democracy appeared early were overwhelmingly agrarian and dominated by small property owners who used their electoral powers to reduce, not raise, taxes (Dich 1973). In contrast, ruling classes in authoritarian polities were better positioned to impose high taxes on an unwilling populace.

Social class as a political agent

We have noted that the case for a third approach to analyzing the welfare state, the class mobilization thesis, flows from social democratic political economy. It differs from structuralist and institutional analyses by its emphasis on the social classes as the main agents of change and its argument that the balance of class power determines distributional outcomes. To emphasize active class mobilization does not necessarily deny the importance of structured or hegemonic power (Korpi 1983). But it is held that parliaments are, in principle, effective institutions for the translation of mobilized power into desired policies and reforms. Accordingly, parliamentary politics are capable of over-riding hegemony, and may be made to serve interests that are antago-nistic to capital. Further, the class mobilization theory assumes that welfare states do more than simply alleviate the current ills of the system; a "social democratic" welfare state will, in its own right, establish critical power resources for wage earners and, thus, strengthen labor movements. As Heimann (1929) originally held, so-cial rights push back the frontiers of capitalist power and prerogatives.

The question of why the welfare state itself is a power resource is vital for the theory's applicability. The answer is that wage earners in the market are inherently atomized and stratified, compelled to com-pete, and are insecure and dependent on decisions and forces beyond their control. This limits their capacity for collective solidarity and mobilization. The social rights, income security, equalization of in-come, and eradication of poverty that a universalistic welfare state pursues are necessary preconditions for the strength and unity that collective power mobilization demands (Esping-Andersen 1985a).

The single most difficult problem for this thesis is to specify the conditions for power mobilization. Power depends on the resources that flow from the unity of electoral numbers and from collective bar-gaining. Power mobilization, in turn, depends on the levels of trade union organization and voter shares and the number of parliamentary and cabinet seats held by left or labor parties. But how long a period of sustained power mobilization is required in order to produce decisive effects? If power is measured over a brief time span (five to ten years), we risk the fallacy of a "Blum/Mitterand" effect: a brief spell of leftist power that proves ineffectual because the left is ousted before having had a chance to act.

There are several valid objections to the class mobilization thesis. Three, in particular, are quite fundamental. One is that in advanced capitalist nations, the locus of decision making and power may shift from parliaments to neocorporatist institutions of interest intermediation (Shonfield 1965; Schmitter and Lembruch 1979). A second criticism is that the capacity of labor parties to influence welfare state development is circumscribed by the structure of rightist party power. Castles (1978; 1982) has argued that the degree of unity among the rightist parties is more important than is the activated power of the left. Other authors have emphasized the fact that denominational (usually social catholic) parties in countries such as the

Netherlands, Italy, and Germany mobilize large sections of the working classes and pursue welfare state programs not drastically at variance with their socialist competitors (Schmidt 1982; Wilensky 1981). The class mobilization thesis has, rightfully so, been criticized for its Swedocentrism, that is, its inclination to define the process of power mobilization too much on the basis of the rather extraordinary Swedish experience (Shalev 1983).

These objections address a basic fallacy in the theory's assumptions about class formation: we cannot assume that socialism is the natural basis for wage-earner mobilization. Indeed, the conditions under which workers become socialists are still not adequately documented. Historically, the natural organizational bases of worker mobilization were precapitalist communities, especially the guilds, but also church, ethnicity, or language. A ready-made reference to false consciousness will not do to explain why Dutch, Italian, or U.S. workers continue to mobilize around nonsocialist principles. The dominance of socialism in the Swedish working class is as much a puzzle as is the dominance of confessionalism in the Dutch.

The third and, perhaps, most fundamental objection has to do with the model's linear view of power. It is problematic to hold that a numerical increase in votes, unionization, or parliamentary seats will translate into more welfare statism. First, for socialist as for other parties, the magical "50 percent" threshold for parliamentary majorities seems practically insurmountable (Przworski 1985). Second, if socialist parties represent working classes in the traditional sense, it is clear that they will never succeed in their project. In very few cases has the traditional working class been numerically a majority, and its role is rapidly becoming marginal.[6]

Probably the most promising way to resolve the combined linearity—and working class minority—problem lies in recent applications of Barrington Moore's path-breaking class coalition thesis to the transformation of the modern state (Weir and Skocpol 1985; Gourevitch 1986; Esping-Andersen 1985a; Esping-Andersen and Friedland 1982). Thus, the origins of the Keynesian full employment commitment and the social democratic welfare state edifice have been traced to the capacity of (variably) strong working-class movements to forge a political alliance with farmers' organizations; in addition, it is arguable that sustained social democracy has come to depend on the formation of a new working class–white collar coalition.

The class coalitional approach has additional virtues. Two nations, such as Austria and Sweden, may score similarly on working-class mobilization variables, and yet produce highly unequal policy results. This can be explained by differences in the two countries' historical coalition formation: The breakthrough of Swedish social democratic hegemony stems from its capacity to forge the famous "red-green" alliance; the comparative disadvantage of the Austrian socialists rests in the "ghetto" status assigned to them by virtue of the rural classes being captured by a conservative coalition (Esping-Andersen and Korpi 1984).

In sum, we have to think in terms of social relations, not just social categories. Whereas structural-functionalist explanations identify convergent welfare state outcomes, and class-mobilization paradigms see large, but linearly distributed, differences, an interactive model such as the coalitions approach directs attention to distinct welfare state regimes.

What is the welfare state?

Every theoretical paradigm must somehow define the welfare state. How do we know when and if a welfare state responds functionally to the needs of industrialism, or to capitalist reproduction and legitimacy? And how do we identify a welfare state that corresponds to the demands that a mobilized working class might have? We cannot test contending arguments unless we have a commonly shared conception of the phenomenon to be explained.

A remarkable attribute of the entire literature is its lack of much genuine interest in the welfare state as such. Welfare state studies have been motivated by theoretical concerns with other phenomena, such as power, industrialization, or capitalist contradictions; the welfare state itself has generally received scant conceptual attention. If welfare states differ, how do they differ? And when, indeed, is a state a welfare state? This turns attention straight back to the original question: what is the welfare state? A common textbook definition is that it involves state responsibility for securing some basic modicum of welfare for its citizens. Such a definition skirts the issue of whether social policies are emancipatory or not; whether they help system legitimation or not; whether they contradict or aid the market process; and what, indeed, is meant by "basic"? Would it not be more appropriate to require of a welfare state that it satisfies more than our basic or minimal welfare needs?

The first generation of comparative studies started with this type of conceptualization. Its authors assumed, without much reflection, that the level of social expenditure adequately reflects a state's commitment to welfare. The theoretical intent was not really to arrive at an understanding of the welfare state, but rather to test the validity of contending theoretical models in political economy. By scoring nations with respect to urbanization, level of economic growth, and the share of aged in the demographic structure, it was believed that the essential features of industrial modernization were adequately captured. Alternatively, by scoring nations on left party strength, or working-class power mobilization (with complex weighted scores of trade unionism, electoral strength, and cabinet power), others sought to identify the impact of working-class mobilization as formulated in the social democratic model.

The findings of the first generation of comparativists are extremely difficult to evaluate. No convincing case can be made for any particular theory. The shortage of nations for comparisons statistically restricts the number of variables that can be tested simultaneously. Thus, when Cutright (1965) or Wilensky (1975) finds that economic level, with its demographic and bureaucratic correlates, explains most welfare state variations in "rich countries," relevant measures of working-class mobilization or economic openness are not included. A conclusion in favor of a logic of industrialism view is therefore in doubt. And, when Hewitt (1977), Stephens (1979), Korpi (1983), Myles (1984), and Esping-Andersen (1985b) find strong evidence in favor of a working-class mobilization thesis, or when Schmidt (1982; 1983) finds support for a neocorporatist, and Cameron (1978) for an economic openness argument, it is without fully testing against the strongest alternative explanation.[7]

Most of these studies claim to explain the welfare state. Yet, their focus on spending may be irrelevant or, at best, misleading. Expenditures are epiphenomenal to the theoretical substance of welfare states. Moreover, the linear scoring approach (more or less power, democracy, or spending) contradicts the sociological notion that power, democracy, and welfare are relational and structured phenomena. By scoring welfare states on spending, we assume that all spending counts equally. But, some welfare states, Austria for example, spend a large share on benefits to privileged civil servants. This is normally not what we would consider a commitment to social citizenship and solidarity.

Other nations spend disproportionally on means-tested social assistance. Few contemporary analysts would agree that a reformed poor relief tradition qualifies as a welfare state commitment. Some nations spend enormous sums on fiscal welfare in the form of tax privileges to private insurance plans that mainly benefit the middle classes. But these tax expenditures do not show up on expenditure accounts. In the United Kingdom, total social expenditure has grown during the Thatcher period; yet, this is almost exclusively a function of very high unemployment. Low expenditures on some programs may signify a welfare state more seriously committed to full employment.

Therborn (1983) is right when he holds that we must begin with a conception of state structure. What are the criteria with which we should judge whether, and when, a state is a welfare state? There are three approaches to this question. Therborn's proposal is to begin with the historical transformation of state activities. Minimally, the majority of a genuine welfare state's daily routine activities must be devoted to servicing the welfare needs of households. This criterion has far-reaching consequences. If we simply measure routine activity in terms of spending and personnel, the result is that no state can be regarded as a real welfare state until the 1970s! And, some that we normally label as welfare states will still not qualify because the majority of their routine activities concern defense, law and order, administration, and the like (Therborn 1983). Social scientists have been too quick to accept nations' self-proclaimed welfare state status. They have also been too quick to conclude that the presence of the battery of typical social programs signifies the birth of a welfare state.

The second conceptual approach derives from Richard Titmuss's (1958) classical distinction between residual and institutional welfare states. The former assumes that state responsibility begins only when the family or the market fails; its commitment is limited to marginal groups in society. The latter model addresses the entire population, is universalistic, and implants an institutionalized commitment to welfare. It will, in principle, extend welfare commitments to all areas of distribution vital for societal welfare. This approach has fertilized a variety of new developments in comparative welfare state research (Myles 1984; Korpi 1980; Esping-Andersen and Korpi 1984; 1986; Esping-Andersen 1985b; 1987). And it has forced researchers to move away from the black box of expenditures and toward the content of welfare states: targeted versus universalistic programs, the conditions of eligibility, the quality of benefits and services, and, perhaps most importantly, the extent to which employment and working life are encompassed in the state's extension of citizen rights. This shift to welfare state typologies makes simple linear welfare state rankings difficult to sustain. We might in fact be comparing categorically different types of states.

The third approach is to select theoretically the criteria on which to judge types of welfare states. This can be done by measuring actual welfare states against some abstract model and then by scoring programs, or entire welfare states, accordingly (Day 1978; Myles 1984). The weakness of this approach is that it is ahistorical, and does not necessarily capture the ideals or designs that historical actors sought to realize in the struggles over the welfare state. If our aim is to test causal theories that involve actors, we should begin with the demands that were actually promoted by those actors that we deem critical in the history of welfare state development. It is difficult to imagine that anyone struggled for spending per se.

A respecification of the welfare state

Few people can disagree with T. H. Marshall's (1950) proposition that social citizenship constitutes the core idea of a welfare state. What, then, are the key principles involved in social citizenship? In our view, they must involve first and foremost the granting of social rights. This mainly entails a decommodification of the status of individuals vis-à-vis the market. Second, social citizenship involves social stratification; one's status as a citizen will compete with, or even replace, one's class position. Third, the welfare state must be understood in terms of the interface between the market, the family, and the state. These principles need to be fleshed out prior to any theoretical specification of the welfare state.[8]

Rights and decommodification

As commodities in the market, workers depend for their welfare entirely on the cash-nexus. The question of social rights is thus one of decommodification, that is, of granting alternative means of welfare to that of the market. Decommodification may refer either to the service rendered, or to the status of a person, but in both cases it signifies the degree to which distribution is detached from the market mechanism. This means that the mere presence of social assistance or insurance may not necessarily bring about significant decommodification if it does not substantially emancipate individuals from market dependence. Means-tested poor relief will possibly offer a security blanket as a last resort. But if benefits are low and attached with social stigma, the relief system will compel all but the most desperate to participate in the market. This was precisely the intent of the nineteenth-century poor laws. Similarly, most of the early social insurance programs were deliberately designed to maximize labor market performance (Ogus 1979). Benefits required long contribution periods and were tailored to prior work effort. In either case, the motive was to avert work-disincentive effects.

There is no doubt that decommodification has been a hugely contested issue in welfare state development. For labor, it has always been a priority. When workers are completely market dependent, they are difficult to mobilize for solidaristic action. Since their resources mirror market inequalities, divisions emerge between the ''ins'' and the ''outs,'' making labor movement formation difficult. Decommodification strengthens the worker and weakens the absolute authority of the employer. It is for exactly this reason that employers have historically opposed decommodification.

Decommodified rights are differentially developed in contemporary welfare states. In welfare states dominated by social assistance, rights are not so much attached to work performance as to demonstrable need. Needs-tests and typically meager benefits, however, serve to curtail the decommodifying effect. Thus, in nations where this model is dominant (mainly in the Anglo-Saxon countries), the result is actually to strengthen the market since all but those who fail in the market will be encouraged to contract private sector welfare.

A second dominant model espouses compulsory state social insurance with fairly strong entitlements. Yet, again, this may not automatically secure substantial decommodification, since this hinges very much on the fabric of eligibility and benefit rules. Germany was the pioneer of social insurance but over most of the twentieth century can hardly be said to have brought about much in the way of decommodification through its social programs. Benefits have depended almost entirely on contributions and, thus, work and employment. In fact, before World War II, average pensions in the German insurance system for workers were lower than prevailing poverty assistance rates (Myles 1984). The consequence, as with the social assistance model, was that most workers chose to remain at work rather than retire. In other words, it is not the mere presence of a social right, but the corresponding rules and preconditions that dictate the extent to which welfare programs offer genuine alternatives to market dependence.

The third dominant model of welfare, namely the Beveridge-type citizens' benefit, may, at first glance, appear the most decommodifying. It offers a basic, equal benefit to all irrespective of prior earnings, contributions, or work performance. It may indeed be a more solidaristic system, but not necessarily decommodifying since only rarely have such schemes been able to offer benefits of such a standard that they provide recipients with a genuine option to that of working.

Decommodifying welfare states are, in practice, of very recent date. A minimalist definition must entail that citizens can freely, and without potential loss of jobs, income, or general welfare, opt out of work under conditions when they, themselves, consider it necessary for reasons of health, family, age, or even educational self-improvement; when, in short, they deem it necessary for participating adequately in the social community.

With this definition in mind, we would, for example, require of sickness insurance that individuals have a guarantee of benefits equal to normal earnings, the right to absence with minimal proof of medical impairment and for the duration that the individual deems necessary. These conditions, it is worth noting, are those usually enjoyed by academics, civil servants, and higher echelon white-collar employees. Similar requirements would be made of pensions, maternity leave, parental leave, educational leave, and unemployment insurance.

Some nations have moved toward this level of decommodification, but only recently and, in many cases, with significant exemptions. Thus, in almost all nations, benefits were upgraded to almost equal normal wages in the late 1960s and early 1970s. But, in some countries, for example, prompt medical certification in case of illness is still required; in others, entitlements depend on long waiting periods of up to two weeks; in others, the duration of entitlements is very short (in the United States, for example, unemployment benefit duration is maximally six months, compared to thirty months in Denmark). Overall, the Scandinavian welfare states tend to be the most decommodifying; the Anglo-Saxon ones the least.

The welfare state as a system of stratification

Despite the emphasis given to it in both classical political economy and in T. H. Marshall's pioneering work, the relationship between social citizenship and social class remains severely neglected, both theoretically and empirically. Generally speaking, the issue has either been assumed away (it has been taken for granted that the welfare state creates a more egalitarian society), or it has been approached narrowly in terms of income distribution or in terms of whether education promotes upward social mobility. A more basic question, it seems, is: What kind of stratification system is promoted by social policy? The welfare state is not just a mechanism that intervenes in, and possibly corrects, the structure of inequality; it is, in its own right, a system of stratification. It actively and directly orders social relations.

Comparatively and historically, we can easily identify alternative systems of stratification embedded in welfare states. The poor relief tradition and its contemporary means-tested social assistance offshoot were conspicuously designed for purposes of stratification. By punishing and stigmatizing recipients, it promotes severe social dualisms, especially within the ranks of the working classes. It comes as no surprise that this model of welfare has been a chief target of labor movement attacks.

The social insurance model promoted by conservative reformers such as Bismarck and von Taaffe was also explicitly a form of class politics. It sought, in fact, to achieve two simultaneous stratification results. The first goal was to consolidate divisions among wage earners by legislating distinct programs for different class and status groups, each with its own conspicuously unique set of rights and privileges designed to accentuate the individual's appropriate station in life. The second objective was to tie the loyalties of the individual directly to the monarchy, or central state authority. This was Bismarck's motive when he promoted a direct state supplement to the pension benefit. This state-corporativist model was pursued mainly in nations such as Germany, Austria, Italy, and France and often resulted in a labyrinth of status-specific insurance funds (in France and Italy, for example, there exist more than one hundred status-distinct pension schemes).

Of special importance in this corporatist tradition was the establishment of particularly privileged welfare provisions for the civil service (*"Beamten"*). In part, this was a means of rewarding loyalty to the state and in part, a way of demarcating this group's uniquely exalted social status. We should, however, be careful to note that the corporatist status-differentiated model springs mainly from the old guild tradition. The neoabsolutist autocrats, such as Bismarck, saw in this tradition a means to combat the rising labor movements.

The labor movements were as hostile to the corporatist model as they were to poor relief—in both cases for obvious reasons. Yet, the alternatives first espoused by labor were no less problematic from the point of view of uniting the workers as one solidaristic class. Almost invariably, the model that labor first pursued was that of the self-organized friendly societies or equivalent union- or party-sponsored fraternal welfare plan. This is not surprising. Workers were obviously suspicious of reforms sponsored by a hostile state, and saw their own organizations not only as the basis of class mobilization, but also as embryos of an alternative world of solidarity and justice, as a microcosm of the socialist haven to come. Nonetheless, these micro-socialist societies often became problematic class ghettos that divided rather than united workers. Membership was typically restricted to the strongest strata of the working-class and the weakest—who needed protection most—were most likely outside. In brief, the fraternal society model contradicted the goal of working-class mobilization.

The socialist ghetto approach was an additional obstacle when socialist parties found themselves forming governments and having to pass the social reforms they so long had demanded. For reasons of political coalition building and broader solidarity, their welfare model had to be recast as welfare for the "people." Hence, the socialists came to espouse the principle of universalism and, borrowing from the liberals, typically designed their welfare model on the lines of the democratic flat-rate, general revenue–financed, Beveridge model.

As an alternative to means-tested assistance and corporatist social insurance, the universalistic system promotes status equality. All citizens are endowed with similar rights, irrespective of class or market position. In this sense, the system is meant to cultivate cross-class solidarity, a solidarity of the nation. But, the solidarity of flat-rate universalism presumes a historically peculiar class structure, one in which the vast majority of the population are the "little people" for whom a modest, albeit egalitarian, benefit may be considered adequate. Where this condition no longer exists, as occurs with growing working-class prosperity and the rise of the new middle classes, flat-rate universalism inadvertently promotes dualism because the better-off turn to private insurance and to fringe-benefit bargaining to supplement modest equality with their accustomed standards of welfare. Where this process unfolds (as in Canada or the United Kingdom), the result is that the wonderfully egalitarian spirit of universalism turns into a dualism similar to that of the social assistance state: the poor rely on the state, and the remaining groups on the market.

It is not only the universalist, but in fact all historical welfare state models, that have faced the dilemma of class structural change. But, the response to prosperity and middle-class growth has been varied and, therefore, so has the stratificational outcome. The corporatist insurance tradition was, in a sense, best equipped to manage new and loftier welfare state expectations since the existing system could technically be upgraded quite easily to distribute more adequate benefits. Konrad Adenauer's 1957 pension reform in Germany was a pioneer in this respect. Its avowed purpose was to restore status differences that had eroded due to the old insurance system's incapacity to provide benefits tailored to expectations. This it did simply by moving from contribution- to earnings-graduated benefits without altering the framework of status-distinctiveness.

In nations with either a social assistance— or a universalistic Beveridge-type system, the option was whether to allow the market or the state to furnish adequacy and satisfy middle-class aspirations. Two alternative models emerged from this political choice. The one typical of the United Kingdom and most of the Anglo-Saxon world was to preserve an essentially modest universalism in the state and allow the market to reign for the growing social strata demanding superior welfare. Due to the political power of such groups, the dualism that emerges is not merely one between state and market, but also between forms of welfare state transfers: in these nations, one of the fastest growing components of public expenditure is tax-subsidies for so-called private welfare plans. And the typical political effect is eroding middle-class support for what is less and less a universalistic public sector transfer system.

Yet another alternative has been to seek a synthesis of universalism and adequacy outside the market. This road has been followed in the countries where, by mandate or legislation, the state includes the new middle classes by erecting a luxurious second-tier, universally inclusive, earnings-related insurance scheme on top of the flat-rate egalitarian one. Notable examples are Sweden and Norway. By guaranteeing benefits tailored to expectations, this solution reintroduces benefit inequalities, but effectively blocks off the market. It thus succeeds in retaining universalism and, therefore, also the degree of political consensus required to preserve broad and solidaristic support for the high taxes that such a welfare state model demands.

Welfare state regimes

Welfare states vary considerably with respect to their principles of rights and stratification. This results in qualitatively different arrangements among state, market, and the family. The welfare state variations we find are therefore not linearly distributed, but clustered by regime types.

In one cluster, we find the ''liberal'' welfare state, in which means-tested assistance, modest universal transfers, or modest social insurance plans predominate. These cater mainly to a clientele of low-income, usually working-class, state dependents. It is a model in which, implicitly or explicitly, the progress of social reform has been severely circumscribed by traditional, liberal work-ethic norms; one where the limits of welfare equal the marginal propensity to demand welfare instead of work. Entitlement rules are therefore strict and often associated with stigma; benefits are typically modest. In turn, the state encourages the market, either passively, by guaranteeing only a minimum, or actively, by subsidizing private welfare schemes.

The consequence is that this welfare state regime minimizes decommodification effects, effectively contains the realm of social rights, and erects a stratification order that blends a relative equality of poverty among state welfare recipients, market-differentiated welfare among the majorities, and a class-political dualism between the two. The archetypical examples of this model are the United States, Canada, and Australia. Nations that approximate the model are Denmark, Switzerland, and the United Kingdom.

A second regime cluster is composed of nations such as Austria, France, Germany, and Italy. Here, the historical corporatist-statist legacy was upgraded to cater to the new ''postindustrial'' class structure. In these ''corporativist'' welfare states, the liberal obsession with market efficiency and commodification was never preeminent and, as such, the granting of social rights was hardly ever a seriously contested issue. What predominated was the preservation of status differentials; rights, therefore, were attached to class and status. This corporativism was subsumed under a state edifice perfectly ready to displace the market as a provider of welfare; hence, private insurance and occupational fringe benefits play a truly marginal role in this model. On the other hand, the state's emphasis on upholding status differences means that its redistributive effects are negligible.

But, the corporativist regimes are also typically shaped by the church, and therefore influenced by a strong commitment to the preservation of traditional family patterns. Social insurance typically excludes nonworking wives and family benefits encourage motherhood. Day care, and similar family services, are conspicuously underdeveloped, and the "subsidiarity principle" serves to emphasize that the state will only interfere when the family's capacity to service its members is exhausted. An illustrative example is German unemployment assistance. Once a person has exhausted his or her entitlement to normal unemployment insurance, eligibility for continued assistance depends on whether one's family commands the financial capacity to aid the unfortunate; this applies to persons of any age.

The third, and clearly smallest, regime cluster is composed of those countries in which the principles of universalism and decommodifying social rights were extended to the new middle classes. We may call it the "social democratic" regime type since, in these nations, social democracy clearly was the dominant force behind social reform. Norway and Sweden are the clearest cases, but we should also consider Denmark and Finland. Rather than tolerate a dualism between state and market, between working class and middle class, the social democrats pursued a welfare state that would promote an equality of the highest standards, rather than an equality of minimal needs as was pursued elsewhere. This implied, first, that services and benefits be upgraded to levels commensurable to even the most discriminate tastes of the new middle classes, and, second, that equality be furnished by guaranteeing workers full participation in the quality of rights enjoyed by the better-off.

This formula translates into a mix of highly decommodifying and universalistic programs that, nonetheless, are tailored to differentiated expectations. Thus, manual workers come to enjoy rights identical to those of salaried white-collar employees or civil servants; all strata and classes are incorporated under one universal insurance system; yet, benefits are graduated according to accustomed earnings. This model crowds out the market and, consequently, inculcates an essentially universal solidarity behind the welfare state. All benefit, all are dependent, and all will presumably feel obliged to pay.

The social democratic regime's policy of emancipation addresses both the market and the traditional family. In contrast to the corporatist-subsidiarity model, the principle is not to wait until the family's capacity to aid is exhausted, but to preemptively socialize the costs of family-hood. The ideal is to maximize not dependence on the family, but capacities for individual independence. In this sense, the model is a peculiar fusion of liberalism and socialism. The result is a welfare state that grants transfers directly to the children, and takes direct caring responsibilities for children, the aged, and the helpless. It is, accordingly, committed to a heavy social service burden, not only to service family needs, but also to permit women to chose work outside the household.

Perhaps the most salient characteristic of the social democratic regime is its fusion of welfare and work. It is, at once, a welfare state genuinely committed to a full employment guarantee and a welfare state entirely dependent on its attainment. On the one side, it is a model in which the right to work has status equal to the right of income protection. On the other side, the enormous costs of maintaining a solidaristic, universalistic, and decommodifying welfare system means that it must minimize social problems and maximize revenue. This is obviously best done with the most people working, and the fewest possible people living off social transfers.

While it is empirically clear that welfare states cluster, we must recognize that no single case is pure. The social democratic regimes of Scandinavia blend crucial socialist and liberal elements. The Danish and Swedish unemployment insurance schemes, for example, are still essentially voluntarist. Denmark's labor movement has been chronically incapable of pursuing full employment policies due in part to trade union resistance to active labor market policy. And in both Denmark and Finland, the market has been allowed to play a decisive role in pensions.

Nor are the liberal regimes pure. The U.S. social security system is redistributive, compulsory, and far from actuarial. At least in its early formulation, the New Deal was as social democratic as was contemporary Scandinavian social democracy. In contrast, the Australian welfare state would appear exceedingly close to the bourgeois-liberal ideal type, but much of its edifice has the coresponsibility of Australian labor. And, finally, the European corporatist regimes have received both liberal and social democratic impulses. Social insurance schemes have been substantially destratified and unified in Austria, Germany, France, and Italy. Their extremely corporativist character has thus been reduced.

Notwithstanding the lack of purity, if our essential criteria for defining welfare states have to do with the quality of social rights, social stratification, and the relationship between state, market, and family, the world is composed of distinct regime clusters. Comparing welfare states on scales based on more or less or, indeed, better or worse, will yield highly misleading results.

The causes of welfare state regimes

If welfare states cluster into three distinct regime types, we are confronted with a substantially more complex task of identifying the causes of welfare state differences. What is the explanatory power of industrialization, economic growth, capitalism, or working-class political power in accounting for regime types? A first superficial answer would be: very little. The nations we study are all more or less similar with regard to all but the working-class mobilization variable. And we find very powerful labor movements and parties in each of the three clusters. A theory of welfare state developments must clearly reconsider its causal assumptions if we wish to explain clusters. The hope to find one single powerful causal motor must be abandoned; the task is to identify salient interaction effects. Based on the preceding arguments, three factors in particular should be of importance: the nature of (especially working-) class mobilization; class-political coalition structures; and the historical legacy of regime institutionalization.

As we have noted, there is absolutely no compelling reason to believe that workers will automatically and naturally forge a socialist class identity; nor is it plausible that their mobilization will look especially Swedish. The actual historical formation of working-class collectivities will diverge, and so also will their aims and political capacities. Fundamental differences appear both in trade unionism and party development. A key element in trade unionism is the mix of craft and industrial unions. The former is prone to particularism and corporativism; the latter is inclined to articulate broader, more universal objectives. This blend decisively affects the scope for labor party action and also the nature of political demands. Thus, the dominance of the American Federation of Labor (AFL) in pre–World War II United States was a major impediment to social policy development. Likewise, the heavily craft-oriented Danish labor movement, compared to its Norwegian and Swedish counterparts, blocked social democracy's aspirations for an active labor market policy for full employment. In the United States, craft unions believed that negotiating occupational benefits was a superior strategy, given their privileged market position. In Denmark, craft unions jealously guarded their monopoly on training and labor mobility. Conversely, centralized industrial unionism tends to present a more unified and consolidated working-class clientele to the labor party, making policy consensus easier, and power mobilization more effective. It is clear, therefore, that a working-class mobilization thesis must pay attention to union structure.

Equally decisive is political or denominational union fragmentation. In many nations, for example, Finland, France, and Italy, trade unionists are divided between socialist and communist parties; white-collar unions are politically unaffiliated or divide their affiliation among several parties. Denominational trade unionism has been a powerful feature in the Netherlands, Italy, and other nations. Since trade unionism is such a centrally important basis for party mobilization, such fragmentation will weaken the left and thus benefit the nonsocialist parties' chances of power. In addition, fragmentation may entail that welfare state demands will be directed to many parties at once. The result may be less party conflict over social policy, but it may also mean a plurality of competing welfare state principles. For example, the subsidiarity principle of Christian workers will conflict with the socialists' concern for the emancipation of women.

The structure of trade unionism may or may not be reflected in labor party formation. But, under what conditions are we likely to expect certain welfare state outcomes from specific party configurations? There are many factors that conspire to make it virtually impossible to assume that any labor or left party will ever be capable, single-handedly, of structuring a welfare state. Denominational or other divisions aside, it will be only under extraordinary historical circumstances that a labor party alone will command a parliamentary majority long enough to impose its will. We have noted that the traditional working class has, nowhere, ever been an electoral majority. It follows that a theory of class mobilization must look beyond the major leftist party. It is a historical fact that welfare state construction has depended on political coalition building. The structure of class coalitions is much more decisive than are the power resources of any single class.

The emergence of alternative class coalitions is, in part, determined by class formation. In the earlier phases of industrialization, the rural classes usually constituted the single largest electorate. If social democrats wanted political majorities, it was here that they were forced to look for allies. Therefore, it was ironically the rural economy that was decisive for the future of socialism. Where the rural economy was dominated by small, capital-intensive family farmers, the potential for an alliance was greater than if it depended on large pools of cheap labor. And, where farmers were politically articulate and well organized (as in Scandinavia), the capacity to negotiate political deals was vastly superior.

The role of the farmers in coalition formation and, hence, in welfare state development is clear. In the Nordic countries, the conditions provided for a broad red-green alliance for a full employment welfare state in return for farm price subsidies. This was especially true in Norway and Sweden, where farming was highly precarious and dependent on state aid. In the United States, the New Deal was premised on a similar coalition (forged by the Democratic party) but with the important difference that the labor-intensive South blocked a truly universalistic social security system and opposed further welfare state developments. In contrast, the rural economy of continental Europe was very inhospitable to red-green coalitions. Often, as in Germany and Italy, much of agriculture was labor-intensive and labor unions and left parties were seen as a threat. In addition, the conservative forces on the continent had succeeded in incorporating farmers into "reactionary" alliances, helping to consolidate the political isolation of labor.

Political dominance was, before World War II, largely a question of rural class politics. The construction of welfare states in this period was, therefore, dictated by which force captured the farmers. The absence of a red-green alliance does not necessarily imply that no welfare state reforms were possible. On the contrary, it implies which political force came to dominate their design. The United Kingdom is an exception to this general rule because the political significance of the rural classes eroded before the turn of the nineteenth century. In this way, the United Kingdom's coalition logic showed at an early date the dilemma that faced most other nations later, namely that the new white-collar middle classes constitute the linchpin for political majorities. The consolidation of welfare states after World War II came to depend fundamentally on the political alliances of the new middle classes. For social democracy, the challenge was to synthesize working-class and white-collar demands without sacrificing the commitment to solidarity.

Since the new middle classes have, historically, enjoyed a relatively privileged position in the market, they have also been quite successful in meeting their welfare demands outside the state or as civil servants by privileged state welfare. Their employment security has tradition-ally been such that full employment has been a peripheral concern. Finally, any program for drastic income equalization is likely to be met with great hostility among a middle-class clientele. On these grounds, it would appear that the rise of the new middle classes would abort the social democratic project and strengthen a liberal welfare state formula.

The political position of the new middle classes has, indeed, been decisive for welfare state consolidation. Their role in shaping the three welfare state regimes described earlier is clear. The Scandinavian, or social democratic, model relied almost entirely on social democracy's capacity to incorporate the middle class in a new kind of welfare state: one that provided benefits tailored to the tastes and expectations of the middle classes, but nonetheless retained universalism of rights. Indeed, by expanding social services and public employment, the welfare state participated directly in manufacturing a middle class instrumentally devoted to social democracy.

In contrast, the Anglo-Saxon nations retained the residual liberal welfare state model precisely because the new middle classes were not wooed from the market into the state. In class terms, the consequence is dualism. The welfare state caters essentially to the working class and the poor. Private insurance and occupational fringe benefits cater to the middle classes. Given the electoral importance of the latter, it is quite logical that further extensions of welfare state activities are resisted. Indeed, the most powerful thrust in these countries is an accent on fiscal welfare; that is, on tax expenditures and deductions for private sector welfare plans.

The third, or corporativist welfare regime of continental Europe, has also been patterned by the new middle classes, but in a different way. The cause is historical. Developed by conservative political forces, these regimes institutionalized a middle-class loyalty to the preservation of both occupationally segregated social insurance programs and, ultimately, to the political forces that brought them into being. Adenauer's great pension reform in 1957 was explicitly designed to resurrect middle-class loyalties.

Conclusion

We have presented an alternative to a simple class mobilization theory of welfare state development. It is motivated by the analytical necessity of shifting from a linear to an interactive approach with regard to both welfare states and their historical foundations. If we wish to study welfare states, we must begin with a set of criteria that define their role in society. This role is certainly not to spend or tax, nor is it necessarily that of creating equality. We have presented a framework for comparing welfare states that takes into consideration the principles for which the historical actors willingly have struggled and mobilized. And, when we focus on the principles embedded in welfare states, we discover distinct regime clusters, not merely variations of "more" or "less" around a common denominator.

The salient forces that explain the crystallization of regime differences are interactive. They involve, first, the pattern of working class political formation and, second, the structure of political coalitions with the historical shift from a rural economy to a middle-class society. The question of political coalition formation is decisive.

Third, past reforms have contributed decisively to the institutionalization of class preferences and political behavior. In the corporatist regimes, hierarchical status-distinctive social insurance cemented middle-class loyalty to a peculiar type of welfare state. In the liberal regimes, the middle classes became institutionally wedded to the market. And, in Scandinavia, the fortunes of social democracy after World War II were closely tied to the establishment of a middle-class welfare state that benefited both its traditional working-class clientele and the new white-collar strata. In part, the Scandinavian social democrats were able to do so because the private welfare market was relatively undeveloped and, in part, because they were capable of building a welfare state with features of sufficient luxury to satisfy the tastes of a more discriminating public. This also explains the extraordinarily high cost of Scandinavian welfare states.

But, a theory that seeks to explain welfare state growth should also be able to understand its retrenchment or decline. It is typically believed that welfare state backlash movements, tax revolts, and rollbacks are ignited when social expenditure burdens become too heavy. Paradoxically, the opposite is true. Anti–welfare state sentiments over the past decade have generally been weakest where welfare spending has been heaviest, and vice versa. Why?

The risks of welfare state backlash depend not on spending, but on the class character of welfare states. Middle-class welfare states, be they social democratic (as in Scandinavia) or corporatist (as in Germany), forge middle-class loyalties. In contrast, liberal, residualist welfare states found in the United States, Canada, and, increasingly, the United Kingdom depend on the loyalties of a numerically weak, and often politically residual social stratum. In this sense, the class coalitions in which the three welfare states were founded explain not only their past evolution but also their future prospects.

Notes

An earlier version of this chapter appeared in the *Canadian Review of Sociology and Anthropology* 2, 1 (February 1989):10–36.

1. Adam Smith is often cited but rarely read. A closer inspection of his writings reveals a degree of nuance and a battery of reservations that substantially qualify a delirious enthusiasm for the blessings of capitalism.

2. In the *Wealth of Nations* (Smith 1961, vol. 2, 236), Smith comments on states that uphold the privilege and security of the propertied as follows: ". . . civil government, so far as it is instituted for the security of property, is in reality instituted for the defense of the rich against the poor, or of those who have some property against those who have none at all."

3. This tradition is virtually unknown to Anglo-Saxon readers, since so little has been translated into English. A key text, which greatly influenced public debate and later social legislation, is Adolph Wagner's *Rede über die Soziale Frage* (1872). For an English language overview of this tradition of political economy, see Schumpeter (1954), and especially Bower (1947).

From the Catholic tradition, the fundamental texts are the two Papal Encyclicals, *Rerum Novarum* (1891), see Rutten 1932, and *Quadrogesimo Anno* (Pius XI 1938). The social Catholic political economy's main advocacy is a social organization where a strong family is integrated in cross-class corporations, aided by the state in terms of the subsidiarity principle. For a recent discussion, see Richter (1987).

Like the liberals, the conservative political economists also have their contemporary echoes, although they are substantially fewer in number. A revival occurred with Fascism's concept of the Corporative ("Ständiche") state of Ottmar

Spann in Germany. The subsidiary principle still guides much of German Christian Democratic politics (see Richter 1987).

4. Chief proponents of this analysis are members of the German "state derivation" school (Müller and Neusüss 1973; Offe 1972; O'Connor 1973; Gough 1979; see also the work of Poulantzas (1973). As Skocpol and Amenta (1986) note in their excellent overview, the approach is far from one-dimensional. Thus, Offe, O'Connor, and Gough identify the function of social reforms as also being concessions to mass demands and as potentially contradictory.

Historically, socialist opposition to parliamentary reforms was principled less by theory than by reality. August Bebel, the great leader of German social democracy, rejected Bismarck's pioneering social legislation, not because he did not favor social protection, but because of the blatantly anti-socialist and divisionary motives behind Bismarck's reforms.

5. This realization came from two types of experiences. One, typified by Swedish socialism in the 1920s, was the discovery that not even the working-class base showed much enthusiasm for socialization. In fact, when the Swedish socialists established a special commission to prepare plans for socialization, it concluded after ten years of exploration that it would be practically quite impossible to undertake. A second kind of experience, typified by the Norwegian socialists and Blum's Popular Front government in 1936, was the discovery that radical proposals could easily be sabotaged by the capitalists' capacity to withhold investments and export their capital abroad.

6. This is obviously not a problem for the parliamentary class hypothesis alone; structural Marxism faces the same problem of specifying the class character of the new middle classes. If such a specification fails to demonstrate that it constitutes a new working class, both varieties of Marxist theory face severe (although not identical) problems.

7. This literature has been reviewed in great detail by a number of authors. See, for example, Wilensky et al. (1985). For excellent and more critical evaluations, see Uusitalo (1984), Shalev (1983), and Skocpol and Amenta (1986).

8. This section derives much of its material from earlier writings (see, especially Esping-Andersen (1985a; 1985b; 1987).

References

Bell, D. 1978. *The Cultural Contradictions of Capitalism.* New York: Basic Books.

Bendix, R. 1964. *Nation-Building and Citizenship.* New York: Wiley.

Block, F. 1977. "The Ruling Class does not Rule." *Socialist Revolution* 7 (May–June):6–28.

Bower, R. H. 1947. *German Theories of the Corporate State.* New York: Russel and Russel.

Bowles, S. and Gintis, H. 1986. *Democracy and Capitalism.* New York: Basic Books.

Cameron, D. 1978. "The Expansion of the Public Economy: A Comparative Analysis." *American Political Science Review* 72:1243–61.

Castles, F. 1978. *The Social Democratic Image of Society.* London: Routledge and Kegan Paul.

————. ed. 1982. *The Impact of Parties*. London: Sage.

Cutright, P. 1965. "Political Structure, Economic Development, and National Social Security Programs." *American Journal of Sociology* 70:537–50.

Day, L. 1978. "Government Pensions for the Aged in 19 Industrialized Countries." In R. Tomasson, ed., *Comparative Studies in Sociology*. Greenwich, CT: JAI Press.

Dich, J. 1973. *Den Herskende Klasse*. Copenhagen: Borgen.

Dobb, M. 1946. *Studies in the Development of Capitalism*. London: Routledge and Kegan Paul.

Esping-Andersen, G. 1985a. *Politics against Markets*. Princeton: Princeton University Press.

————. 1985b. "Power and Distributional Regimes." *Politics and Society* 14:223–56.

————. 1987. "Citizenship and Socialism: De-commodification and Solidarity in the Welfare State." In M. Rein, G. Esping-Andersen, and L. Rainwater, eds., *Stagnation and Renewal*. Armonk, NY: M. E. Sharpe.

Esping-Andersen, G., and Friedland, R. 1982. "Class Coalitions in the Making of West European Economies." *Political Power and Social Theory* 3:1–52.

Esping-Andersen, G., and Korpi, W. 1984. "Social Policy as Class Politics in Postwar Capitalism." In J. Goldthorpe, ed., *Order and Conflict in Contemporary Capitalism*. Oxford: Oxford University Press.

————. 1987. "From Poor Relief to Institutional Welfare States." In R. Erikson et al., eds., *The Scandinavian Model*. Armonk, NY: M. E. Sharpe.

Flora, P., and Alber, J. 1981. "Modernization, Democratization and the Development of Welfare States in Europe." In P. Flora and A. Heidenheimer, eds., *The Development of Welfare States in Europe and America*. London: Transaction Books.

Flora, P., and Heidenheimer, A., eds. 1981. *The Development of Welfare States in Europe and America*. London: Transaction Books.

Gough, I. 1979. *The Political Economy of the Welfare State*. London: Macmillan.

Gourevitch, P. 1986. *Politics in Hard Times*. Ithaca, NY: Cornell University Press.

Heimann, E. 1929. *Soziale Theorie des Kapitalismus*. Reprint 1980. Frankfurt: Suhrkamp.

Hewitt, C. 1977. "The Effect of Political Democracy and Social Democracy on Equality in Industrial Societies." *American Sociological Review* 42:450–64.

Jessop, B. 1982. *The Capitalist State*. Oxford: Martin Robertson.

Katzenstein, P. 1985. *Small States in World Markets*. Ithaca, NY: Cornell University Press.

Korpi, W. 1980. "Social Policy and Distributional Conflict in the Capitalist Democracies." *West European Politics* 3:296–316.

————. 1983. *The Democratic Class Struggle*. London: Routledge and Kegan Paul.

Marshall, A. 1920. *Principles of Economics*. 8th ed. London: Macmillan.

Marshall, T. H. 1950. *Citizenship and Social Class*. Cambridge: Cambridge University Press.

Myles, J. 1984. *Old Age in the Welfare State*. Boston: Little, Brown, and Co.

Myrdal, A., and Myrdal, G. 1936. *Kris i Befolkningsfrågan*. Stockholm: Tiden.

O'Connor, J. 1973. *The Fiscal Crisis of the State*. New York: St. Martin's Press.
Offe, C. 1972. "Advanced Capitalism and the Welfare State." *Politics and Society* 2, no. 4:479–88.
———. 1985. *Disorganized Capitalism*. Cambridge, MA: MIT Press.
Ogus, A. 1979. "Social Insurance, Legal Development and Legal History." In H. F. Zacher ed., *Bedingungen für die Entstehung von Sozialversicherung*. Berlin: Duncker and Humboldt.
Okun, A. 1975. *Equality and Efficiency: The Big Trade-Off*. Washington DC: Brookings Institute.
Pius XI. 1938. *On Reconstruction of the Social Order (Q.A.) Encyclical of His Holiness Pope Pius XI*. New York: The America Press.
Polanyi, K. 1944. *The Great Transformation*. New York: Rhinehart.
Poulantzas, N. 1973. *Political Power and Social Classes*. London: New Left Books.
Pryor, F. 1969. *Public Expenditures in Communist and Capitalist Nations*. London: Allen and Unwin.
Przworski, A. 1980. "Material Bases of Consent: Politics and Economics in a Hegemonic System." *Political Power and Social Theory* 1:21–66.
———. 1985. *Capitalism and Social Democracy*. Cambridge: Cambridge University Press.
Richter, E. 1987. "Subsidiarität und Neoconservatismus." *Politische Vierteljahresschrift* 28 (September):293–314.
Robbins, L. 1976. *Political Economy Past and Present*. London: Macmillan.
Rokkan, S. 1970. *Citizens, Elections, Parties*. Oslo: Universitetsforlaget.
Rutten, G. 1932. *La doctrine sociale de l'Eglise resumee dans les ensycliques Rerum novarum et Quadragesimo anno*. Paris: Editiones du Cerf.
Schmidt, M. 1982. "The Role of Parties in Shaping Macro-economic Policies." In F. Castles, ed., *The Impact of Parties*. London: Sage.
———. 1983. "The Welfare State and the Economy in Periods of Economic Crisis." *European Journal of Political Research* 11:1–26.
Schmitter, P., and Lembruch, G. 1979. *Trends Toward Corporatist Intermediation*. London: Sage.
Schumpeter, J. 1954. *History of Economic Analysis*. New York: Oxford University Press.
Shalev, M. 1983. "The Social Democratic Model and Beyond." *Comparative Social Research* 6:315–51.
Shonfield, A. 1965. *Modern Capitalism*. Oxford: Oxford University Press.
Skocpol, T., and Amenta, E. 1986. "States and Social Policies." *Annual Review of Sociology* 12:131–57.
Smith, A. 1961. *The Wealth of Nations*. Edited by E. Cannan. London: Methuen.
Stephens, J. 1979. *The Transition from Capitalism to Socialism*. London: Macmillan.
Therborn, G. 1983. "When, How and Why does a Welfare State become a Welfare State?" Paper presented at the European Consortium for Political Research (ECPR) Workshops, Freiburg, March.
———. 1986. "Karl Marx Returning. The Welfare State and Neo-Marxist, Corporatist and Statist Theories." *International Political Science Review* 7, no. 2:131–64.

Titmuss, R. 1958. *Essays on the Welfare State*. London: Allen and Unwin.

Tufte, E. 1978. *Political Control of the Economy*. Princeton: Princeton University Press.

Uusitalo, H. 1984. "Comparative Research on the Determinants of the Welfare State: The State of the Art." *European Journal of Political Research* 12, no. 4:403–22.

Wagner, A. 1872. *Rede über die Soziale Frage*. Berlin: Wiegandt und Grieben.

———. 1962. *Finanzwissenschaft (1883)*. Reproduced partly in R. A. Musgrave and A. Peacock, eds., *Classics in the Theory of Public Finance*. London: Macmillan.

Weir, M., and Skocpol, T. 1985. "State Structures and the Possibilities for Keynesean Responses to the Great Depression in Sweden, Britain, and the United States." In P. Evans et al., eds., *Bringing the State Back In*. New York: Cambridge University Press.

Wilensky, H. 1975. *The Welfare State and Equality*. Berkeley: University of California Press.

———. 1981. "Leftism, Catholicism, and Democratic Corporatism." In P. Flora and A. Heidenheimer, eds., *The Development of Welfare States in Europe and America*. London: Transaction Books.

Wilensky, H., and Lebeaux, C. 1958. *Industrial Society and Social Welfare*. New York: Russel Sage.

Wilensky, H., et al. 1985. "Comparative Social Policy: Theory, Methods, Findings." Research Series no. 62. Berkeley: International Studies.

5

The Interaction of Welfare States and Labor Markets: The Institutional Level

KÅRE HAGEN

Introduction

In the international social policy literature, it is widely assumed that the Scandinavian welfare states resemble each other so much that they collectively constitute one distinct model. However, the essential core of this model can be identified from at least three perspectives.

In one popular view, the Scandinavian model is identified by policy ambitions. A broad consensus exists across party and class cleavages that the state should neutralize the social inequalities created by markets, and thus achieve a high level of welfare and social security for all individuals (Erikson 1987; Alestalo and Kuhnle 1984). Hence, the Scandinavian model is characterized by the nearly universal acceptance of state intervention. Welfare politics is dominated by the struggle over means, rather than ends.

A second position characterizes the Scandinavian model by its welfare achievements. All countries share a high level of social security and individual welfare, exemplified by full employment, an even distribution of economic growth, and legislation concerning individual social rights. Poverty is largely eradicated, and the societies achieve a successful balance between individual freedom, equality, and social security (Brox 1988; Vogel 1984). The Scandinavian model is a noncommunist way to achieve the allocation of benefits "to all according to needs; by all according to ability."

Finally, a third point of view defines the Scandinavian model in terms of its institutional characteristics. To a considerable extent, public social policy has replaced markets and bargaining as the principal mechanisms of benefit allocation. Universal programs provide benefits both in cash and kind, irrespective of position in the labor market, and the financing of benefits is integrated into the general system of taxation. Private insurance is strongly regulated and of limited importance. Distributional considerations have been built into the tax system as well as into employment policies and social security programs. Thus, the Scandinavian model constitutes a distinct social security regime (Esping-Andersen 1985).

The similarities have been explained using different approaches. Esping-Andersen and Korpi (1987) emphasize the political power structure of the countries, having a consolidated, revisionist labor movement and a rural-based petty bourgeoisie which represent their class interests through separate political parties. The profound role of the state is based on an informal center-left alliance, supported by groups who see their social interests better represented within democratic politics than through other systems of allocation, such as markets or bargaining. Kuhnle (1983) has emphasized the role of "political learning"; that social security legislation has diffused from one country to the others. Since World War II, a comprehensive system of collaboration exists among the Scandinavian countries, between politicians and civil servants, but also among political "sister parties," and other private organizations. This extensive formal as well as informal coordination of policies naturally has contributed to the perception of the Scandinavian countries as a model group of states.

Whether the notion of a Scandinavian model is meaningful depends both on the point of departure and the very concept of a welfare state. However, as will be shown, also in the traditional core areas of the welfare state, significant differences exist between the countries, which are often overlooked by the Swedocentric bias of most comparative welfare state literature, in which the other countries are implicitly assumed to be copies of Sweden (Olafsson 1989).

The ambition of this chapter is to make a systematic comparison of the public welfare programs in the Scandinavian countries, by looking specifically at the systems of income maintenance provided by social security cash transfers. The period covered is 1960 to 1985, and the general question to be addressed is: To what extent have the institutional parameters of the social security systems expanded in such a way that they may shape and alter the behavior of individuals in the labor market?

The postwar "Keynesian welfare state" is based on two principal assumptions. First, the state is responsible for the guarantee of each citizen's welfare, and second, the means to accomplish this should not interrupt the production process of the capitalist economy. Hence, the obligations of the state have been fulfilled through interventions in the allocation of income (from production), whereas production itself has been left to the market. This constellation has been labeled a class compromise between labor and capital (Mjøset 1986), and as a socially acceptable equilibrium between the capitalist demand for efficiency and a political call for distributional justice (Kolberg 1983).

The separation of production and distribution has made both the labor market and the welfare state sources of individual income: the first by participation in paid work, the second through rights to a social wage, "paid nonwork." The concern that the social wage could become an alternative source of income is as old as the first welfare programs, and this contention has gained renewed support by the revival of neoclassical economics in the 1970s. The basic argument is that any political interference (by state or collective action) in the sphere of distribution will affect—that is, reduce—total output. The existence of an alternative income to wages provides a temptation for labor to reduce its participation in the market. High levels of social transfers (and correspondingly high taxes) will tend to erode the motivation to work, to lower investment, and to reduce long term growth. Thus, the first welfare programs provided only a modest level of benefits, according to very restrictive conceptions of "needs." The ambition of these programs was to ensure a minimum purchasing power; not to compensate for the loss of market wage, or the ability to participate in paid work.

During the postwar years a tacit but significant redefinition of the work-welfare relation took place. Participation in paid work has been seen as an important component of individual welfare in its own right. State subsidized wages, integration of disabled persons in sheltered jobs, and employment creation programs are all examples of this ideology. Another change, contrary to the previous, is the idea of permanent exit and temporary absence from work as welfare gains. The lowering of the pensionable age, the extension of maternity leave, and the establishment of early retirement programs all substantiate the theory that the alleviation of the work compulsion is a policy device to increase individual welfare.

Our point of departure is the concept of paid nonwork, by which we mean a temporary or permanent exit from ordinary gainful employment in the labor market, compensated through a system of legal rights to income transfers. Three categories of temporary absence will be addressed: sickness, childbirth, and unemployment. As regards permanent exit from work, the different kinds of public retirement schemes pertaining to employees below the age of sixty-five will be covered. Ordinary old age pension is excluded from our analysis.

Paid nonwork, as well as paid work, is an "activity" that takes place within an institutional setting. This setting includes, first, a comprehensive system of social rights which contain the conditions to be met in order to be entitled to absence and the regulations of the economic transfers during the period of absence. This legal system will be denoted as the social policy regime. Second, through participation in the labor market, manifested by the work contract, the individual is subordinated to a set of formal as well as informal norms regulating his or her economic behavior, a production regime. Both the social policy regime and the production regime will constrain, and create options for, individual behavior. How individual characteristics such as physical ability to work, family obligations, motivation, and preferences affect actual economic behavior must be understood in terms of the individual's interaction with both the social policy regime and the production regime.

The combination of social rights, formal and informal norms at work, and individual characteristics constitutes a setting in which the individual may have the option to choose between work and nonwork. In the neoclassical tradition, the assumption is that the rational person will opt out of work if the value of alternative activities approaches wages. Rising levels of sickness absence, unemployment, and early retirement are interpreted as part of the attractive effect of the economic compensation in these programs. The alternative perspective of this chapter is to consider the levels of temporary and permanent exit from work as the (intended) effects of a deliberate policy. By defining more needs and transforming them to individual rights, the legislators make it possible for workers to exit from paid work in specific circumstances.

The time span covered is undoubtedly the most expansive period of public welfare effort in all the Scandinavian countries (Iceland excluded). It is characterized by two major changes in the relationship between the state and the labor market. The first is the growth that occurred in public sector employment within education, health, and other welfare services. This expansion implies a transfer of work often done previously (by women) in the households to paid work in the formal economy which has created a new labor market in which total production (i.e., employment) is determined not by market demand, but by policy decisions. As a consequence of higher labor force participation, a growing proportion of the population has been integrated into the programs of social citizenship developed and designed for wage earners.

Second, as will be substantiated, the period 1960–85 is characterized by a significant liberalization of the rights for wage earners to leave work, temporarily or permanently, and still maintain high levels of income. We may also assume that generous unemployment and early retirement schemes from the mid-1970s, as well as high levels of temporary absence, were accepted as policy measures to clear the labor market by reducing the total supply of labor.

Thus, our period of analysis saw two significant changes in the relationship between the welfare state and the labor market: an increasing participation (by women) in paid work and rising levels of permanent and temporary exit from paid work and entry into paid nonwork.

Any social security scheme, legislated or negotiated, that makes paid absence from work possible is a concrete expression of specific normative priorities, defined by a range of legitimate causes of absence. Social needs are not transformed to social rights unless a process of needs definition has taken place (Titmuss 1958, 39; Hansen 1981). Some actors, within democratic politics, bargaining systems, or markets, have to decide who shall benefit, in what cases, and how the costs are to be distributed. Hence, a social security scheme must be recognized as a policy outcome that reflects the intentions and needs conceptions of the actors creating the specific program (Myles 1984). The postwar welfare states have not necessarily expanded because social needs have swelled in some objective sense, as much as because the definitions of which, and whose, needs are to be met by social rights have widened.

For the workers, a set of social rights is a parameter that affects their decision of whether or not to work. Thus, both the definitions of legitimate cases of absence and the qualifying conditions (e.g., working time or income thresholds) are meant to affect the labor market behavior of wage earners. The programs, therefore, are significant for the degree to which participation in the labor market may be combined with satisfying social needs without loss of income (Polyani 1957). Social rights make it possible for wage earners, under a set of specified conditions, to consume without participating in current production. That is why the rights exist. As such, they provoke the core logic of capitalist systems of production, where wages should be the exclusive source of income (and welfare). The right to a social wage through institutional transfers reduces the importance of the wage as a unique parameter of labor market behavior, making it possible for individuals to satisfy needs independently, or less affected by, the work compulsion which otherwise would have existed. It is this quality of social security rights that Esping-Andersen (1981) has denoted as a "decommodification of labor." However, the shield provided by welfare rights includes several dimensions. First, most cash benefits, both in the case of temporary and permanent exit from work, require that the recipient is, or has been, in employment. The closer the link between participation requirements and social benefits, the more plausible it is to consider the rights to be a reward from the market, rather than a protection from it. Also, the financing of benefits must be taken into account. If the insured person has to pay his or her own benefits, the cash benefit should be recognized as deferred wage (or enforced savings). Third, the protection from the market cannot be considered as related to labor as such, but to specific needs. The concept of decommodification is most fruitful when it is applied to the specific elements in the social security scheme that allow the individual to choose between work or income through the social wage. For example, if sickness pay or early retirement pension is provided only after a thorough medical verification of the ability to work, an option hardly exists, whereas if the decision is left to the individual, the concept of decommodification is clearly relevant.

Whether labor market participation in the Scandinavian countries has become more strongly affected by decommodifying elements of the welfare programs must be answered through three steps. First: Have the institutional arrangements actually expanded in such a way that they provide greater options for wage earners to prefer absence to work? The second step is to use indicators of potential decommodifying properties as explanatory variables to test the effects of social policy on patterns of labor market participation. We cannot assume that more generous social rights automatically lead to decommodified behavior. There may be costs linked to exploiting a social right, such as a possible lowering of the quality of one's labor due to absence and a consequent reduction in career or employment opportunities. The assumption of an inverse relationship between unemployment and sickness absence is an example of this (Sundboe et al. 1982). Correspondingly, some studies of maternity leave (Lindroos 1984; Kaul 1982) suggest that generous rights are not fully used, especially by men. Third, proper control for other intervening variables is essential. High levels of exit from work may be caused or influenced by factors not related to social security programs, like the demographic composition of the labor force, business cycles, or industrial structure.

In the rest of this chapter, the first of these three questions will be addressed: To what extent is it possible to see the development of a welfare state that provides more generous options of paid nonwork? And, is there a convergence between the different countries that supports the notion of a Scandinavian model, or have intercountry variations emerged or been enlarged? In order to answer these questions, we must first discuss the problems of comparing welfare state programs across countries and time.

Comparing social security programs

Any comprehensive comparison of social security programs across countries (and/or time) is faced with two major questions. The first is what to compare; the second is how to compare. What to compare has already been addressed; we are concerned with cash benefit programs that potentially affect the labor market behavior of wage earners. The second question is more complex: What are the institutional parameters that are likely to influence behavior?

First, any legal right to paid absence may be anchored in legislation or by bargained arrangements covering employees in specific occupations, industries, or even single firms. In some segments of the labor market, absence may be compensated economically through different programs at the same time, for example, a public (basic) benefit combined with occupational benefits. Thus, the relevant parameter for the individual is naturally the sum of benefits, not the distribution between programs. This complicates the comparison of institutions at the national level, since different groups of employees within the country are covered by separate schemes. Second, wage earners may in some instances choose between different programs to meet the same social problem. For example, in all the Scandinavian countries it is more economically favorable to receive sickness pay than to enter into early retirement, or to extend the period of maternity absence by reporting sick prior to confinement. Hence, the incentive concerning when or if to use a program is dependent not only upon the actual scheme intended for use in the specific case, but also by alternative options of paid nonwork.

A systematic empirical comparison of social security schemes requires a definition of the theoretical dimensions on which we are able to rank assumed behavioral parameters. Any scheme, public or private, is characterized by three sets of rules. First, those regulating access: Who has the right to absence and in what cases? The second set determines the level of cash benefits: How are they calculated and what is their duration? Third, the financial structure of the scheme: How are the costs distributed? These three sets of rules can be viewed as three independent dimensions, and serve as organizing guidelines for the compilation of the data and the subsequent presentation.

The right to absence

The first dimension, eligibility, consists of two filters. The first is the set of conditions to be met in order to be covered (or insured) by the program. The second screen is the specification of legitimate cases of absence. There is no logical interrelation between these two filters. They address separate political decisions, and any potential user of a social right has to pass them both.

We can distinguish four separate principles of coverage. The first is universalism, in which social insurance is an integrated part of legal citizenship. The next two are both related to the position of the individual in the labor market: either by linking coverage to market participation (like time in employment or wage level), or by membership in an occupational collective, a trade union, or an insurance scheme. The fourth principle is to link insurance to (monetary) contribution, compulsory or voluntary. The more restrictive the coverage conditions, and the harder they are to satisfy for ordinary employees, the smaller is the proportion of wage earners who are covered. Conversely, programs based on universalism, or openhanded participation or contribution requirements will cover all or a large majority of the employees, and potentially make decommodified behavior an option for a larger proportion of the wage earners.

The next filter is represented by the set of legitimate causes of absence. Basically, the underlying variable is the conception of man. On one extreme, narrow economic criteria reflect the notion of man as manpower: only if the quality of this commodity is below a defined limit is absence legitimate in order to restore the quality of the labor or to permit a permanent pension. This is the logic behind medical verification of absence and of invalidity pensions. On the other hand, we have the notion of man as a social being who is capable of defining his or her own needs. Therefore, the most liberal rights are those that accept self-certification of absence. In between, and most relevant in the case of early retirement, are schemes that require a verification of need, but emphasize a total evaluation of health, social concerns, and future employment opportunities of the individual.

The extent to which a social program encourages decommodified behavior must be linked to the interaction between the insurance principle (determining the number of potential users) and the cases in which a social right may be used (determining the actual number of beneficiaries). If universalism is combined with very restrictive concepts of needs, there is no reason to assume that this principle itself will affect behavior. Conversely, generous rights to self-determined absence may be of less importance to explain overall labor market behavior, if the rights are limited only to small segments of the work force. Hence, the most liberal programs are those that combine universalism with broad definitions of needs. In analytical terms, the eligibility dimension is a variable composed of the interaction between the principles of insurance and the needs definitions applied.

The economic compensation level

The second dimension is the relation between the level of cash benefits during a period of absence and the wage while at work. This ratio is frequently used as the independent variable in economic studies, and is implicitly assumed to be the prime parameter of individual choice. In fact, there are several (often ignored) problems involved in determining the actual empirical ratio. For one thing, a duration period of ab-

Figure 5.1. **The Eligibility Dimension**

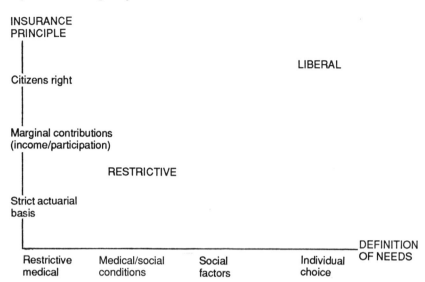

INSURANCE
PRINCIPLE

|

                                                    LIBERAL

Citizens right

Marginal contributions
(income/participation)

                RESTRICTIVE

Strict actuarial
basis

                                                        DEFINITION

| Restrictive | Medical/social | Social | Individual | OF NEEDS |
| medical | conditions | factors | choice | |

sence must be stipulated, and the effects of waiting days, taxation, and even individual characteristics such as income and family situation must be taken into account. All these variables affect the actual benefit-wage ratio of a given person, which in turn implies that compensation levels have to be calculated for ideal types of households with identical behavior in order to be comparable across time and countries.

How the principles of benefit calculation are combined determines the distributional effects of the scheme. Full wage continuation will reproduce market wage differentials in the social wage, whereas a flat-rate benefit provides higher benefit-wage ratios for low income levels. Proportional benefits, combined with a maximum limit on daily allowance, produce a declining compensation level for (very) high income earners. On the other hand, for the single recipient, the principle of benefit calculation is of minor importance. What matters is the actual amount the person receives, which implies that we have to take into account the duration of absence, since daily benefits may vary according to the length of the absence. The significance of duration is not only a question of making accurate calculations of benefit-wage ratios, but is also highly relevant for predicting the incentive effect of short-term versus long-term absence. The total level of absence is a sum of short- and long-term, and an aggregate result of individual decisions both on whether or not to work, and on when to return to work. A program providing a high compensation level for a short period may result in the same compensation level as a scheme with low benefits paid for a longer period, but their effects on short-term versus long-term absence are likely to differ considerably.

The relevant measure of the benefit-wage ratio is the purchasing power of the benefit compared to wages. Hence, taxes have to be deducted. In all the Scandinavian countries during the period we address, social security transfers have become taxable, and are usually added to income from work. A progressive income tax is levied on the yearly income, which makes the calculation of tax on benefit and tax on wage interdependent if absence is compensated by less than full wage continuation. Absence will reduce total yearly income, and with progressive income tax, the average tax ratio is dependent on total income. Again, we need specifications of the duration of absence in order to make correct estimates of total yearly income and taxes.

For the data presented in this chapter, compensation levels have been calculated for a single worker and for a breadwinner with two children below the age of fifteen and an economically inactive spouse. In both households, we assume the worker earns an average production-worker income through full-time employment. The procedure applied in the calculations will answer the following question: What is the value of the total cash benefit received by the household relative to wages in the different countries for the various years, if the individual is absent from work for a specified period?

Distributional effects and the private-public mix

In presenting the development of social rights and benefits for an average employee, two important dimensions are necessarily omitted. The first is the distributional ambitions and effects of various public programs, and the second is the impact of possible private—including bargained—schemes. Both factors manifest themselves by producing differences in both eligibility and generosity among groups of employees; the first (mainly) according to wage level, the second by position (occupation, firm) in the labor market.

Any public flat rate benefit given to all, or compulsory insurance only for low income earners, causes a decrease in the compensation level as income rises. Limitations of the maximum (daily) benefit to be paid from income-related benefit calculation reduce the compensation level for (very) high income groups. In both cases an incentive is created for the best paid groups of employees to establish additional benefits. Hence, both eligibility and generosity restrictions in the public scheme may serve as incentives for certain (excluded) groups to invent their own, more generous, programs. And historically, the existence of occupational schemes for privileged and well-organized groups was a major argument for compulsory and universal insurance for all workers. Of the programs covered in this chapter, maternity leave and unemployment insurance are areas where bargained rights never played a significant role. However, cash sickness and early retirement pension are historically two core areas for private schemes, and a more comprehensive analysis of the total system of social security protection should include the development of private programs.

Financing

All systems of income transfers have a revenue side. Each scheme may have its own financial structure, or be integrated in a comprehensive system, which is financing a number of (or all) social benefits, or it may simply be financed by general state taxes. The financial structure contains two dimensions: First, who pays (and how much), and second, how the technical transfer of income from production to social wages takes place—through funds or by a pay-as-you-go system.

Whereas both the eligibility and the generosity dimensions may be assumed to have direct incentive effects on work-exit choices, the effects of the financial structure are probably of a more complex and indirect nature. The financial structure determines the cost-benefit ratio of the scheme for the two main contributing parties, the employers and the workers. From the early phases of welfare state development, there are examples of workers who opposed more generous social security legislation because they were forced to pay the costs by imposed wage deductions. The contributions were regarded as a special tax on wage earners only. In general, the way in which benefits are financed may influence the actors' interest in expansion or retrenchment of a program, in terms of both eligibility and generosity.

Hence, the decisive issue is to what extent the financial structure establishes a direct link between the cost and the incidence of absence for any of the contributing parties. For example, if it is possible for a firm to reduce its sickness pay outlay by reducing the rates of absence among its employees, it has an incentive to improve working conditions and other factors related to sickness absence, or to not employ workers with high probabilities of absence. On the other hand, if firms have to pay a fixed payroll premium irrespective of absence in its own production, this incentive is removed. Rold-Andersen's (1984) contention that social rights are not fully universalist unless the financing is entirely incorporated in the general tax system may in this respect be given a proper argument. Disconnecting employer contributions from the social security scheme can be regarded as a deliberate policy to prevent differences in production regimes to interfere with the actual use of social rights among employees. Conversely, when employers are compelled to pay at least a part of the costs of absence in their own firms, this must be regarded as an imposed incentive to reduce absence.

For each of the programs, we will try to identify changes in eligibility criteria and in the concepts of social needs. The financial structure will be treated as a whole, since a profound feature of the Scandinavian countries is the development of a comprehensive revenue system that finances most of the benefits we are addressing.

Sickness insurance

Eligibility

By 1960, all Scandinavian countries except Finland had introduced compulsory sickness insurance for all wage earners. The main principle of coverage applied was that of automatic insurance through a required minimum of participation in paid work. In Norway and Sweden, the new programs replaced a system of compulsory insurance only for employees with low income, while in Denmark they replaced means testing. The Finnish reform in 1964 replaced bargained rights for parts of the working class. This was also the case in the other countries, in which occupational programs coexisted with the more residual public programs prior to the great reforms (Table 5.1[1]). However, these systems of bargained rights were not abolished.

But the introduction of universal coverage reduced the effect of (stratificational) position in the labor market on the rights to paid absence due to sickness.

As Olsson (1986) argues, it does not make much sense to calculate

Table 5.1

**Major Institutional Reforms in Sickness Insurance;
Four Scandinavian Countries**

Reform	Denmark	Finland	Norway	Sweden
First state intervention	1892	1897	1909	1891
Universal coverage	1961	1964	1953	1955
Present scheme	1973	1982	1978	1974

Sources: Kuhnle (1983); Flora (1986); national legislation; and NSS (1955–89). (For full references of NSS, see Reference list Nordisk Statistisk Skriftserie.)

the proportion of insured employees in encompassing universalist programs. A (marginal) part of the employees are not covered, because they have not participated in paid work for the required period (or earned income above the stipulated minimum level). This is in most practical cases a temporary period. In Norway and Sweden the length of the qualifying period is defined in terms of a minimum income, and in Denmark and Finland by weeks in employment (see Table 5.2). With the possible exception of Finland, these participation requirements must be regarded as liberal. Although insurance is not universalist in the strict sense of the term, all wage earners are covered automatically by cash sickness insurance after a relatively short period of time. As is evident, there have been no dramatic changes in the last twenty years.

On the other hand, the definition of legitimate causes of absence has been liberalized remarkably. The original (and still prevailing) requirement was that sickness absence must be the result of a certified physical reduction in the capacity to work. This has been changed in two ways: first by accepting children's sickness as a legitimate cause of absence, and second by giving workers the right to judge the need for absence themselves, that is, self-certification of absence.

Parents' right to absence in the case of their children's sickness was introduced in all the Scandinavian countries with the exception of Denmark in the mid-1970s. In Finland this right was first introduced as a part of an incomes policy, and varied during the first years within specific industries. In Norway and Sweden, and later in Finland, this right became an integrated part of the general sickness leave legislation.

This innovation within the sickness scheme can be evaluated from two angles: First, as an extension of the concept of eligibility; an

Table 5.2

Minimum Working Requirements (weeks) in Order to be Entitled to Paid Sickness Absence; Four Scandinavian Countries, 1960–85

Year	Denmark	Norway	Finland	Sweden
1960	6	4 (1,000)	n.s.	5 (1,200)
1965	1	3 (1,000)	13	3 (1,800)
1970	1	7 (4,000)	13	mis.
1975	1	4 (4,000)	13	5 (4,500)
1980	1	3 (4,000)	13	4 (6,000)
1985	1	5 (12,700)	13	3 (6,000)

Sources: National legislation; Kangas and Palme (1987); and NSS (1955–89). (For full references of NSS, see Reference list Nordisk Statistisk Skriftserie.)

Notes: For Norway and Sweden, the minimum income is transformed to weeks by assuming an average production worker income; Finland's workers after 1970 gained bargained rights within segments of the labor market which give rights to absence from four weeks. n.s. = no scheme/program.

employee does not only have a need to exit from paid work in the case of his or her own sickness, but also when special care obligations occur within his or her family. Second: The change means that the legal system has accepted that the fulfillment of these obligations shall not imply a loss of wage (see Table 5.3). Finland and Sweden have experienced a considerable liberalization of working parents' right to absence. Finnish data (Lindroos 1984) show that 71 percent of all cases of absence in the case of child sickness is among women, while in Sweden this figure has dropped from 64 percent to 55 percent over the period 1975–84 (RFV 1985). In the same period, the total number of absence days compensated by sickness pay have increased fivefold. In Norway there is no data on who uses this right. Denmark is an exception: there is no general right, but state employees are permitted to stay at home for one (the first) day in case of a sick child.

Self-certification of absence, both in the case of one's own or one's child's sickness, was introduced in Norway as a part of the major 1978 reform. Employees were entitled to six periods of self-certified absence (none of them exceeding three days) per year. The argument for the reform was to relieve the burden of physicians to verify short-term sickness. In 1984, the rights were reduced to four times per year, on the assumption that abuse had developed. In Sweden (since 1974),

Table 5.3

**The Right to Paid Absence in Case of Child Sickness;
Four Scandinavian Countries, 1974–84**

Year	Finland	Norway	Sweden	Denmark
1974			10 (10)	
1976	1–4 (10)			No
1977			12 (10)	general
1978		20 (10)		right
1979			60 (12)	
1983	30 (12)			
1984	45 (16)			

Sources: National legislation; Kangas and Palme (1987); NSS (1955–89). (For full references of NSS, see Reference list Nordisk Statistisk Skriftserie.)
Note: Data shown is number of allowed days per couple, per year, until the child passes the age shown in parentheses.

medical verification must be presented after one week of absence, while Denmark has no fixed regulations. Instead, employers have the right to claim medical certification after three days. Even in Finland there is no general rule, and practice varies according to bargained agreements. However, the norm is that an employee must verify the absence after two to three days. Self-certified absence implies for the individual that he or she is free to assess his or her own capacity to work, and thereby control the decision of whether to work or to make use of a social right. A criterion which allows the individual self-determined absence must be regarded as the most liberal criterion for the allocation of social benefits. On the other hand, medical verification (which is required in all countries in case of long-term absence) does not imply that individuals do not have any influence at all, but that the judgment of a physician is the basis for the formal decision.

Generosity

The rationale behind a waiting day is to impose a loss of income upon the worker by nonparticipation in production, and thereby make absence costly. Hence, a waiting period is an institutionally created incentive for employees to minimize (short-term) absence. As displayed in Table 5.4, all countries except Finland have gradually reduced the

Table 5.4

**Number of Absence Days before Benefits Are Paid in the Public Cash
Sickness Insurance; Four Scandinavian Countries, 1960–87**
(year of change in parentheses)

Country	1960	1965	1970	1975	1980	1985	1987
Denmark	3 (1960)	6 (1961)	6	0 (1973)	0	1 (1983)	0 (1986)
Finland	n.s.[a]	15 (1964)	7 (1967)	7[b]	7[b]	7[b]	7[b]
Norway	3 (1956)	3	3	3	0 (1978)	0	0
Sweden	3 (1955)	3	1 (1967)	1	1	1	0 (1987)

Sources: National legislation; Kangas and Palme (1987); and NSS (1955–89). (For
full references of NSS, see Reference list Nordisk Statistisk Skriftserie.)
[a]n.s. = no public scheme.
[b]Employers pay wage continuation the first week.

waiting period, and benefits are paid from the first day of absence.
Even in a broader international comparison, Finland has kept a long
waiting period (OECD 1985). On the other hand, since 1971, employers have paid wage continuation the first week. Regarding duration (of
cash sickness benefits), Sweden has had an unlimited period since the
1955 reform. The same applies to Denmark (since 1973), while Norway and Finland, since 1953 and 1964, respectively, have a maximum
duration of one year. However, it could be argued that the maximum duration of cash sickness benefits is of minor importance as a
characteristic of the sickness scheme since other forms of benefits
directed to long-term illness (like rehabilitation and disability schemes)
have been developed. It is important to note that the duration period of
illness may "inflate" the aggregate level of sickness absence, in countries (and periods) where long-term illness is compensated with higher
benefits than programs for permanent exit from paid work (compare
Table 5.5 with Table 5.15).

Waiting days and restricted duration limit the period in which an
absentee receives economic benefits, by denying compensation for the
first days and for the period of absence that exceeds the duration limit.
The effect of waiting days is most important, since the majority of
absences due to one's own or one's children's sickness are of short
duration. A Danish study (referred to in Sundboe et al. 1982) found
that of all cases of sickness absence in 1966/67, only 35 percent were
compensated economically, because the rest fell within the (then six-

Table 5.5

Cash Sickness Benefits as Percent of Wage for a Worker with Average Production Worker (APW) Income; Four Scandinavian Countries, 1960–85

		1960	1965	1970	1975	1980	1985
1-Week Absence							
Norway	single	19	17	25	27	100	100
	married	26	21	31	31	100	100
Sweden	single	37	29	71	77	77	77
	married	39	32	64	77	77	77
Denmark	single	8	0	0	64	78	75
	married	9	0	0	66	78	75
Finland	single	n.s.	0	0	0	0	0
	married	n.s.	0	0	0	0	0
26-Week Absence							
Norway	single	38	34	49	53	100	100
	married	46	40	60	60	100	100
Sweden	single	63	50	82	90	90	90
	married	67	55	74	90	90	90
Denmark	single	15	37	52	64	78	74
	married	18	40	60	66	78	75
Finland	single	n.s.	59	50	31	37	77
	married	n.s.	73	68	42	43	77
52-Week Absence							
Norway	single	38	34	50	54	100	100
	married	47	41	61	61	100	100
Sweden	single	64	51	83	90	90	90
	married	68	59	75	90	90	90
Denmark	single	7	19	55	64	78	74
	married	9	20	63	66	78	75
Finland	single	n.s.	55	45	27	37	77
	married	n.s.	68	61	38	43	77

Sources: National legislation; NSS (1955–89). (For full references of NSS, see Reference list Nordisk Statistisk Skriftserie; and Kangas and Palme [1987].)

Notes: n.s. = no public scheme; compensation levels are calculated by combining duration and per-day benefits given. The APW incomes are from Kangas and Palme (1987); taxes are estimated by figures given in NSS and national tax regulations. See also note 1.

day) waiting period. Hence, in order to get a proper measure of the compensation level, it is essential to include the effects of a waiting period and of duration. The calculations of actual benefit-wage ratios are given in Table 5.5. Below is a review of the development of the principles of benefit calculation.

Finland was the first Scandinavian country to adopt income proportional sickness pay (1964), by paying a daily benefit of 0.15 percent of yearly wage. This implies a compensation level at about 50 percent of wage. Since 1982, the sickness benefit has been 80 percent of wage, and taxable. Norway and Sweden sustained (until 1971 and 1974 respectively) the old system of dividing the wage earners into classes by income, and paying a flat cash benefit for all in the same income class. This system was in reality a mix of a flat rate and an income proportional calculation. The increase in the compensation level for these two countries during the 1960s was an effect of higher daily benefits, not a change in the principle of calculation. Norway experienced a gradual introduction of income proportional calculation, with a (taxable) daily benefit of 0.14 percent of wage plus four kroner per day since 1971 until full wage continuation was introduced in 1978. Sweden adopted income proportional benefits in 1974, by fixing the cash sickness pay to 90 percent of wage. The Danish story is somewhat different. The compensation level has been regulated by the combination of a maximum benefit-wage ratio (80 percent since 1963 and 90 percent since 1974) and a maximum daily pay subject to yearly regulation. As mentioned, the maximum amount has been increased less than wages, and only employees below an average income in fact receive or approach the maximum compensation level.

As is clearly seen, a considerable increase in the compensation levels has taken place, mostly so with respect to cases of short-term illness. Finland is an exception, with zero compensation for short-term absence due to the long waiting period. However, as mentioned, since 1971 employees have received benefits from the employer through bargained agreements. This was also the case in Norway until the 1978 reform. Thus, the actual compensation level for a significant proportion of the workers during short-term illness was higher than the Finnish and Norwegian data for the early 1970s indicate. The development of cash sickness benefits can be summarized by pointing out four general trends seen in all countries: The first is the implementation of earnings-graduated benefits, and making sickness pay subject to taxation. Taxing the benefits could be regarded as a logical consequence of benefits close to, or equal to, full wages, but it is also a manifestation of a change in the character of the benefits from compensation for income lost due to sickness, to a system of wage continuation.

Table 5.6

Cash Sickness Pay for an Average Production Worker (APW) and Year When Sickness Pay Became Taxable; Four Scandinavian Countries, 1960–85

	1960	1970	1980	1985	Year Taxable
Norway	140	132	100	100	1971
Sweden	105	102	100	100	1974
Finland	110	135	135	112	1982
Denmark	123	131	100	100	1960

Sources: National legislation; NSS (1955–89). (For full references of NSS, see Reference list Nordisk Statistisk Skriftserie; and Kangas and Palme [1987].)

Notes: Pay shown is for APW with two children below age fifteen as percent of pay for APW with no children. Compensation levels are calculated by combining duration and per-day benefits given. The APW incomes are from Kangas and Palme (1987); taxes are estimated by figures given in NSS and national tax regulations.

The second, related, trend is the abolition of additional benefits related to family characteristics (number of children). While they played a significant role in the 1960s in all countries except Sweden, family-related benefits now exist only in Finland (see Table 5.6).

The third trend, equalization of the economic compensation between short-term and long-term illness, has significantly reduced income (loss) as a parameter for individual choice, and has made absence less costly.

The fourth trend, the general improvement of the compensation levels, combined with the right to self-certification and absence in case of children's sickness, has made it possible for workers to include their own need for absence and caring obligations vis-à-vis their children into their labor market behavior, without being punished by the market in terms of income loss.

Maternity leave

Eligibility

Paid maternity leave was introduced in all the Scandinavian countries as a part of making general cash sickness insurance universal. The need for (female) workers to stay at home after childbirth was a social need not recognized or institutionalized as a social right prior to these

Table 5.7

Fathers' Right to Maternity Leave; Four Scandinavian Countries, 1974–85

	Maximum Number of Paid Days	Year of Introduction	Percent of Total Paid Leave
Sweden	150	1974	56
Finland	12	1978	
increasing to	100	1982	43
Norway	72	1978	55
Denmark	60	1985	42

Sources: National legislation; Kangas and Palme (1987); and NSS (1955–89). (For full references of NSS, see Reference list Nordisk Statistisk Skriftserie.)

reforms. In all the Scandinavian countries the entitlements to paid absence are regulated within the general cash sickness legislation. In Denmark and Finland, eligibility criteria are the same as for sickness, whereas in Norway and Sweden longer participation in paid work is required in order to receive cash benefits. In the period 1956–77 Norwegian women had to work ten months prior to leave; since 1978 they have to have worked six of the last ten months to obtain the right to paid leave. Sweden requires nine months of employment—an unchanged requirement since 1955.

The need for a parent to exit from work in order to provide care for a newborn child is not controversial. Thus, the basic question is the length of the period of benefits, and the cost of the absence for the parent in terms of income loss for a given period.

Within two areas there has been an extension of generosity, which may be regarded as a liberalization of the accepted needs. The first is the acceptance of adoption as a change in the social situation of an employee equal to the birth of one's own child; the worker therefore, in principle, should have the same rights as in the case of birth. This need was accepted in all countries in the 1970s, although the permitted duration of parental leave in these cases is not as long as for one's own child. Second, and more important, is the acceptance of fathers' need to parental leave. As shown in Table 5.7, this option is relatively new. Sweden and Finland allow the father a considerably longer leave than do Denmark and Norway, both in terms of number of days, and as a proportion of the total leave per couple. The Scandinavian countries

Table 5.8

Number of Paid Maternity Days, and Year of Change; Four Scandinavian Countries, 1955–87 (all figures adjusted to six days per week)

Year	Denmark	Finland	Norway	Sweden
1955	0	0	0	44
1956	84		72	
1963				180
1964		54		
1971		72		
1973	98			
1974		174		210
1978		198	108	270[a]
1979		210		
1980	108	234		360
1981		258[b]		
1985	144			
1986			120	
1987			132	

Sources: National legislation; Kangas and Palme (1987); and NSS (1955–89). (For full references of NSS, see Reference list Nordisk Statistisk Skriftserie.) See also note 1.
[a]Sweden: 180 full paid days, 90 (later 180) days with flat rate.
[b]Finland: 148 full paid days, 110 days with flat rate.

clearly split: Sweden has been most expansionist, and has extended the period of paid leave from forty-four days in 1955 to more than a year since 1980. Finland started ten years later, but experienced a dramatic improvement during the 1970s. Denmark and Norway have lagged behind, with a much slower extension of duration. These countries are also more restrictive regarding fathers' rights. The variation is considerable, with Swedish women having a right to absence almost three times as long as that for Norwegian women. However, Sweden and Finland seem to have stopped the expansion around 1980, whereas Denmark and Norway extended the duration in the mid-1980s (see Table 5.8).

Generosity

In all the Scandinavian countries, the development of maternity benefits is parallel to sickness pay; income proportional, taxable benefits were introduced in the 1970s. Along with the extension of the compensated period, the income loss for a worker who stays at home with a newborn child has been dramatically reduced. As a consequence, this has created a greater income difference between women eligible for cash benefits, and women and families who do not enjoy the right to paid leave.

In Denmark and Norway, the economic benefit of maternity leave is calculated like that for sickness. This was also the case in Finland and Sweden until 1978 and 1979, respectively, when a system of income proportional benefit calculation (as with sickness benefits) for the first part of the period was combined with a daily flat-rate allowance for the exceeded period. The duration period was extended, but the per-day benefit was lowered.

The compensation levels presented in Table 5.9 reflect the combined effect of benefit per compensated day and the duration period. When the duration period is exceeded, we assume the women have no other income. Thus, the figures should be read as a worker's total income from maternity cash benefits as a percent of (alternative) wage, if she decides to stay at home for twenty-six or fifty-two weeks. However, these figures do not necessarily represent the actual economic situation of a woman who stays at home with a newborn child. In all countries a general child allowance is paid irrespective of the employment status of the mother, and there are special tax deductions dependent on her marital status, as well as other social security benefits if she is a single parent. On the other hand, our aim is to present the "pure" effect of the maternity leave program.

In case of an absence of twenty-six weeks, the differences among the countries has diminished: the high level of compensation combined with a short duration in Denmark and Norway provide roughly the same compensation level as in Finland and Sweden. However, if a woman decides to take one year off, the effect of the duration period in Finland and Sweden produces a significant dissimilarity.

Paid maternity leave is probably the kind of absence that most clearly reflects the confrontation of participation in the labor market with social obligations. The extent to which the maternity program also includes elements of choice for the parents as to how they prefer to allocate their time between work and child care is important. Again we find a clear distinction between Denmark and Norway on the one hand and Finland and Sweden on the other. In Finland and Sweden, the duration period is conceived of as a "quota" within which parents are

Table 5.9

**Cash Maternity Benefits as Percent of Wage for a Worker with APW
Income; Four Scandinavian Countries, 1960–85**

	1960	1965	1970	1975	1980	1985
At home 26 weeks						
Norway	20.1	18.8	18.8	23.4	87.8	83.1
Sweden	14.6	63.8	66.8	92.0	92.0	92.0
Finland	n.s.	16.2	16.2	46.8	43.6	77.3
Denmark	7.7	16.0	28.6	48.3	62.3	83.1
At home 52 weeks						
Norway	10.1	11.1	11.1	11.6	43.9	43.2
Sweden	7.3	31.9	33.4	51.8	72.9	72.1
Finland	n.s.	8.1	8.1	26.1	37.2	61.1
Denmark	3.9	8.0	14.3	24.2	31.2	41.5

Sources: National legislation; Kangas and Palme (1987); and NSS (1955–89). (For full references of NSS, see Reference list Nordisk Statistisk Skriftserie.)
Note: n.s. = no public scheme.

allowed to allocate time for work and absence until the child reaches the age of seven. In Denmark and Norway, the right to paid absence is cut off if the parent (mother) goes back to work before the maximum allowed period is terminated.

Sweden is the only country to allow parents to combine part-time work and part-time benefits, which in effect is a right to reduced working hours with marginal cost in terms of income loss. Norwegian women, in contrast, also have a right to reduced working hours, but without economic compensation.

By necessity, such elements of flexibility create problems for employers. Labor is more unstable because the employees themselves may decide when, and how much, to work. A fear of devaluing one's position in the labor market may occur; this explains the findings of empirical studies that paid maternity-leave rights are not fully used by those who are entitled (Lindroos 1984; Kaul 1982). Hence, even if the scheme as such allows decommodified behavior, we cannot assume that it actually induces it.

To summarize, Sweden and Finland have clearly been more responsive to the needs of economically active parents of small children, by allowing a longer period of absence, a more generous policy for fathers to leave work, and the parents' right to decide when to make use of the right to paid absence. In addition, the rights to paid leave in cases of child sickness (cf. Table 5.3) are extremely generous in Sweden and Finland compared to Denmark and Norway. The Danish and Norwegian schemes are more rigid, and are in fact nothing but a right to cash sickness benefits in a defined period after childbirth.

Unemployment insurance

Unemployment insurance differs from sickness and maternity benefits in several respects. Whereas these transfers are rights within the work contract, unemployment benefits pertain to those who are excluded from paid work. The historical conflicts about unemployment insurance have been deeper. Basically, they have been battles of how unemployment should be interpreted: as a manifestation of eroded individual willingness to work, or as the individual consequence of labor surplus. This ideological dimension may explain why unemployment insurance has been, and still is, the most controversial of the social security benefits provided by modern welfare states. Even if unemployment insurance is based on universal coverage, the actual possibility of becoming, or remaining, unemployed is closely related to qualifications and class. Empirical research regularly finds that unemployment benefits have less prestige value than other social transfers (Coughlin 1980; Hernes 1985).

Second, because unemployment is a function of market demand for labor, it varies according to business cycles and is therefore less predictable than other forms of labor market exit. Thus, for unemployment insurance to be reliable, state participation or a guarantee from the state on the income side is required. The first state interventions into unemployment insurance came by way of contributions to voluntary insurance schemes, not by regulating eligibility.

Third, it is necessary to distinguish between two types of unemployed individuals: those who lost jobs and those who never had one. This makes the role of trade unions ambivalent. Their interest is to protect those in employment, not those outside the market.

Fourth, job creation by political means is always an alternative strategy to unemployment benefits, and the Scandinavian countries

Table 5.10

Major Reforms in Scandinavian Unemployment Insurance
(year of reform)

Reform	Denmark	Finland	Norway	Sweden
First state intervention	1907	1917	1906	1934
Present structure	1966	1960	1959	1934
Last major reform	1974	1985	1971	1974
Taxable benefits	1970	1985	1971	1974

Sources: Kuhnle (1983); Flora (1986); national legislation; and NSS (1955–89). (For full references of NSS, see Reference list Nordisk Statistisk Skriftserie.)

differ considerably in this respect.[2] These traditions, as well as differences in historical levels of unemployment, are the main factors underlying the development of unemployment insurance schemes in the different countries. For example, Olsson (1986) explains the relatively "institutionally underdeveloped" Swedish system of cash unemployment insurance by stating that a successful employment policy has eroded the need for modernizing the cash benefit program (see Table 5.10).

Unemployment insurance has retained a close connection to trade unions in all the Scandinavian countries except Norway. The eligibility dimension is closely linked to union membership, which implies that in principle, unemployment insurance is voluntary in Denmark, Finland, and Sweden. Only Norway has (since 1959) developed a scheme to cover all who are economically active.

This makes a national comparison more difficult, as rights may vary across unions in terms of both eligibility and generosity. The data in the following sections aim to portray the rules relevant for an "average" unionized employee.

Eligibility

Norway is the only Scandinavian country where participation in paid work is the only requirement for coverage by unemployment insurance. Unemployment insurance was incorporated in the National Insurance Scheme in 1971, and has since been administered like all other public social transfers. In the other countries, insurance is based on

Table 5.11

Minimum Labor Market Participation Required for Unemployment Insurance; Four Scandinavian Countries, 1960–85

Norway	1960–70	Minimum income; 30 weeks of employment
	1971–	Minimum income (equals approximately 8 weeks)
Sweden	1960–	12 months of membership; 20 weeks of employment
Denmark	1960–	Membership; 26 weeks of employment
Finland	1960–64	52 weeks of membership; 50 weeks of employment
	1965–	26 weeks of membership; 26 weeks of employment

Sources: National legislation; Kangas and Palme (1987); and NSS (1955–89). (For full references of NSS, see Reference list Nordisk Statistisk Skriftserie.)

trade union membership, combined with extensive state participation in regulating the cash benefits, financing, and administration. The most important difference between Norway and the other countries is, however, that since the mid-1970s, Denmark, Finland, and Sweden have had an additional flat-rate benefit for unemployed who are not eligible in the ordinary union-based program. On the other hand, with the high rates of unionization that characterize these countries, the actual difference between the Norwegian system of automatic coverage, and the other countries' should not be overestimated. The group of economically active individuals most affected by these differences is the self-employed who are automatically included in the Norwegian scheme, but not in the more typical wage-earner profile of the programs in the other countries.

All countries require some minimum labor market participation to qualify for cash benefits. This requirement has been liberalized in Norway and Finland but has remained unchanged in Denmark and Sweden for the last twenty-five years.

Table 5.11 shows Norway to have the most liberal requirement, regulating access to unemployment insurance by a minimum income (as for cash sickness benefits). In the period 1959–71, only employees with average and below average wages were insured on a compulsory basis. Since 1971, the average production worker can earn the minimum income required and be eligible after approximately eight weeks of employment. All the other countries still require a

Table 5.12

Percent of Labor Force Covered by Unemployment Insurance; Four Scandinavian Countries, 1960–85

	1960	1965	1970	1975	1980	1985
Norway	59.6	61.1	60.7	91.8[a]	90.0	90.0
Sweden	41.1	45.8	63.6	74.9	70.9	75.0
Finland	16.6	22.6	37.5	52.7	65.1	63.5
Denmark	35.2	35.9	34.9	44.2	62.0	80.0

Sources: National legislation; Kangas and Palme (1987); and NSS (1955–89). (For full references of NSS, see Reference list Nordisk Statistisk Skriftserie.)

[a]From 1971, the figure is approximately 90 percent, which equals the proportion of economically actives with (taxable) income above the minimum income. However, this is not a valid measure of the excluding effect of the eligibility conditions.

working period of about six months to qualify for benefits.

Working requirements automatically exclude young people who never had a job; the qualifying condition of membership in trade unions excludes the self-employed. Table 5.12 shows that the proportion of the labor force covered has grown considerably in all the countries during the past twenty-five years. However, this increase is not caused by the liberalization of eligibility criteria alone. The rates of unionization and the proportion of self-employed individuals in the labor force are also important components. In the formally voluntary systems of Denmark, Finland, and Sweden, even individual motives may influence the figures (e.g., if workers enter trade unions in order to become insured because of an increased probability of becoming unemployed).

The definition of "unemployed" is the same in all the Scandinavian countries. Three conditions have to be met: First, the person must be "involuntary" unemployed, that is, they must have left their previous job involuntarily; second, the person must be registered at an employment office; and third, he or she must be "disposable" for the labor market. This last requirement implies that the person may lose the right to benefits if a vacant job is refused. In Norway (since 1971), an unemployed person may refuse a vacant job if the work is not "suitable" or if the pay is below normal wages in the industry. In general, these conditions leave room for discretion at the level of implementation (for example, the extent to which a person may be de-

Table 5.13

Maximum Duration of Unemployment Benefits (weeks); Four Scandinavian Countries, 1960–85

	1960	1965	1970	1975	1980	1985
Norway	20	20	40	40	40	40
Sweden	26	30	60	60	60	60
Finland	9	25	25	40	40	100
Denmark	45	45	130	130	130	130

Sources: National legislation; Kangas and Palme (1987); and NSS (1955–89). (For full references of NSS, see Reference list Nordisk Statistisk Skriftserie.)

prived of the right to benefits if he or she refuses to move geographically to fill a vacant job).

In 1984, the proportion of actually unemployed individuals with no right to cash benefits was estimated at approximately 30 percent in Norway and Sweden, 20 percent in Denmark, and 10 percent in Finland (NU 1985), which reflects that the working requirements have a significant exclusionary effect.

In the early 1960s, all Scandinavian countries had a one-week waiting period between the onset of unemployment and the remuneration of benefits. This period was abolished in Denmark by the end of that decade, and reduced to three days in Norway in 1971. It still exists in Sweden and Finland.

The waiting period affects the actual compensation level less in this case than in that of sickness insurance because unemployment periods are generally longer. Therefore, the duration period is more important (see Table 5.13).

Denmark has historically had, and still has, the longest unemployment benefit period. In fact, since 1968 it has not been formally restricted, but indirectly limited by the need for an unemployed person to work for twenty-six new weeks every third year in order to become reeligible for a new benefit period. In the other three countries, older workers have been entitled to extended duration: in 1974, both Finland and Sweden allowed eligible workers over 55 years of age to stay on unemployment benefits for 180 and 90 weeks respectively, whereas Norway introduced an 80-week period for those over 55 years of age in 1983. In 1986, duration was extended to eighty weeks for all.

Generosity

Norway is the only country to fully adopt the principle of income proportional calculation of unemployment benefits. From 1959 to 1975, the daily cash benefit was calculated as sickness compensation. For a short period (1975–79), the benefits paid per day amounted to 0.1 percent of yearly income plus 15 NOK, until the present system of a daily taxable benefit of 0.2 percent of yearly income was introduced.

In the other countries, the role of public intervention is somewhat different. These three countries fix an upper and a lower limit of the daily amount and a maximum percentage of wage which the compensation level cannot exceed. This system implies income-related, but not entirely proportional, calculation of unemployment benefits.

Denmark has the highest compensation level. As early as 1962, the maximum compensation level was increased to 67 percent of wage for single persons, and 75 percent for breadwinners. In 1968, the maximum level was set at 80 percent, and the present 90-percent level was adopted as early as 1972. In Finland, the maximum compensation level was limited to 67 percent in the early 1960s, increased to 75 percent in 1971, and to the present 90 percent in 1985. After this last reform, no formal upper limit on the daily amount applies, but the benefit is reduced by 20 percent after one hundred days of unemployment. The Swedish system resembles the old sickness insurance scheme, by dividing the workers into income classes, and by specifying an upper and lower limit for the daily benefit within each income class, yielding an increase in the compensation level (see Table 5.14). The Danish system was already very generous by the late 1960s; the compensation levels in Norway and Sweden rose significantly during the 1970s; and those in Finland rose by the 1985 reform. An inflationary reduction of the maximum benefit reduced the compensation in Denmark in the 1980s. This amount was kept constant in nominal value for the period 1982–86. In fact, it is the most dramatic decrease of a temporary cash benefit in the period we discuss. However, workers with income below the average wage still receive compensation close to the general level of 90 percent.

As for sickness, the importance of family-related allowances has vanished; they still exist only in Finland and Norway. For the whole period we discuss, the eligibility criteria for unemployment insurance have been more restricted than those that apply to sickness insurance in

Table 5.14

Unemployment Benefits: Net Compensation as Percent of Net Wage in Case of Unemployment; Four Scandinavian Countries, 1960–85

	26 Weeks		52 Weeks	
	Single	Married	Single	Married
Norway				
1960	32.9	46.1	19.1	26.7
1965	25.2	35.3	14.6	20.5
1970	47.9	61.0	27.8	35.4
1975	42.4	52.9	32.8	40.9
1980	61.2	67.9	47.4	52.6
1985	61.2	65.5	61.8	66.1
Sweden				
1960	46.8	60.8	23.4	30.4
1965	39.9	45.2	19.9	22.6
1970	43.8	47.8	25.4	27.7
1975	72.8	72.8	75.8	75.8
1980	64.2	64.2	66.8	66.8
1985	72.1	72.1	73.6	73.6
Finland				
1960	6.0	8.0	3.0	4.0
1965	43.4	64.4	21.7	32.2
1970	41.1	52.0	20.5	26.0
1975	38.6	52.3	30.1	40.8
1980	30.7	46.9	23.9	35.9
1985	56.4	73.4	51.9	68.8
Denmark				
1960	40.6	56.2	27.7	41.4
1965	38.6	46.7	27.4	34.5
1970	80.0	80.0	80.0	80.0
1975	80.5	80.5	80.5	80.5
1980	77.9	77.9	77.9	77.9
1985	59.2	59.2	59.2	59.2

Sources: National legislation; Kangas and Palme (1987); and NSS (1955–89). (For full references of NSS, see Reference list Nordisk Statistisk Skriftserie.)

Note: Figures are for persons under the age of fifty-five, receiving average production worker income. Married persons are assumed to have two children under the age of fifteen.

all countries. An interesting shift has taken place with respect to one specific item: the compensation level. In the 1960s, only marginal differences existed between sickness and unemployment benefits, and if a difference endured, unemployment benefits were higher. Since the mid-1970s, the compensation for sickness absence has escalated vis-à-vis unemployment in all countries. It is hard to justify more generous compensation for sickness absence than for absence due to unemployment, that is, to imply that one is more voluntary than the other. A possible explanation is that the fear of creating work disincentives has been greater for unemployment schemes than for sickness benefits. Alternatively, it could be that benefits to the unemployed have less legitimacy than those to the sick.

Early retirement programs

Definition of retirement

Early retirement is a far more complex phenomenon than the temporary benefits we have addressed so far. The concept does not necessarily mean the same thing in all countries. In our discussion, early retirement is defined as a permanent or partial exit from paid work at an age lower than the ordinary pensionable age, and the term *early retirement program* denotes all schemes that distribute economic transfers on a permanent basis to persons who leave paid work.

While there has been progress in temporary benefits policies toward the integration of occupational and status-related schemes into one main program for all employees, the trend is opposite in the case of early retirement. Since the mid-1960s, new social needs for permanent exit from paid work have been accepted, through both liberalized criteria within existing schemes and institutional innovations, which makes a systematic comparison across countries difficult. In all countries except Norway, there are several programs that make it possible for older workers not only to leave the labor market, but to choose among different programs as well.

Early retirement programs may be conceptualized in at least three different ways, reflecting elements of other social security programs. First, an early retirement pension may be regarded as an extension of temporary benefits. The pension program takes care of those cases of sickness or unemployment that seem to be permanent. Second, early retirement can be regarded as early entry into ordinary old-age pension. Third, early retirement can be seen as an extension of invalidity benefits, namely, of income provision for those who, for various reasons, are unable to earn their living by participating in paid work. As public policy, early retirement programs are a means to obtain welfare goals. Yet, early retirement has important effects on labor supply, and can be used as a policy device to reduce labor supply when there is an excess of (young) unemployed people.

In the following section, we address the development of rights to leave paid work and receive an early retirement pension. Our purpose is to identify the principal changes in the conditions under which employees are given the right to paid exit.

Eligibility

Since the 1950s, four significant changes in the early retirement programs have occurred in the Scandinavian countries. First, invalidity programs based on restrictive criteria of needs testing have been transformed into universal programs that cover the whole population. Second, we have seen a marked redefinition of the concept of inability to work, from a medical toward a more social understanding. Third, new programs targeted at older workers who are unemployed for long periods have been introduced, and fourth, options that make it possible for workers to exit partially from paid work have been instituted.

A universal early retirement pension was introduced in all Scandinavian countries around 1960 as an extension of the invalidity benefits enacted in Sweden in 1913 and in the other countries in the interwar period. The core of the new programs was the right for all citizens to a permanent cash benefit in the case of a medically caused reduction in the capacity to work, defined as a percentage of full ability to work. This degree of disability was fixed at one-half in Denmark and Sweden, and at two-thirds in Finland and Norway. The introduction of graded pensions in the mid-1960s implied that benefits were provided according to the degree of disability. At the same time, the minimum incapacity to work in order to obtain a graded pension was reduced (see Table 5.15).

The concept of incapacity to work was redefined in all the countries at the end of the 1960s. Medical factors in a strict sense were no longer

Table 5.15

Major Reforms in Disability Programs; Four Scandinavian Countries

Reform	Denmark	Finland	Norway	Sweden
Invalidity benefit	1922	1936	1936	1913
Universal coverage	1960	1956	1961	1963
Degree of disability	50	67	67	50
Graded pensions	1965	1970	1967	1963
New minimum				
degree of disability	33	20	50	50

Sources: Kuhnle (1982); Flora (1986); national legislation; and NSS (1955–89). (For full references of NSS, see Reference list Nordisk Statistisk Skriftserie.)

the exclusive criteria in evaluating the ability to work. Other socially caused factors like alcoholism or psychiatric problems were included as restrictions on a person's ability to participate in paid work. The extension of the concept of ability to work implied a political acceptance that an individual's need for a stable income in cases of involuntary nonparticipation in paid work should be secured by the state, with less emphasis on the causes of nonparticipation.

At the same time, in both Denmark and Sweden, the right to enter the general old-age pension program prior to pensionable age was liberalized, making it possible for workers to exit from work (with a reduced pension) without passing through the medicalized schemes. The introduction of "general weakness caused by aging" in the Norwegian disability pension scheme as a separate "diagnosis," could be interpreted as fulfilling much the same function as the new flexibility of the old-age pension in Sweden and Denmark.

From medically caused incapacity to work to the actual ability to work, it was a marginal step to also include a person's actual possibility to get paid work. But again, this was a principal extension of the obligations of the welfare state. To determine the "actual possibility" to get work, characteristics of the labor market situation had to be taken into account as a separate criterion when evaluating a person's need for early retirement pension. In this case, the distinctions between an early retirement scheme and a permanent unemployment benefit tend to evaporate, as both programs provide the individual with a social wage on a permanent basis due to the lack of demand for labor in the market. Sweden accepted explicitly "labor market causes" as a separate criterion for persons above sixty years of age in 1970, Finland the year after for workers older than fifty-five years (increased to sixty years in 1985). In both cases, this "unemployment pension" required that the person had received unemployment benefits and had exceeded the duration period. In Denmark, no such liberalization within the disability pension took place; instead it seems that both the longer duration period of unemployment benefits and the right to early old-age pension (from sixty years of age in 1967 and fifty-five years of age in 1977) played a similar role (Socialministeriet 1980). However, the introduction of the "after wage" program in Denmark in 1979 is the most remarkable program innovation to provide a social wage to the older part of the work force with employment troubles. Here, a person who has been covered by unemployment insurance in ten of the previous fifteen years, and is above sixty years of age, has the possibility to retire within this program. The other conditions are that the recipient of "after wage" does not work more than two hundred hours per year, and maintains his or her trade union membership. Norway is the only country with no formal acceptance of long-term unemployment as a criterion for early retirement pension. This has been explained both by less severe employment problems among older workers, and by the understanding that a significant part of the entry into early retirement in fact is related to employment problems, but hidden by the medicalized image of the program (Halvorsen 1977).

As already mentioned, a social security program that allows voluntary entry must be considered liberal. None of the programs we have accounted for contain this right explicitly. But the rights to early entry into both the old-age pension and even more so, the "after wage" program, come close to legitimating voluntary exit from the labor market. By implication, because the applicant's own assessment of his or her social and economic situation must be taken into account, an element of individual choice is introduced.

The right to voluntary exit from paid work is fully implemented in the Swedish partial pension program which was introduced in 1976. Workers above the age of sixty have the right to reduce their weekly working hours to a minimum of seventeen hours if they are covered by unemployment insurance and have worked for five of the previous ten months. Similar schemes were adopted in Finland and Denmark in 1987. These programs entitle older workers to voluntary exit from work on a partial basis. Like the rights to partial maternity leave, they represent a loosening of traditionally rigid boundaries between those who are economically active and those who are not.

In summary, four conclusions seem to be warranted: First, the early retirement schemes have changed, and can increasingly be characterized as income security systems for wage earners with labor market problems. Second, this implies that early retirement programs have become more responsive vis-à-vis the labor market. As more roads lead from paid work into early retirement, closer relationships have been established between labor market change and the obligations of the welfare state. Labor market changes, whether related to demography or to market demand for more qualified labor are imported into the welfare state as expenditure pressure and into the social structure as disemployment. Third, by the liberalization of eligibility conditions and the introduction of new schemes, labor market exit has become a more concrete alternative to paid work for larger proportions of the labor force, rendering their economic welfare interests less dependent on the labor market. Problems that previously had to be solved by a job search, geographical mobility, or wage reduction, can now be solved by exit. In other words, "the whip of the market" has been restrained considerably. Fourth, different country profiles have emerged. As already mentioned, all countries have developed their present early retirement programs from roughly similar systems of state disability pension, and a redefinition of the concept of inability to participate in paid work. Since the early 1970s, different patterns have emerged. Norway has typically the most restrictive system, by formally maintaining a medicalized scheme in which all applicants for early retirement pension have to pass a medical examination. There are neither criteria with specific reference to the long-term unemployed, nor specific options for those who are not far below the pensionable age, such as a flexible age limit or a partial pension. Sweden, like Norway, has maintained nearly full employment (in an international perspective), but has clearly liberalized the access to early exit through the flexibility of the pensionable age, the explicit recognition of "labor market causes" in the disability pension scheme for individuals above sixty years of age, and the partial pension schemes. The Finnish development is quite similar to the Swedish: both countries have introduced schemes, which, taken together, provide a menu of options for the older part of the work force to leave paid work or to reduce their working hours. Denmark is the only country where unemployment most directly leads to a new program. At the international level, Sweden and Norway have been most successful in combining very low unemployment rates with high (and growing) participation in paid work. But they have developed completely different early retirement options. As mentioned, Sweden and Finland have cultivated similar schemes, but at radically different unemployment levels. Finland and Denmark experienced a rise in unemployment from 2 percent to 8 percent over the years 1974 to 1978 and both made the options of early retirement more accessible for older workers. Denmark introduced an extension of the unemployment insurance equivalent to a voluntary early retirement program; Finland expanded the existing pension system. Hence, the experience of these four countries scarcely supports the notion that early retirement options are uniformly introduced in order to clear the labor market.

Compensation level

Since we cannot speak of one early retirement program in each country (except Norway), it is not possible to present a single figure to represent the economic benefits for early retirees. In addition, special tax rules and various (means tested) supplements play a role, as well as marital status and economic position of the spouse. And a considerable number of the early retirees have additional income from part-time work, former savings, benefits from occupational schemes, severance pay, and the like.

Three principles of calculation are applied with respect to early retirement pensions in the Scandinavian countries: (1) the pension equals (or is related to) the ordinary old-age pension the retiree would have enjoyed if he or she had stayed in paid work until retirement age; (2) the compensation is a fixed proportion of the wage decrease due to reduced working hours (applied in the partial pension programs); and, (3) the calculation of unemployment benefits is applied (in the Danish "after wage" system).

In all countries, disability and unemployment (in Finland and Sweden) pensions equal the old-age pension. With the exception of Denmark, this consists of a basic flat rate and a supplementary pension

Table 5.16

Early Retirement Pension as Percent of APW Income after Taxation; Four Scandinavian Countries, 1960–84

	Denmark		Norway		Sweden		Finland	
Year	1	2	1	2	1	2	1	2
1960	35	55	29	25	53	54	24	29
1962	34	55	34	42	37	48	25	31
1964	34	53	33	40	44	59	27	32
1968	73	82	40	48	60	70	38	39
1970	77	90	41	48	85	92	48	54
1972	80	88	43	56	80	90	51	53
1974	71	82	39	61	73	76	62	65
1978	70	82	75	81	68	72	61	82
1981	76	88	75	85	81	87	65	83
1984	80	89	73	82	73	76	70	85

Sources: NSS (1965–86). (For full references of NSS, see Reference list Nordisk Statistisk Skriftserie.)

Notes: 1: single person; 2: married persons with one income.

related to one's working career (number of years and income). In Denmark, the public old-age pension is a flat-rate benefit given to all, and employment-related supplementary pensions are provided by occupational schemes.

Table 5.16 presents the compensation levels in the public disability pension, calculated by the Nordisk Statistisk Sekretariat. By the mid-1980s, all countries had reached fairly similar levels of compensation. While Denmark and Sweden had already reached this level in the early 1970s, the Norwegian expansion came in the 1970s, and in Finland even later.

The Danish "after wage" program pays benefits equal to unemployment compensation for the first thirty months, then 80 percent of unemployment benefits for the next year, and 70 percent for the period until the recipient is eligible for old-age pension. Thus, the economic compensation in the after wage scheme is lower than the alternative, but not fully "voluntary," programs.

The partial pension in Sweden compensates 65 percent of the income loss of reduced working hours (50 percent in the years 1981–86), and the Finnish, 50 percent. Therefore the benefit-wage ratio depends on the number of hours actually worked; still, these schemes provide a

Table 5.17

Acceptance of Needs by Institutional Reforms in the Scandinavian Countries after 1960

Needs	Institutional Change	Exceptions
Sickness		
Short-term absence	Reduced waiting period	
Own assessment of health	Right to self-certification	
Child sickness	Treated as own sickness	Denmark
Maternity leave		
Time to care	Right to paid leave	
Adoption	As own child	
Fathers' right	Right to part of period	
Long-term absence	Extended duration	Denmark, Norway
"Save" leave	Postpone use	Denmark, Norway
Combine benefit/work	Right to partial benefit	Denmark, Norway, Finland
Unemployment benefits		
Employment problems among elderly	Extended duration	
Early retirement		
Nonmedical causes of inability to work	Redefinition of "inability"	
Employment problems	Separate schemes	Norway
Voluntary exit	Early old-age pension	Norway
Combine work/pension	Partial pension	Norway

higher total income for the (partially) retired than for "ordinary" early retirees. A worker reducing his or her working week to twenty hours receives 82 percent of a full-time income in Sweden and 75 percent in Finland (before taxes). In Denmark, a fixed amount (one-thirty-ninth of maximum daily sickness pay) is received per hour reduced, which provides a lower compensation level. On the other hand, the use of a flat-rate amount provides higher compensation levels for the low-income earners.

Hence, as for the temporary benefits, the compensation levels of the early retirement programs have increased considerably. These levels are so high that the income consequences for workers who leave the labor market have been reduced dramatically, if not entirely removed.

Conclusions

Table 5.17 summarizes the welfare reforms. A general trend that applies to all the Scandinavian countries is the shift from a general policy of somewhat fixed benefit entitlements for all workers (in the 1950s and 1960s) toward more sensibility ("needs acceptance") for the social needs of specific groups. However, the target groups are defined in terms of phases in the life cycle, through which the overwhelming majority of wage earners will pass or have passed. This is of no small importance for the legitimacy of the welfare reforms in question.

The development of economic generosity follows a parallel pattern in all four countries: benefits were at first a supplement to market wages. Over time, however, all the programs have provided a compensation level which is not only proportional to wages, but close to full income replacement for the large majority of the wage earners. This means that the traditionally most important parameter in explaining labor market behavior (the wage/income) has, in wide areas of human needs, been largely removed, or become irrelevant for individual decisions. Patterns of behavior that would have been associated with considerable loss of income thirty years ago, are now not only legal but involve no costs. Certain types of behavior have become "decommodified" in the sense that eligibility conditions and entitlements have replaced market wage.

A higher level of compensation implies that the relative importance of the social wage has increased relative to market wage over the life cycle. It is of course impossible to construct a comprehensive and comparable measure of the overall compensation of absence from paid work. In order to illustrate the effect of the increase in the social wage, a ratio between the total income from social transfers and market wage can be estimated for an assumed life cycle. In the estimation of the social wage presented in Figure 5.2, we imagine a (single) twenty-year-old who enters employment at average pay and leaves work through early retirement pension at the age of fifty-seven. During these thirty-seven active years, our "person" has been unemployed one year, has had a year off on maternity leave, and has had a yearly average of fifteen days off due to sickness. Based on these assumptions, and the compensation levels presented in this chapter, we are able to illustrate the relative importance of the improvement of the compensation of paid nonwork.

Although this assumed life cycle is neither typical nor average, it is

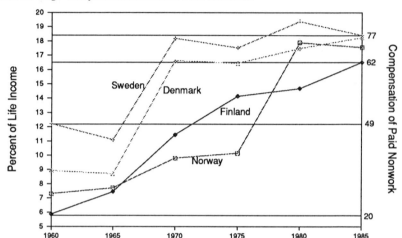

Figure 5.2. The Social Wage as Percent of Estimated Life Income, and Average Compensation Level of Paid Nonwork

not totally unrealistic. And it provides a comparative measure of the overall improvement in the compensation levels of various programs. It summarizes fairly well the developments we have reported. In all countries, the programs provided marginal benefits in the early 1960s. This was a period characterized by the extension of eligibility, rather than by higher benefits for those eligible. Denmark and Sweden were the first countries to increase benefit levels, and have experienced a remarkably parallel development. Norway and Finland increased benefit levels later, but since the mid-1980s, their overall compensation levels have not differed significantly when compared to the two other countries. However, in both Norway and Finland, the impact of occupational sickness pay (for short-term absence) is not included, and the figures overestimate the actual differences between workers in Finland and Norway on the one hand, and in Denmark and Sweden on the other during the early 1970s.

Hence, the conclusion is that the Scandinavian welfare states have become more similar with respect to the compensation of absence from paid work. They provide ordinary workers with an income of approximately 70–85 percent of former wages in cases where they are entitled to leave paid work. The tremendous growth in the social wage is clearly evident when we compare these figures with the compensation levels of 6 percent to 12 percent in 1960.

Figure 5.2 summarizes two significant and general developments.

First, the increase in the social wage, from supplementary allowances to market wage, then to income continuation is clearly charted. Second, it reflects how the income maintenance programs of the welfare state have become more important as a source of income. From this we see that all those who participate in paid work have become increasingly dependent on public welfare policies, extending far beyond the traditional target groups of the welfare state. A nexus between social rights, public expenditures, and individual components of welfare for all wage earners has been established. This is probably an important factor underlying the ability of the Scandinavian welfare states to resist the cutbacks found in other Western countries.

In this study we have addressed the development of the options for wage earners to exit from paid work, and the economic compensation of this withdrawal. In the case of temporary benefits, all the Scandinavian welfare states have liberalized both eligibility and compensation levels in a similar way. There is remarkably less institutional variation in the temporary absence programs in the mid-1980s than there was twenty-five years ago. As for the programs of early retirement, there is also a trend towards convergence. All countries began to modernize this policy area from quite analogous disability schemes via a redefinition of the object of the program. However, since the mid-1970s, Norway has neither followed Sweden and Finland in a continued liberalization, nor developed any separate program for voluntary exit for older workers with employment problems as has Denmark.

All countries have introduced the principle of proportional income calculation of the social wage (except the Danish disability pension). Along with the extension of options to paid nonwork, this means that differences in the market wage are (within certain limits) reproduced in the social wage, making for more stable income differences among households. Thus, to a large extent, the distributional effects of the cash transfer system have been undermined, and left to the tax system. The income and behavior of individuals have become more independent of the logic of markets, but on the other hand, the benefits provided by the welfare state have been more closely tied to the rewards of market participation. Whereas labor has become decommodified, some important elements of state welfare policies have been "commodified," and reflect, rather than reduce, the importance of labor market participation for individual income and welfare.

Notes

1. The information for the tables is compiled from a number of different sources. The main sources used fall into four categories: (1) national legislation in the different countries from 1960 to 1987; (2) the publication "Social Security in the Nordic Countries" published (irregularly, ten times between 1960 and 1986) in the series *Statistical Reports of the Nordic Countries* by the Nordic Statistical Secretariat (NSS), Copenhagen, which contains systematic comparisons of social security legislation and expenditures; for full reference of this source, see reference list, Nordisk Statistisk Skriftserie (NSS); (3) official reports from public institutions in the various countries; and, (4) data collected and presented by other researchers. In the last category, two sources have been of major importance: First the collection of welfare state regime characteristics for all OECD countries done by Olli Kangas and Joakim Palme at the Swedish Institute for Social Research, and second, the contributions of Sven Olsson, Lars Nørby Johansen, Stein Kuhnle, Matti Alestalo, and Hannu Uusitalo in Flora (1986).

The APW incomes applied in the calculations are (national currencies):

	Denmark	Finland	Norway	Sweden
1960	13,065	4,873	13,682	12,823
1965	18,866	7,299	17,868	18,814
1970	31,720	10,525	27,539	25,580
1975	67,018	24,107	52,625	44,595
1980	107,827	41,059	82,514	70,075
1985	176,300	67,420	129,000	104,000

2. See chapter 6, "Unemployment Regimes," in J. E. Kolberg, ed., *Between Work and Social Citizenship*. Armonk, NY: M. E. Sharpe.

References

Alestalo, M., and Kuhnle, S. 1984. *The Scandinavian Route*. Research Reports no. 31. Helsinki: Research Group for Comparative Sociology, University of Helsinki.

Brox, O. 1988. *Ta Vare På Norge*. Oslo: Universitetsforlaget.

Coughlin, R. 1980. *Ideology, Public Opinion and Welfare Policy*. Research Series no. 42. Berkeley: University of California.

Erikson, R., et al. eds., 1987. *The Scandinavian Model*. Armonk, NY: M. E. Sharpe.

Esping-Andersen, G. 1981. *Politics Against Markets: Decommodification in Social Policy*. Stockholm: Institute for Social Research.

———. 1985. "Power and Distributional Regimes." *Politics & Society* 14, no. 2:223–56.

Esping-Andersen, G. and Korpi, W. 1987. "From Poor Relief to Institutional Welfare States: The Development of Scandinavian Social Policy." In R. Eriksson et al., eds., *The Scandinavian Model*. Armonk, NY: M. E. Sharpe.

Flora, P. 1986. *Limits to Growth: The Western European Welfare States Since World War II*. Berlin: de Gruyter.
Halvorsen, K. 1977. *Arbeid eller Trygd*. Oslo: Pax.
Hansen, T. 1981. "Transforming Needs into Expenditure Decisions." In K. Newton, ed., *Urban Political Economy*. London: Frances Pinter.
Hernes, G. 1985. "Velferdsstatens Akser." In J. Hippe, ed., *Ny Kurs For Velferdsstaten*. Oslo: FAFO.
Kangas, O., and Palme, J. 1987. Databank on Welfare State Regime Characteristics. Stockholm: Institute for Social Research.
Kaul, H. 1982. *Når Fravær Er Nærvær. Småbarnsforeldres Bruk av Omsorgspermisjoner*. Trondheim: IFIM.
Kolberg, J. E. 1983. *Farvel til Velferdsstaten?* Oslo: Cappelen.
Kuhnle S. 1983. *Velferdsstatens Utvikling: Norge i Komparativt Perspektiv*. Oslo: Universitetsforlaget.
Lindroos, K. 1984. *Faderna som moderskapspenningtagare*. Helsinki: Ministry of Social Affairs and Health.
Mjøset, L., ed., 1986. *Norden Dagen Derpå*. Oslo: Universitetsforlaget.
Myles, J. 1984. *Old Age and the Welfare State*. Toronto: Little, Brown and Co.
Nordisk Statistisk Skriftserie (NSS). 1955. *Samordning af de nordiske landes statistik vedrørende den sociale lovgivning*. Copenhagen: Nordisk Statistisk Sekretariat, no. 2.
Nordisk Statistisk Skriftserie (NSS). 1959. *Statistikk vedrørende den sociale lovgivning i de nordiske land 1956 (1956/57)*. Oslo: Nordisk Statistisk Sekretariat, no. 6.
Nordisk Statistisk Skriftserie (NSS). 1961. *Samordnad nordisk statistik rörande sociallagstiftningen 1958 (1958/59)*. Stockholm: Nordisk Statistisk Sekretariat, no. 8.
Nordisk Statistisk Skriftserie (NSS). 1965. *Sosial Trygghet i de nordiske land. Utgifter til og omfanget av visse sociale tiltak 1962 (1962/63)*. Oslo: Nordisk Statistisk Sekretariat, no. 11.
Nordisk Statistisk Skriftserie (NSS). 1967. *Social Trygghet i de nordiska länderna. Utgifter och verksamhetens omfattning 1964 (1964/65)*. Stockholm: Nordisk Statistisk Sekretariat, no. 13.
Nordisk Statistisk Skriftserie (NSS). 1971. *Sosial Trygghet i de nordiske land. Utgifter til og omfanget av visse sociale tiltak 1968 (1968/69)*. Oslo: Nordisk Statistisk Sekretariat, no. 22.
Nordisk Statistisk Skriftserie (NSS). 1973. *Social Trygghet i de nordiska länderna. Utgifter och verksamhetens omfattning 1970 (1970/71)*. Stockholm: Nordisk Statistisk Sekretariat, no. 24.
Nordisk Statistisk Skriftserie (NSS). 1975. *Social Tryghed i de nordiske lande. Udgifter og virksomhedens omfattning 1972 (1972/73)*. Copenhagen: Nordisk Statistisk Sekretariat, no. 29.
Nordisk Statistisk Skriftserie (NSS). 1978. *Sosial Trygghet i de nordiske land. Utgifter og virksomhetens omfang 1974 (1974/75)*. Bergen: Nordisk Statistisk Sekretariat, no. 34.
Nordisk Statistisk Skriftserie (NSS). 1980. *Social Trygghet i de nordiska länderna. Verksamhetens omfattning, utgifter och finansiering 1978*. Stockholm: Nordisk Statistisk Sekretariat, no. 37.

Nordisk Statistisk Skriftserie (NSS). 1984. *Social Trygghet i de nordiska länderna. Omfattning, utgifter och finansiering 1981.* Helsingfors: Nordisk Statistisk Sekretariat, no. 43.

Nordisk Statistisk Skriftserie (NSS). 1986. *Social Tryghed i de nordiske lande. Omfang, udgifter og finansiering 1984.* Copenhagen: Nordisk Statistisk Sekretariat, no. 47.

Nordisk Statistisk Skriftserie (NSS). 1989. *Social Tryghed i de nordiske lande. Omfang, udgifter og finansiering 1987.* Copenhagen: Nordisk Statistisk Sekretariat, no. 50.

Nordiska Utredningar. 1985. *Arbejdsløshetens Omkostninger i Norden.* Stockholm: Nordiska Ministerrådet, no. 2.

Olafsson, S. 1989. *The Making of the Icelandic Welfare State. A Scandinavian Comparison.* Reprint Series no. 12. Reykjavik: Social Science Research Institute.

Olsson, S. 1986. "Sweden." In P. Flora, ed., *Growth to Limits: The Western European Welfare States Since World War II.* Berlin: de Gruyter.

Organization for Economic Cooperation and Development (OECD). 1985. *Measuring Health Care 1960–1983.* Paris: OECD.

Polyani, K. 1957. *The Great Transformation.* Boston: Beacon Press.

Riksforsäkringsverket. 1985. *Socialförsäkringsfakta.* Stockholm: Riksförsäkringsverket.

Rold-Andersen, B. 1984. *Kan Vi Bevare Velfærdsstaten.* Copenhagen: Amtskommunernes og Kommunernes Forskningsinstitut.

Socialministeriet. 1980. *Betenkning om Førtidspensjon.* Betenkning no. 898. Copenhagen: Socialministeriet.

Sundboe, J., et al. 1982. *Arbejdsfravær.* Research Report no. 44. Copenhagen: Socialforsikringsinstituttet.

Titmuss, R. 1958. *Essays on the Welfare State.* London: Allen and Unwin.

———. 1974. *Social Policy: An Introduction.* London: Allen and Unwin.

Vogel, J., ed. 1984. *Level of Living and Inequality in the Nordic Countries.* Stockholm: Nordic Council.

6

Sick-Leave Regimes: The Private-Public Mix in Sickness Provision

SVEN BISLEV and RAFAEL LINDQVIST

Sickness insurance and the welfare state

If labor power were an ordinary commodity, sold at its commercial value, any absence from the place of work would cost the worker a full loss of wages during a period of absence, no matter how short: a dollar for a visit to the toilet, a dime for a sneeze. In many places, conditions like that exist, and draconian surveillance ensures that no cheating occurs. A welfare state, on the other hand, can be seen as society's recognition of the fact that labor power is a human and social thing, and can be sold only under special circumstances (Polanyi 1957). Sickness insurance, or more broadly, the provision of income during sickness, is one important facet of the welfare state. It provides a means of livelihood during the many unavoidable absences from the workplace which occur as a result of a temporary disability to work.

The welfare state can be seen as having a double function in relation to the commodity character of labor power. On the one hand, the welfare state is part of the commodification process: the working ability of people has to be separated from their social existence before it can be sold as labor power. "Archaic" processes like the eviction of peasants and the forceful repression of workers secure part of that, but the welfare state helps in transforming the sale of labor power into an orderly and peaceful process, and in extending the labor market by including women (Offe and Lehnhardt 1984). In this perspective, sickness provision is a way of helping the workers through periods of sickness without losing their association with the labor market and having to rely on nonmarket institutions.

On the other hand, the welfare state is a vehicle for decommodification: the provision of income during periods of nonwork means that the immediate dependence on the market is lessened. Decommodification, defined as the extent to which individuals and families can uphold a normal and socially acceptable standard of living regardless of their performance in the labor market (Esping-Andersen and Korpi 1987), is usually connected with a highly developed welfare state where public social benefits and services take the main responsibility for the welfare of its citizens. An ideal-type institutional (or universalist) welfare state is characterized by: (1) large parts of the population covered by its welfare policies, (2) a high range of entitlements, (3) a high degree of income replacement, (4) long duration periods, (5) short waiting periods, and (6) automatic entitlement independent of subjective factors. A welfare state organized along these lines is considered to have the strongest decommodifying effects on the working class. It becomes, in itself, a nonmarket institution, giving workers a partial autonomy from the dictatorship of the workplace (Esping-Andersen 1981).

A well-organized working class can be seen as a political product of the workers' collective striving for autonomy. The autonomous workers can be assumed to be better able to withstand the pressures from the market (Esping-Andersen and Korpi 1987). Providing the workers with a livelihood during sickness is under this aspect an enhancement of dignity and probably of health: one can remain passive and relax until full recovery, instead of struggling through long workdays made worse by poor health.

The provision of income during sickness can be done in several ways, some of which are specified below. In the Nordic countries, the main institutions for this purpose are the public sickness insurance systems. Our task here is to look at those public systems[1] with the following goals of (1) determining their relationship with the general welfare state regimes of the Nordic countries, (2) analyzing the way that public resources, private resources and institutions interact in the sickness area, and (3) finding the effects of the private-public mix upon the social structure.

Sickness insurance (SI) systems are part of the welfare state. As such, the specific construction of a sickness insurance system is influenced by the general features of the welfare state that encompasses it. On

Figure 6.1. **A Causal Model of the Role of Sickness Insurance**

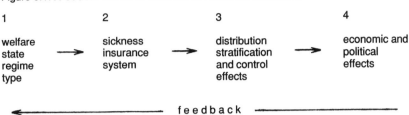

1	2	3	4
welfare state regime type	→ sickness insurance system	→ distribution stratification and control effects	→ economic and political effects

← ——————————— f e e d b a c k ——————————— →

the other hand, SI systems produce social effects in the form of mechanisms for (re-)distribution and social control. These effects, in turn, influence general features of a society such as the labor market and the political system. A causal model of the role of SI is shown in Figure 6.1.

The Nordic countries, with the exception of Iceland, are rather alike in their historical and structural backgrounds. Therefore, their welfare states are alike, as so many treatises on the Scandinavian model have shown. They can be said to be one regime type, but one type with variations: All of them are universalistic or institutional, and they all build on a strong relationship between social and labor market policy. But there are differences among them in terms of: (a) degree of universalism, (b) general level of benefits, (c) the relationship between social and labor policies, and (d) the role of nonstate agents.

Sickness insurance systems are again alike, but with interesting variations, partly in response to the divergences of welfare states, partly for specific, historical reasons. SI systems differ in terms of (a) their generosity in regard to coverage, eligibility, and compensation; and (b) their institutional characteristics: private or public, insurance or no insurance, relation to other areas, and methods of finance.

A sickness insurance system is a mechanism for distributing specific benefits in accordance with certain controlled criteria. In that sense, it will have the following distribution, stratification, and control effects on the thinking and behavior among those concerned: (a) SI impinges on the distribution among occupational groups, income strata, and the public and private sectors. (b) SI, therefore, is part of a struggle over status differentials. It affects the expectations of actors within social divisions. It influences the stratificational structure; softens old divisions of interest and perhaps creates new ones, molds the workings of public institutions and policies, and so forth. (c) SI is part of the system of social control. It is connected with other private and public systems that serve to regularize and control the life of the working class. Its specific function is to formalize the role and function of sickness and to regularize the reproduction of workers during periods of absence from work. (d) The direct effects of altering distribution, stratification, and social control are general societal effects and have implications for macro-social processes and structures. (e) Social implications, the processes of commodification and decommodification, are furthered or restricted according to the nature of the SI system. More generally, the choices between market- and nonmarket institutions for provision during sickness are one important part of a household's general "income packaging behavior" (Rein and Rainwater 1986). (f) The concept of economic efficiency is usually defined as being neutral in relation to some given distribution. On the other hand, many economists argue that the changes in incentives caused by welfare state redistribution endanger efficiency. In a Keynesian perspective, welfare state expansion has effects on aggregate demand. For Marxists, the welfare state helps capital accumulation by underwriting part of the costs for the reproduction of labor power. (g) In the political arena, a more equal distribution can create both solidarity (support for labor reformism), legitimacy (acceptance of the bourgeois state), and, possibly, a welfare backlash.

Such social, economic, and political implications have a feedback effect on the development of the state in general and the welfare state specifically.

This chapter focuses especially on the characteristics of the SI systems and their direct effects, or what one could call the narrow causal loop. More specifically, we focus on the respective roles of public and private institutions and organizations in sickness insurance. The private-public distinction is not a clear-cut one, and the distributional effects of public versus private arrangements may not be great. But the political implications of, say, comprehensive national insurance versus collectively bargained sick pay may be very different. Our main interest is in the social implications mentioned above, but with unavoidable attention to economic and political questions.

Private provision and the need for collective assistance

The need for a sickness insurance system is classically a typical labor question because only workers are totally dependent on every piece of

Figure 6.2. The Need for a Collective Institution to Assist during Sickness

Mode of Provision	Need for Sickness Insurance
Wage work	High/Immediate
Small Property/own work or specialized skills	Medium
Large property or privileged employment	Low/Long-term

work they deliver for their reproduction. None of the other classes—peasants, bourgeoisie, salaried employees—endanger their daily reproduction immediately by being passive for a short time. They possess some of the means of livelihood of which the workers were deprived during the process of original accumulation (Polanyi 1957, Thompson 1968). The need for a collective institution to assist during sickness is presented in Figure 6.2.

Besides being a simple scheme of notions about classes and their reproduction, Figure 6.2 also denotes a historical process: like social policy in general, SI starts as a labor question, either for the hegemonic classes concerned about social unrest or for the workers concerned about securing themselves against misery.[2] Later, it develops from an isolated concern for small groups of active workers to include the whole working class. The state gets involved and eventually universalist aspirations may develop.[3]

If sickness provision were subjugated to market criteria, entitlement and benefit levels should be determined by criteria similar to those that influence wages, that is, bargaining strength and economic position (Taylor-Gooby and Lakeman 1988). The emergence of welfare programs for income protection is a way of supplanting the market—of producing things that the market, given its atomizing effect, does not willingly provide.

In this way, collective arrangements substitute for the market on different levels. In the end, four different forms of income protection in case of sickness have come into existence, defined by their sectoral organization and the locus of control of the benefits in question (see Figure 6.3).

First, *private, individual forms* of income protection are those that individuals possess as a consequence of their general social status as

Figure 6.3. **Forms of Sickness Insurance (SI)**

Control	Sector	
	Private	Public
Individual	property savings; privileges; private insurance	voluntary SI within public SI
Collective	benefit funds; group insurance; wage continuation	cash benefits

farmers, capitalists, or privileged employees. This group also includes the actuarial sickness insurance forms, which still exist. They have been consistently aimed at the better-off, primarily propertied classes, and now serve as complements to the collective and public forms.[4]

Second, *private, collective forms* of income protection developed early in the history of capitalist industry. It is possible to make a distinction between at least three different forms. First, benefit funds or benefit societies were voluntarily organized on the basis of a variety of economic and cultural interests. Many of them were initiated by employers, who wanted to provide their workers with safer conditions to ensure their loyalty and productivity. Worker-established benefit funds were often integrated with trade unions and political organizations. Second, sick pay or wage continuation to private and public employees was started. Governments stimulated much of the early growth in wage continuation programs by extending benefits to new groups of workers who moved into the public sector. These benefits are occupational in nature. They reflect the government's role as employer and reflect status privileges rather than legislated social rights. Third, group insurance, by which individuals and corporate bodies obtain protection in the private market against income loss in case of sickness, developed. Protection is given to members of a contractual sharing group and the risks are supposed to be pooled and shared.

The general tendency in the Scandinavian countries has been first to establish state control and support of the benefit funds and then to eliminate them. Some, such as the following, still exist: (a) workplace funds, integrated in the public system (Finland) (b) group insurances by branch or profession, to supplement public systems (Sweden), and (c) collective wage continuation agreements for some strong trade unions (all countries).

Third, *public, collective forms* are publicly organized forms of income protection, where the conversion of benefits into goods is done by individual disposal—through cash benefits. By and large, these are organized as social insurance. Social insurance is compulsory insurance, but can vary according to: (a) coverage: most wage earners, all wage earners, or the whole adult population (with exceptions) (b) benefits: flat-rate, wage-related, or income-related, and (c) own contribution: existing or not, equal or differential.

Fourth, *public, individual forms* of income protection within the public SI system exist for a small fraction of the population. Public income protection schemes were frequently constructed according to the principle of universal coverage. Also, the self-employed were allowed to be members, since the living conditions for the majority of the self-employed, like farmers, artisans, small business people, and shopkeepers were considered to be more and more similar to those of wage laborers. The fact that employers and the self-employed contributed to the financing of the public schemes motivated a certain freedom of choice within the public SI concerning, for example, number of waiting days and replacement levels. Occasionally this freedom of choice has been extended to homemakers and students.

The above four types of income protection have grown historically in the Scandinavian countries and still exist, although the public, collective forms is the dominant type. Alongside these types, another set of institutions has grown up: the institutions for delivering health services. In the days of benefit funds, the two programs were integrated, but today, there are systems for income protection outside the health service system. They are complementary systems but are constructed on different principles: income protection is social policy and great care is taken not to produce adverse effects on the labor market; health service is health policy and the free provision of especially hospital services is supposed to have no effect on the labor market. In a few areas, the two principles overlap, and divergent or contradictory results emerge: while Sweden charges a fee for doctors' services, Denmark does not; dentists' and opticians' services are in general only partially covered; the payment for medical supplies is very different for hospital patients and outpatients. In this chapter, we cover the income protection field, but we will occasionally touch on institutional health services.

The development of Nordic sickness insurance

Until World War II, the welfare state was in what Heclo (1981) called its experimental phase. Different models of social policy competed. In the Nordic countries, most social programs had needs tests, covered narrow target groups, and yielded low benefits. Differences among the countries were mainly in the role of benefit funds: in the sickness area, the Danish and Swedish funds had state support since 1891/92; Iceland had state support dating from 1911; while Norway had social insurance for low-paid workers since 1909. In Finland, benefit funds were first regulated in 1897 without any substantial state support until 1963, when public sickness insurance was instituted.

For most of the interwar period, social legislation was a highly controversial subject, touching on the very basics of the relationship between individuals and society. The social democratic parties increasingly supported an extension of social policy, emphasizing its decommodifying aspects. The conservative parties supported some of it from a paternalistic angle, while the liberalists strongly denounced any interference with pure market forces, deliberately neglecting the commodifying or market-supporting aspects of social policy. But during the 1930s the picture gradually changed in Denmark, Norway, Sweden, and Iceland. Long periods of Social Democratic growth and government participation led to attempts at systematic social reforms. Denmark in 1933, Norway in 1933–38, and Sweden in 1935–38, saw attempts at homogenizing the organizational structure of the welfare state.

The substantial effects of these reforms in Denmark and Sweden were not great, they sought rather to integrate the benefit funds and other independent branches into state policies.[5] The Norwegian reforms were substantially more important, while the Finnish working class was too weak to press for better social policies. In Iceland, Worker's General Insurance was legislated in 1936 (Olafsson 1989). In both sickness and unemployment insurance, coverage in the three Scandinavian countries and Iceland was gradually extended to cover most of the working class. But programs were still residual, with strict categorical limits, needs tests, and substantial individual contributions.

The shift to the universalist tendencies of the post–World War II period came with the reformist programs of the Norwegian and Swedish Social Democratic parties of 1944. Inspired by various sources, mainly the specific political situation during the war but also the British Beveridge report, these programs called for a broad-based, universalist welfare state with adequate benefits and no stigmas attached to its services. During the 1950s, the parties won political power (or entered suitable alliances) to implement these ideas. Iceland instituted compulsory social insurance in 1951, Sweden exchanged its benefit funds for full, compulsory coverage in 1955, Norway extended its coverage to the whole population in 1956, Denmark extended its benefit funds to the whole population in 1960, and Finland introduced a sickness insurance law on universalist principles in 1964.

A totally universal or decommodifying sickness insurance not only covers the whole population, it also implies replacement or compensation ratios approaching 100 percent and either very low or nonexistent contributions, so that incentives to buy additional private insurance are removed. A crucial aspect of the SI system, in that respect, is how it treats and compensates groups outside wage labor, like farmers, the self-employed, and homemakers. Does the SI system imply decommodification for wage laborers only or is it decommodifying in a preventive sense? On these points, there were and still are differences among the Nordic countries, as we shall demonstrate.

In Denmark, the situation of wage laborers gradually approached that of the white-collar employees through the improvement of public programs (in 1960, 1970, and 1972) and collective wage agreements (in 1956). The Danish sickness funds were abolished in 1971, and in 1972, benefits for sickness and unemployment were limited to 90 percent of wages, with an upper limit defined as 90 percent of average industrial wage. Full tax financing was introduced and duration limits and waiting days were abolished. Since then, the only changes (apart from two extensions of maternity leave) have been financial cutbacks: a lower, fixed limit reducing the compensation level, implementation of one waiting day, and the setting of a duration limit of ninety-one days in three years—all in 1982/83.[6]

The Danish program has covered the whole active, nonstudent population since 1972—with the exception that housewives and the self-employed have to actively register and pay a fee to be insured. Three causes account for the lack of private supplements: (1) compensation levels arc high, (2) hospitals and doctors are completely tax financed, and (3) all white-collar employees have full wage continuation during sickness.

Table 6.1

Members of *Fortsættelsessygekassen Danmark*
(in thousands)

1974	1976	1978	1980	1982	1984
266	333	361	374	452	652

Sources: Danmark (1975; 1977; 1979; 1981; 1983; and 1985).

The financial cutbacks of 1982–86 reduced the compensation ratio to a level of 60–70 percent, thus recreating large status differentials among manual and nonmanual workers. But private supplements have been growing very slowly, partly because the trade union federation prefers to work for an improvement of state programs instead of a collective agreement on sick-pay arrangements.

The only area where the public program is less generous is in the provision of medical supplies and optician and dental services. In this area there is, a private institution, *Fortsættelsessygekassen Danmark*. Growing out of pre-1970 supplementary benefit funds, it now provides a tax-deductible insurance, covering the lacunae of the public system. The number of members has been growing since 1972, with a spurt during the latest cutback period (see Table 6.1).

In Norway, universalism was gradually introduced from 1949 to 1958, when all the major programs were extended to cover the whole population. In 1966, *Folketrygden* (People's Social Insurance) was established, successively unifying unemployment, sickness, old-age, and accident insurance. It has its own tax-like method of finance, but unlike U.S. Social Security, it is not independent of state budgets (Kolberg 1983; Dølvik and Hippe 1985).

In the 1970s, several different sick-pay systems existed (NOU 1976). All civil servants, that is, 320,000 public employees, had full wage continuation for periods varying from three to twelve months. Private employees (totalling 200,000) had similar arrangements. The rest of the labor force had public social insurance, with a compensation level around 50 percent. But among these, 360,000 workers were covered by a general collective agreement between the trade union and employers' federations, supplementing their sick pay to around 90 percent of wages. Finally, 50,000 workers outside the general agreement

Table 6.2

Private Sickness Insurance in Sweden (number of policies in thousands)

Year	Individual	Group	(Group-AGS)
1960	168	17	—
1965	173	287	—
1970	177	424	—
1975	163	2,566	(2,306)
1980	130	2,629	(2,423)
1985	140	2,682	(2,490)

Sources: Statistiska Centralbyrån 1981, 219 and 1987, 293.
Note: AGS: avtalsgruppsjukförsäkring (negotiated group sickness insurance).

had established local funds to provide themselves with the same supplement as the general one. Since 1978, sick pay has been on a 100-percent compensation level with no waiting days, but with a maximum compensation limit for higher incomes.[7] The difference between manual and nonmanual employees has disappeared in this respect.

Before 1955, Sweden had a system very much like Norway, where large groups had sick-pay arrangements through collective agreements. The universalist arrangement legislated in 1955 made sickness insurance mandatory for all, but with waiting days and a compensation level of 60–70 percent. In 1962, all social insurance (except unemployment compensation) was integrated in a single system, and the benefits of social insurance were gradually improved, until waiting days were abolished (in 1967) and the compensation level reached 90 percent (in 1973) (Lindqvist 1987).

The introduction of public sickness insurance meant a strong reduction in private insurance. Many white-collar employees kept their wage continuation as a complement to sick pay, and although new groups of employees entered the labor market, improvements of the public system shrank the market for private complements. In 1972, a collective agreement introduced avtalsgruppsjukförsäkring (AGS) (negotiated group sickness insurance), an insurance policy that employers can buy in a specific company, which supplements public sick pay for those who have no wage continuation[8] (see Table 6.2).

Lately, a new private element in Sweden has entered the sickness and health sector: private companies are selling sickness insurance to

Table 6.3

Members of *Arbetarsjukkassor*(sick benefit societies) (in thousands)

Year	Number of members
1930	64.3
1950	125.3
1960	160.1
1970	197.7
1980	221.4
1984	219.0

Sources: Ministry of Social Affairs and Health 1933, 88; 1952, 396; 1961a, 480; 1972, 192; and Central Statistical Office of Finland 1986, 193.

employers designed for their top-level employees, which is connected with a private hospital where medical services are provided without the queues of the public system. This reflects a growing general interest from the business community in health for profit (Olsson 1988). Here, privatization takes place in the upper end of the income distribution, where additional benefits are sought in excess of the wage continuation available for upper-level employees. In the lower end, people with a weak connection to the labor market, like part-time workers and the frequently unemployed, have had a low compensation level in the sickness insurance system (Marklund and Svallfors 1987). Homemakers have received extremely low flat-rate benefits.[9] Thus, within a universalistic framework, the Swedish SI treats persons outside wage labor with austerity. A political initiative to improve conditions at that end of the scale was taken in December 1987, but in health services the problem of undercapacity in public hospitals is rising with the exploding costs of hospitals. These problems have led to private initiatives not only in Sweden but in Denmark, too, and the public sector has no ready answer to the undermining of welfare state systems that follows from the private sector cornering the most accessible and profitable part of health service.

The Finnish welfare state has historically developed under a much stronger influence from agrarian interests. The development and character of the Finnish SI system was related to the political power of the Agrarian party and farmers associations.[10] The universalist tendency was there, but benefits were comparatively low until the 1980s

Table 6.4

Sickness Protection through Life Insurance in Finland 1960–84: Number of Insurance Policies with Sickness Benefits (in thousands)

	Insured	% of Population	Hospital Allowances	Daily Allowances
1960	2,006	45	594	836
1965	2,078	45	1.114	937
1970	1,895	41	1.346	849
1975	1,746	37	1.312	781
1984	1,429	29	928	518

Sources: Kangas 1988b; and Ministry of Social Affairs and Health 1961b, 64; 1966, 66; 1971, 84; 1977, 72–73; 1986, 84–87; and Försäkringskasseförbundet 1985, 16.

(Alestalo and Uusitalo 1986). Not until 1982 did the compensation ratio in sick pay reach the level of the other Nordic countries.

A 1934 Relief Fund report on social insurance triggered a decision by the bourgeois government to start building a public pension system. Sickness insurance was postponed, and the existing firm-level workers' benefit funds continued to expand (Kangas 1988). Before the introduction of public sickness insurance in 1963, one great subject for debate was whether municipal and firm-level benefit funds should continue to exist. The result was that they were allowed to continue, but mostly to administer the public benefits for their members. In some places additional, locally negotiated benefits exist (Laurinkari 1979) (see Table 6.3).

Finnish sickness insurance came in two steps: The 1963 reform introduced sickness cash benefits compensation for medical treatment and medicine. In 1967, compensation for doctors' fees was introduced. Employers must pay continued wages during the seven waiting days, according to the Employment Act of 1970, but most employers will pay for three weeks or more. Public civil servants have better terms than most private employees (Laurinkari 1979).

The late introduction of social insurance meant an expansion of private insurance through 1965. Table 6.4 shows the typical crowding-out effect on the private insurance market produced by the establishment of public sickness insurance and pension systems.

Data on Iceland have been sparse but it is clear that until the 1960s

Table 6.5

State-Mandated, Nonpublic Sick Cash Expenditure (wage continuation) as Percent of Total Expenditure for Sick Cash Benefits; Four Scandinavian Countries, 1974–84

Year	Denmark	Finland	Iceland	Norway	Sweden
1974	52.8	43.2	89.2	73.6	0
1976	53.6	44.4	89.6	53.0	0
1978	50.9	77.4	90.5	48.9	0
1980	49.9	80.3	93.4	36.9	0
1982	47.8	55.3	94.3	35.7	0
1984	50.5	54.0	94.8	44.5	0

Source: Recalculation based on NCM 1976, 267; 1979, 272; 1980, 274; 1982, 278–79; 1984, 289–90; and 1986, 313–14.

Notes: Only compulsory contributions are included, except for Iceland where negotiated benefits are also included; Regarding Finland from 1976 on, public sick cash benefits declined because maximum allowances did not keep pace with inflation, which makes the proportion of nonpublic expenditure relatively high. Since 1982, however, public benefits have improved and become taxable. The figure shown for Finland (1989) is from 1983 and the figure shown for Norway (1982) is from 1981.

Iceland was among the leading countries in welfare state development. From then on, development slowed, and as of now, the Icelandic system is much less generous than the other countries as illustrated by compensation ratios in the twenties, ten waiting days, and many private supplements through collective agreements (NSS 1986). Wage continuation through labor negotiations are continuously increasing as the relatively low flat-rate public sickness benefits are being excavated by inflation.

Table 6.5 shows the relation between public (sick cash benefits) and nonpublic (statutory sick pay) expenditures. In Sweden, all statutory cash allowances are public expenditure, deriving from social insurance wage bills. (Swedish civil servants' statutory sick pay also comes from the general financing of the SI system. Expenditure for other white-collar groups is not state-mandated but based on collective agreement.)

Table 6.5 shows that Denmark, Finland, and Norway have a specific private-public mix where a considerable and rather constant part of sickness provision is state-mandated but organized in private collective forms and financed through private firms (in various cost clearing models with the SI system).

Table 6.6

Expenditure for Sick Cash Benefits as a Percent of Total Health Service Expenditure; Four Scandinavian Countries, 1975–85

Year	Denmark	Finland	Iceland	Norway	Sweden
1975	23	38	22	21	40
1981	25	19	22	28	36
1985	19	22	20	31	38

Source: Recalculation based on NCM 1977, 272; 1983, 289; and 1987, 313.
Note: The figure shown for Iceland (1985) is from 1984.

Institutionalism?

In terms of our causal model, we have been describing the SI system (see Figure 6.1). Before proceeding to the effects of the system, we will use the concept of institutionalism to summarize the description and compare the five Nordic countries.

Institutionalism embodies the principle that social protection should be granted as a social right according to the status of citizenship (Marshall 1977). All who possess that status of citizenship are equal with respect to certain rights and duties and are full members of the community. Titmuss's institutional redistributive model is a model of universalist (i.e., extended to everybody independent of contribution) services provided outside the market (i.e., independent of income and status) on the principles of need and social equality (Titmuss 1974, 31). In the absence of a market, there are, however, no universal principles that determine what those rights and duties should be, and the coexistence of the class system and institutionalist social policy creates a conflict between opposing principles (Mishra 1977). In all the Nordic countries, institutionalism (as defined at the beginning of this chapter) is stronger in health services than in income protection. Adequate services in the health sector are directed to the whole population, not only to wage earners, and services are triggered by individual need and financed through general contributions. Compared to cash benefits, health services comprise the larger sector in terms of expenditure, as shown in Table 6.6. Let us look at the various characteristics of universalism in comparing the Nordic SI systems.

Table 6.7

Sickness Insurance (cash benefits) Coverage; Four Scandinavian Countries, 1965–80 (in percent)

	Labor Force		Population 15–65 Years of Age	
	1965	1980	1965	1980
Norway	83	145	50	100
Sweden	138	108	92	87
Finland	138	124	98	90
Denmark	80	100	58	80

Source: Calculated for the Nordic Welfare State Project by Kåre Hagen.
Notes: The Danish percentage of 100 in 1980 should be slightly higher, to account for a few insured housewives; figures for Iceland are not available.

Coverage and compensation level

In general, the Nordic SI systems have a high coverage. As shown in Table 6.7 only Norway has reached full universalism.

We can test for degrees of universalism by looking at how the system compensates people in the upper and lower end of the income distribution, since a universal public SI system should cover and deliver adequate benefits to all of the population, that is, even the self-employed, homemakers, and other non–wage earners. Empirical information is required on the size and character of the proportion of the population that cannot receive substantial sick cash benefits, that is, people unable to qualify for normal income protection. And how many are wealthy people with no real need for sickness insurance? According to Marklund and Svallfors (1987), the Swedish system creates two undercompensated groups: one at the low end of the income scale, consisting of housewives and those with too short a work record (the requirement is six months), and one at the other end, made up of the people who earn more than the maximum of 180,000 SEK. The lower marginal group was 12 percent of the labor force in 1984, the upper was 4 percent in 1986. The upper group has other sources of income protection, the lower most often does not. In this way, the Swedish SI system reproduces the "market" distribution, bringing this segment of the welfare state perhaps closer to Titmuss's industrial achievement model, rather than his institutional redistributive model.

Comparable information on the other countries is not available. However, all the other systems, although they, too, mirror work performances, seem to be more generous at the bottom of the income ladder. The Finnish system is the most generous with a flat-rate amount of about 60 SEK a day in 1986 and no income limit in the upper end of the system (though income replacement is decreasing for high-income earners).

At the core of the Scandinavian SI systems, the size and character of benefits vary although we only have figures for average compensation levels for wage workers. The Danish and Norwegian SI systems cover the self-employed after a waiting period of three weeks and two weeks, respectively (which can be set aside through voluntary insurance). In the other countries, the self-employed are covered on roughly the same conditions as other wage laborers (SOU 1983, 48). Homemakers can be voluntarily insured in Denmark, but they are automatically covered in the other countries.

Table 5.5 shows the compensation levels for the four countries (see chapter 5 in this volume). Currently (in 1985) they vary from 74 percent in Denmark to 100 percent in Norway (see Table 6.8). The data in the figures are calculated as the average production worker's compensation for one week, twenty-six weeks, and fifty-two weeks of sickness, in percent of his or her wage. They *indicate* the difference between low-level manual workers for whom these figures apply (during sickness, they receive no more than the public benefits), and privileged employees of several kinds, who are liable to have wage continuation. They do not show the difference between workers and owners: An insured self-employed Dane gets less than the 74 percent; a self-employed Norwegian gets only 65 percent. But of course the owners of larger enterprises are not dependent on public sickness insurance.

Finland has a specific type of private-public mix where the employers compensate for various time periods (and groups) according to labor contracts. Compared to the Swedish SI system, the Finnish (public) one has higher coverage among the population and higher flat-rate benefits for non–wage laborers but lower compensation level for wage laborers.

Only Norway has instituted full equality for manual workers with white-collar private and public employees. The low Danish compensation level (down to 60 percent in 1986 before tax) is due to financial

Table 6.8

The Compensation Level of Public Sickness Insurance for the Average Production Worker; Four Scandinavian Countries, 1960–84 (in percent)

	1960	1965	1970	1975	1980	1984
Norway	38	34	49	53	100	100
Sweden	63	50	82	90	90	92
Denmark	—	37	52	64	78	74
Finland	59	59	50	(31)	(37)	86

Sources: NC 1963; 1967; 1972; NCM 1977; 1982; and NSS 1986.

cutbacks since 1982. The Swedish private-collective supplements iron out some of the inequality between the different strata, but in Sweden, Denmark, and Finland (and even more Iceland), it is clear that inequality produced through the market status of wage earners is more than reproduced via sickness insurance.

Waiting days and duration of benefits

All five countries have had several waiting days before benefits were paid, but in Norway, Sweden, and Denmark those days have been gradually abolished (Denmark reintroduced them for a brief period). All the countries have had a policy of limited duration of benefits. Three of them have abolished it: Sweden in 1963; Finland in 1964; and Denmark in 1973. Iceland and Norway still have a limit of one year.

Claimant's contribution

No Nordic SI system is financed solely by members' contributions, but in Norway and Finland, contributions are still a major source of financing (see Table 6.9).

None of the systems have any insurance character, with the exception of Denmark, which has the possibility of self-insurance through the public system for housewives and the self-employed. In Norway and Finland, a fund system with individual contributions has been retained but all the insurance elements are gone, as we have shown. The remaining effect of having a separately funded system is the political effect of visibility: some random fraction of the costs of social

Table 6.9

Ratio of Individual's Contribution in the Finance of Sickness Insurance
(in percent)

	1960	1965	1966	1975	1980	1985
Norway	51	48	39	16	08	29
Sweden	46	47	38	00	13	00
Denmark	67	54	54	04	06	01
Finland	—	32	51	44	39	35

Source: Calculated for the Nordic Welfare State Project by Kåre Hagen.
Note: Figures for Iceland are not available.

insurance is separated out as a deficit to be covered through taxes (Kolberg 1983). Portraying the contributions for sickness as a specific payment, separated from the general social insurance premiums, as we have here, is even somewhat artificial.

Automatic entitlement

All the Nordic SI systems have shed most of the stigmatizing effects of public social benefits: needs tests and means tests were abolished in the reforms of the 1960s in all countries in favor of bureaucratic regulations of eligibility and benefits. The SI systems are no longer residual, and in terms of the dual welfare state, they belong to the institutional side (to a high degree reflecting work performance); but in another sense of duality, there is still a definite difference between those welfare states that have full income continuation during sickness as a private right, and those who depend upon a partial compensation from public sources (Jensen 1985). Only the Norwegian system has transcended that division—and it neither bled the public treasury nor emptied the shop floors. Perhaps the effects are smaller than most theorists would expect.

Distribution effects

Of the three sets of direct effects of a social insurance scheme, distribution effects are the most immediate. Distribution can take place horizontally over the life cycle and/or vertically between the better-off and the poorer segments of the population. A substantial part of the transfer payments in SI represents an element of compensation for income loss during sickness. Hence, the immediate distributional effect may be limited, even though income-related SI systems usually have both a floor and a ceiling. One could always argue that if compensation payments were not made at all, the range of inequality would be correspondingly increased. People who otherwise would have been living in poverty due to sickness are being lifted up economically because they are compensated through the SI system.

Redistribution via the welfare state plays a major role in all Scandinavian countries. In Denmark in 1977, 9 percent of total personal incomes were redistributed via the public sector. Seven percent went from the economically active to the nonactive group, corresponding to the fact that pensions constitute the largest part of social expenses. The redistribution effect of the tax system was negligible, but cash transfers were important, making the main routes of redistribution as follows: from wage earners to pensioners, and from all wage earners to workers. Workers were the main recipients of unemployment compensation schemes and sick-pay schemes.[11]

A Swedish study confirms the redistribution effect of sickness insurance: in Sweden, everybody pays for social insurance (through wage bills) proportional to incomes; but benefit ceilings and the relatively higher incidence of sickness among the low-paid means that the lower-paid employees receive proportionately more from the SI system (Ståhlberg 1986). Norwegian and Finnish SI systems rely more on direct contributions from the insured, but the distribution picture remains the same. A major goal for all four countries has been to unify the SI system on a national basis integrating regional and branch-based funds. Unification changes little in the social distribution, but prevents regional and sectoral divergences from growing too large (Stokke 1981).

Stratification effects

The need for SI is related to the notion of classes and their reproduction. Different classes have different interests regarding the types of income protection during sickness. SI systems are best understood as social institutions established through struggles in which governments, employers, employees, and voluntary benefit societies—all with different goals—take part.

In Denmark, prevailing status differentials, formalized in the inter-war period through wage continuation given to white-collar groups, have successively been integrated in the SI system. Proponents for public SI schemes have been striving to improve income protection according to the ideal type instituted for civil servants. However, the recent abolition of sickness benefit funds reflected the important role played by voluntary, broadly class-based forces in constructing SI systems. The vested interests of sickness benefit funds probably delayed a potential working-class solution. Thus, the concrete Danish private public mix is not primarily a solution to the labor question. Rather it can be seen as a coalescing arrangement for a plurality of interests, where the public element has continuously been furthered through reforms in order to keep up with already existing private income protection during sickness.

In the 1980s, the financial cutbacks reduced the compensation ratio to a level of 60–70 percent, re-creating the large status differentials between manual and nonmanual workers. But private supplements have been growing very slowly, partly because the trade union federation prefers to work for an improvement of state programs instead of collective-agreement sick-pay arrangements.

The stratificational effect of the Finnish SI system is closely connected to the ambitions of agrarian interests. The facts that (1) coverage among the population is high, (2) the compensation level for wage earners is relatively low, and (3) compensation for non–wage earners is high, reflect agrarian interests. Firm-level benefit funds, collective agreements on sick pay, and wage continuation by law expanded accordingly. Since the private and the public elements in the mix are not administratively coordinated, employers are accordingly entitled to arrange sickness control in order to further the general goals of the firms.

The Norwegian SI system represents the opposite way of integration, where the existing wage continuation arrangements have been incorporated into and adapted to the public SI system. The dividing line between manual and nonmanual workers has been abolished.

In the Swedish case, too, the labor movement has pursued a SI system capable of covering the entire wage-laboring population on equal terms, that is, income-related sickness benefits. A heavily emphasized Social Democratic ambition in the 1950s was that civil servants and white-collar workers be incorporated into the public schemes. The result was that they were covered but allowed to keep some of the additional services and benefits covered by private schemes, for example, those that covered the income loss not covered by the public schemes.

The current trend in Sweden is that occupational sickness benefits, in addition to the public SI system, are extended to manual workers, reducing the gap between them and their nonmanual colleagues. Trade unions try to expand collective agreement–based wage continuation as well as improve the public SI schemes.[12] Unions have realized that overall spending on income protection during sickness can be maximized more by mixing public and occupational welfare than by relying on public spending alone. Thus, private collective wage continuation can be a route to greater equality in income protection during sickness; it does not have to widen income inequalities and nourish privilege as Titmuss (1963) feared.

Sickness insurance can be viewed as a redistribution of income between periods of work and periods of (sickness) absence. On the microlevel, then, a question remains: What effect does that have on the behavior of labor markets and social institutions? This is where the question of social control must be considered.

Control effects

The opportunity to remain in bed and continue to receive an income could be hypothesized to lead many wage earners into temptation. In rational choice theory, this can be developed into the following hypothesis: the more generous SI systems will produce more sickness absence. The implication is that effective social control is a necessary corollary of any mildly generous sick pay scheme.

All SI systems have various control implications. None of the Scandinavian schemes are restrictive in the immediate sense of controlling the actual existence of sickness. In Denmark, employers decide whether they need a doctor's certification from case to case, and the number of demands for certification is small. In Norway, the employer can restrict the right to self-reporting to three days at a time and three times a year. In Finland and Iceland, control of sickness absence is still more in the hands of the employers. In Sweden, medical certificates are usually required (by the SI bureaucracy) after six days (but from the first day in case of six or more benefit periods in one year). The way insured persons, in case of long-term sickness, are transferred into rehabilitation programs varies among schemes. The Swedish system, with its unlimited benefits, legally requires the Social Insurance Office, after ninety days of employee illness, to investigate the need for more extensive rehabilitation measures, and after approximately one year, to recommend the suitability of disability pension. The SI bureaucracy forces persons to take part in such measures, or threatens withdrawal of sickness benefits.

In a broader sense, control implications arise by the way in which clients in the SI system enter the health bureaucracy, by the length of their sickness, and in the control potential of sickness statistics. The Danish debate about the one waiting day, from 1982 to 1987, clearly showed how statistics could be used to pinpoint branches and social groups where high incidences of sickness absence could be said to indicate problems of climate or morale.

Norwegian sickness absence figures show a limited rise in sickness absence of three days or more, from seven days per year to eight days per year in 1978, when 100 percent compensation was introduced. In Sweden, sickness absence rose from sixteen days per year to twenty days per year per employee when, in 1967, the compensation level was significantly improved. The Danish figures show a change in the pattern of sickness absence toward fewer short-term absences when the waiting days were introduced in 1982 (Holm et al. 1986; Lindqvist 1987).

Several explanations, however, could account for such changes (Holm et al. 1986; Sundbo et al. 1982). A general change in attitude toward reporting sickness may have occurred (for various reasons). There may have been changes in registration and accounting techniques (which often happens along with policy shifts). In addition, the composition of the labor force may have changed, and changes in other policies may have interfered.

The Danish *Karensdagsrapport* (Waiting Day report) concludes, after carefully studying domestic and foreign material on the subject, that changes in program characteristics do affect behavior, but with small and weak effects, which are easily overshadowed by other factors like changes in work climate, general attitudes, and so forth (Holm et al. 1986). This seems to be the general conclusion drawn among policy makers in the Nordic countries, since instituted controls continue to be liberal.

The incentive to control is different for sick pay and wage continuation, and comes from different sectors. Sick-pay systems, operated by the public sector, entail no cost for employers, who have been known to be more liberal in accepting self-reported sickness in slack times than when business is thriving. Wage continuation schemes are paid by employers, who gain an incentive to coordinate the effort toward diminishing sickness with efficiency considerations in the firm (Taylor-Gooby and Lakeman 1988). The institution of public sickness insurance does not contribute immediately to preventing sickness, but serves to decrease the time the workers need to devote toward securing their own financial security. It can also be seen as a buffer between labor and capital in this area (Immergut 1986). For employees, a generous SI system can also be a safety valve in situations where no other options for collective protest are open; both Sweden and Denmark know the phenomenon of police influenza.

Societal effects of sickness insurance

One of the main effects of the welfare state is the way in which it has changed the balance and the relations between the public and private sectors. On a macrolevel, the public sector organizes a large part of societal processes, and on a microlevel, individuals mix a large share of public wages, transfers, and services into their private income sources. Sickness insurance is part of that general picture.

The relationship between public and private elements is different for different countries. In Sweden and Norway, the public systems are completely dominant: existing private schemes were integrated into and subordinated by the public system. In Denmark, like in Sweden, separate wage continuation schemes continue to exist, but in Denmark, the public system was built slightly more on the foundation of the private, preexisting ones. Now, the integration is complete. In Finland, there is less integration on the administrative level: individuals are supposed to know themselves where to claim their benefits—from benefit funds or from public offices. But ordinary benefits are the same. In Iceland, private arrangements dominate the scene.

This growth of the public systems could be expected to create a welfare backlash, a resentment toward the large bureaucracies and high taxes that result from welfare state developments (Wilensky 1975). In turn, this could mean a threat to the legitimacy of the state or of social reformism. However, divided finances, where the employers, as in the

Swedish case, pay the lion's share of the cost, can disperse the pressure on the income tax system as a prime source of tax revolt (Marklund 1988, 88). Another important unifying aspect is that the universal model is considered to have the capacity to create social cohesion. Large groups of income earners are covered under similar conditions.

Recent electoral developments have shown the strength of social democratic parties in Nordic countries to be rather precarious, although no definite setbacks have occurred. But research seems to indicate that resistance toward the welfare state plays no autonomous role in whatever adversity social democrats may experience: support for the welfare state in general is high and the class division in attitudes toward specific programs is rather less than might be expected (Andersen 1982; Pöntinen and Uusitalo 1986; Marklund 1986; Boalt 1985).

Feedback effects on the general level could be expected as a growing division between workers, the main users of sickness systems, and privileged employees, who contribute directly and via taxes, and who use such systems much less. In Denmark especially, where the principled division between manual workers and nonmanual workers still exists, it coincides with a diminishing support for social democracy among white-collar employees. In the Danish context, it fits in with other nonuniversal features like the strong element of status division in pensions and housing, and may be part of the trouble that Social Democrats are experiencing (Esping-Andersen 1985; Jensen 1985). For the other countries, no such coincidence or correlation exists, and the Social Democrats' troubles are less.

Conclusion

The dominant trend in the development of sickness provision in the Nordic countries over the post–World War II period has been to narrow the preexisting gap between classes and strata in regard to benefits. The situations of more groups among the wage workers have come close to that of the traditionally privileged employees.

The principle means of equalization has been to extend the range and coverage of state benefits, but the balance and relationship between private and public elements have developed differently in the five Nordic countries. In all the countries, the end result is one of a decreasing reliance on solidarity mechanisms inside civil society, and an increasing reliance on a mix of market principles and social rights.

Our tentative conclusion is that this mix, in the Nordic context, is itself fragile, but viable: although there are dangers inherent in the contradictions between the two principles, and although the decrease in informal solidarity is a costly and potentially dangerous development, it seems that market principles and social rights can live together in peace if properly groomed and cultivated.

The threat to the sickness insurance part of the Nordic welfare states seems to come less from an inherent contradiction between the two principles of markets and social rights: those two systems have actually been developing together all the time and one could not exist without the other. Rather, the threat seems to come from problems in the interaction between the welfare state and the political system. The unfinished universalism of the Danish SI program is a case in point: in building a relatively generous and costly public SI system while retaining the differences in benefits and status between manual and non-manual employees, it invites political conflicts that might undermine the system.

Notes

1. Some of the institutions that provide their members or clients with livelihood during sickness have lost all or almost all of the insurance character. They have become noncontributory programs. For practical purposes, however, we shall for the rest of the chapter denote all such institutions as SI (sickness insurance).

2. Bismarckian social policy is known as a clear-cut case of hegemonic concerns; later formulations of the purpose of social policy were framed in terms of the differential needs and aspirations of social classes (Cassel 1902; Zeuthen 1948).

3. The universalist formulation claimed that social benefits should be accessible to all and form part of a general egalitarian welfare state (Briggs 1961). That was partly inspired by the Beveridge committee, and partly a link in a general reorientation of European Social Democracy in the 1930s, where the social democracy shred its class appeal and opted for a broader mass basis.

4. Characteristically, early sickness insurance policies often went in combination with life and property insurance (Bergander 1967). They still attract a few, but play a very marginal role in the Nordic countries today.

5. In Denmark, a law was passed at the same time regulating the status of white-collar employees. They were given fringe benefits like paid vacation, wage continuation under sickness, and long notice periods, in a political attempt to separate them from the working class. This law (*Funktionærloven*) still exists and has had political effects which, though ambiguous (it has had a demonstration effect on top of the intended separation effect), are not negligible.

6. The one waiting day was abolished again in 1987. Employers pay their worker's sick pay five weeks, after which the state takes over. A new revision, implemented in 1988, restored to recipients some of the diminished compensation level, and shortened the employer period from five weeks to three weeks.

7. That maximum was lowered in 1988, making about 180,000 NOK (around the next highest decile of income earners) the highest level of full compensation.

8. The Swedish LO (The Federation of Trade Unions) has long been promoting contractual insurance schemes. At all congresses since 1961, the issue has been discussed and the opinion has been in favor of contractual insurances. They have been considered advantageous for several reasons: they may lead to increased membership, they are less expensive than public schemes, and they offer the possibility of exerting a more direct influence on the form of the schemes (Edebalk and Wadensjö 1988).

9. Homemakers' benefits were eight SEK a day until 1986. Since then they can be voluntarily insured within the public SI scheme.

10. As late as the early 1970s, the agrarians argued in favor of flat-rate benefits with high coverage (Kangas 1988a).

11. See figures from the work of the Low Income Commission (1982). Finn Kenneth Hansen has shown that cash transfers had much the same distribution effect in 1981 as in 1977, but that the tax burden has been shifted relatively towards the lower incomes (Hansen 1985). For factor incomes, the ministry of finance recently found a distinctively negative development in the period 1981–85.

12. In the last collective agreement (for 1988/89) practically all trade unions have either instituted new forms of wage continuation or improved existing arrangements.

References

Alestalo, M., and Uusitalo, H. 1986. "Finland." In P. Flora, ed., *Growth to Limits. The West-European Welfare States Since World War II.* Vol. 1. Berlin: de Gruyter.

Andersen, J. G. 1982. "Den folkelige tilslutning til socialpolitikken—en krise for velferdsstaten?" In D. Anckar et al., eds., *Partier, Ideologier, Väljare.* Åbo: Åbo Akademi.

Bergander, B. 1967. *Försäkringsväsendet i Sverige 1814–1914.* Solna: Seelig.

Boalt, G. 1985. *Vad vill väljarna? Åsiktsförskjutningarna 1979–1983.* Stockholm: Almqvist Wiksell International.

Briggs, A. 1961. "The Welfare State in Historical Perspective." *Archives of European Sociology* 11:221–58.

Cassel, G. 1902. *Socialpolitik.* Stockholm: Gebers.

Central Statistical Office of Finland: 1986. *Statistical Yearbook of Finland 1985/86.* Helsinki: Central Statistical Office of Finland, Vol. 81.

Danmark. Various years. *Årsberetning.* Copenhagen: Danmark.

Dølvik, J. E., and Hippe, J. M. 1985. "Velferdsstatens Kostnader." In J. M. Hippe, ed., *Ny kurs for Velferdsstaten.* Oslo: FAFO.

Edebalk, P. G. and Wadensjö, E. 1988. "Contractually Determined Insurance Schemes for Manual Workers." In B. Gustafsson and A. Klevmarken, eds.,

The Political Economy of Social Security. Amsterdam: Elsevier Science Publisher B.V.

Esping-Andersen, G. 1981. "Politics Against Markets: De-commodification in Social Policy." Lund: Department of Economics, University of Lund. Mimeo.

―――. 1985. *Politics against Markets. The Social Democratic Road to Power.* Princeton: Princeton University Press.

Esping-Andersen, G., and Korpi, W. 1987. "From Poor Relief to Institutional Welfare States: The Development of Scandinavian Social Policy." In R. Erikson, E. J. Hansen, S. Ringen, and H. Uusitalo. *The Scandinavian Model: Welfare States and Welfare Research.* Armonk, NY: M. E. Sharpe.

Flora, P., ed., 1986. *Growth to Limits. The West-European Welfare States since World War II.* Vol. 1. Berlin: de Gruyter.

Försäkringskasseförbundet. 1985. *Socialförsäkring.* Stockholm: Försäkringskasseförbundet. No. 10.

Hansen, F. K. 1985. *Fordelingspolitikken og dens virkninger.* Copenhagen: Socialforskningsinstituttet.

Heclo, H. 1981. "Towards a New Welfare State?" In P. Flora and A. Heidenheimer, eds., *The Development of Welfare States in Europe and America.* London: Transaction Books.

Holm, K., et al. 1986. *Sygefravær og Karensdag.* Copenhagen: AKF.

Immergut, E. 1986. "Between State and Market: Sickness Benefits and Social Control." In M. Rein and L. Rainwater, eds., *Public-Private Interplay in Social Protection.* Armonk, NY: M. E. Sharpe.

Jensen, C. V. 1985. *Det tvedelte pensionssystem.* Roskilde: Forlaget Samfundsøkonomi og Planlægning.

Kangas, O. 1988a. Personal communication with authors, February.

―――. 1988b. *Politik och ekonomi i pensionsförsäkringen. Det finska pensionssystemet i ett jämnförande perspektiv.* Stockholm: Institutet för social forskning, Meddelande 5.

Kolberg, J. E. 1983. *Farvel til Velferdsstaten?* Oslo: Cappelen.

Laurinkari, J. 1979. Economic Health Security in Finland, Publications of the University of Kuopio, Kuopio: Community Health Series, Statistics and Reviews, Nr. 3, 1978.

Lindqvist, R. 1987. *Mellan politik och Marknad.* Research Reports no. 91. Umeå: University of Umeå. Department of Sociology.

Low Income Commission. 1982. *Betænkning Nr. 946.* Copenhagen: Statens Trykningskontor.

Marklund, S. 1986. "Missnöje och uppslutning—om välfärdssystemets legitimitet." *Socialmedicinsk Tidskrift* 9:419–26.

―――. 1988. *Paradise Lost? The Nordic Welfare States and the Recession 1975–1985.* Lund: Arkiv.

Marklund, S., and Svallfors, S. 1987. *Dual Welfare—Segmentation and Work Enforcement in the Swedish Welfare System.* Research Reports no. 91. Umeå: Department of Sociology, Umeå.

Marshall, T. H. 1977. *Class, Citizenship and Social Development.* Cambridge: Cambridge University Press.

Ministry of Social Affairs and Health. 1961b. *The Insurance Companies 1960.* Helsinki: Finnish Official Statistics XXII, A:66.

Ministry of Social Affairs and Health. 1966. *The Insurance Companies 1965*. Helsinki: Finnish Official Statistics XXII, A:71.
Ministry of Social Affairs and Health. 1971. *The Insurance Companies 1970*. Helsinki: Finnish Official Statistics XXII, A:76.
Ministry of Social Affairs and Health. 1977. *The Insurance Companies 1975*. Helsinki: Finnish Official Statistics XXII, A:81.
Ministry of Social Affairs and Health. 1986. *The Insurance Companies 1985*. Helsinki: Finnish Official Statistics XXII, A:90.
Ministry of Social Affairs and Health. 1933. *Social Tidskrift*. Helsinki: Ministry of Social Affairs and Health.
Ministry of Social Affairs and Health. 1952. *Social Tidskrift*. Helsinki: Ministry of Social Affairs and Health.
Ministry of Social Affairs and Health. 1961a. *Social Tidskrift*. Helsinki: Ministry of Social Affairs and Health.
Ministry of Social Affairs and Health. 1972. *Social Tidskrift*. Helsinki: Ministry of Social Affairs and Health.
Mishra, R. 1977. *Society and Social Policy. Theoretical Perspectives on Welfare*. London: MacMillan.
Nordic Council (NC). 1963. *Yearbook of Nordic Statistics 1962*. Stockholm: Nordic Council. Vol. 1.
Nordic Council (NC). 1967. *Yearbook of Nordic Statistics 1966*. Stockholm: Nordic Council. Vol. 5.
Nordic Council (NC). 1972. *Yearbook of Nordic Statistics 1971*. Stockholm: Nordic Council. Vol. 10.
Nordic Council of Ministers (NCM). 1976. *Yearbook of Nordic Statistics 1975*. Copenhagen: Nordic Council of Ministers and the Nordic Statistical Secretariat. Vol. 14.
Nordic Council of Ministers (NCM). 1977. *Yearbook of Nordic Statistics 1976*. Copenhagen: Nordic Council of Ministers and the Nordic Statistical Secretariat. Vol. 15.
Nordic Council of Ministers (NCM). 1979. *Yearbook of Nordic Statistics 1978*. Copenhagen: Nordic Council of Ministers and the Nordic Statistical Secretariat. Vol. 17.
Nordic Council of Ministers (NCM). 1980. *Yearbook of Nordic Statistics 1979*. Copenhagen: Nordic Council of Ministers and the Nordic Statistical Secretariat. Vol. 18.
Nordic Council of Ministers (NCM). 1982. *Yearbook of Nordic Statistics 1981*. Copenhagen: Nordic Council of Ministers and the Nordic Statistical Secretariat. Vol. 20.
Nordic Council of Ministers (NCM). 1983. *Yearbook of Nordic Statistics 1982*. Copenhagen: Nordic Council of Ministers and the Nordic Statistical Secretariat. Vol. 21.
Nordic Council of Ministers (NCM). 1984. *Yearbook of Nordic Statistics 1983*. Copenhagen: Nordic Council of Ministers and the Nordic Statistical Secretariat. Vol. 23.
Nordic Council of Ministers (NCM). 1986. *Yearbook of Nordic Statistics 1985*. Copenhagen: Nordic Council of Ministers and the Nordic Statistical Secretariat. Vol. 24.

Nordic Council of Ministers (NCM). 1987. *Yearbook of Nordic Statistics 1986.* Copenhagen: Nordic Council of Ministers and the Nordic Statistical Secretariat. Vol. 26.

Nordisk Statistisk Skriftserie (NSS). 1986. *Social Tryghed i de nordiske lande. Omfang, udgifter og finansiering 1984.* Copenhagen: Nordisk Statistisk Sekretariat, no. 47.

Norges Offentlige Utredninger (NOU). 1976. *Omlegging av sykepengeordningen.* Oslo: Norges Offentlige Utredninger.

Offe, C., and Lehnhardt, G. 1984. "Social Policy and the Theory of the State" In C. Offe, ed., *Contradictions of the Welfare State.* London: Hutchinson.

Olafsson, S. 1989. *The Making of the Icelandic Welfare State. A Scandinavian Comparison.* Reprint Series no. 12. Reykjavik: Social Science Research Institute.

Olsson, S. E. 1988. "Decentralization and Privatization. Strategies against a Welfare Backlash in Sweden." In R. Morris, ed., *Testing the Limits—International Perspectives on Social Welfare Changes in Nine Countries.* Hanover, NH: University of New England Press.

Polanyi, K. 1957. *The Great Transformation.* Boston: Beacon Press.

Pöntinen, S., and Uusitalo, H. 1986. *The Legitimacy of the Welfare State: Social Security Opinions in Finland 1975–85.* Report no. 15. Helsinki: Finnish Gallup.

Rein, M., and Rainwater, L., eds. 1986. *Public/Private Interplay in Social Protection.* Armonk, NY: M. E. Sharpe.

Ringen, S. 1981. *Hvor Går Velferdsstaten?* Oslo: Gyldendal.

Ståhlberg, A-C. 1986. "Socialförsäkringarna är inkomstomfördelande." *Ekonomisk Debatt* 6:481–88.

Statens Offentliga Utredningar (SOU). 1983. *Egenföretagares sjukpenning m.m.* Stockholm: Ministry of Social Affairs, 1983:48.

Statistiska Centralbyrån. 1981. *Statistical Abstract of Sweden 1981.* Stockholm: Statistiska Centralbyrån.

Statistiska Centralbyrån. 1987. *Statistical Abstract of Sweden 1988.* Stockholm: Statistiska Centralbyrån.

Stokke, S. 1981. *Fra Sykeforsikring til Folketrygd.* Oslo: Hovedoppgave i Statsvitenskap, Institutt for Statsvitenskap, Universitetet i Oslo.

Sundbo, J., et al., eds. 1982. *Sygefravær.* Copenhagen: Socialforskningsinstituttet.

Taylor-Gooby, P., and Lakeman, S. 1988. "Back to the Future: Statutory Sick Pay, Citizenship and Social Class." *Journal of Social Policy* 17, pt. 1:23–39.

Thompson, E. P. 1968. *The Making of the English Working Class.* Harmondsworth: Penguin.

Titmuss, R. 1963. *Essays on the Welfare State.* Boston: Beacon Press.

———. 1974. *Social Policy.* London: Allen and Unwin.

Wilensky, H. 1975. *The Welfare State and Equality.* Berkeley: University of California Press.

Zeuthen, F. 1948. *Social sikring.* Copenhagen: Nyt Nordisk Forlag.

7

The Private-Public Mix in Pension Policy

OLLI KANGAS and JOAKIM PALME

Introduction

Historically, pensions have been provided by a wide variety of institutions: friendly societies, insurance companies, employers, local municipalities, and the state have given support to widows, orphans, the disabled, and the elderly on the basis of insurance or need. However, the relative importance of these institutions has varied widely over time and between nations. The post–World War II era has seen a huge increase in public spending on social security programs. While there is a great deal of research on welfare state expansion, there are few comparative studies on private social security provisions.

The concepts of *public* and *private* in welfare provision have several dimensions and the borderlines between them are not easily defined (Rein and Rainwater 1986, 1987; Tamburi and Mouton 1987). Public pensions have been distinguished from private pensions by different criteria: legislated or contractual/voluntary, universal or exclusive, obligatory or voluntary, state administered or privately organized, financed by taxes or by contributions. Nor do the private pensions constitute a homogeneous universe: some are more "private" than others. Private pensions can be individually subscribed or they can be collective and based on contractual agreements. They can be negotiated centrally among the labor market organizations, or they can cover certain occupational groups, or provide benefits at the company level. It is therefore important to bear in mind what aspect of pensions is at stake and that the issue of private versus public is one of importance (see, e.g., Øverbye 1988).

In Scandinavia we find examples of this institutional variety. For example, in Denmark basic pensions are legislated, universal, obligatory, state-administered and tax-financed. Statutory supplementary pensions in Finland are also legislated, universal, and obligatory but mainly privately organized and financed by contributions. In Sweden the contractual pension programs (ITP,[1] KPA,[2] SPV,[3] and STP[4]) have a near universal coverage of the labor force, but their legislative status, administration, and financing are different. And in Norway, local municipalities often organize pension programs for their employees via private insurance companies.

Social policy in the Scandinavian countries is often associated with the concept of a Scandinavian model. The data that will be presented below indicate that there is some justification in applying such a model to basic pensions, but that the model's utility is weaker in other parts of the pension systems—both public and private.

The working hypothesis in this chapter is that the relative size of private pensions has significant consequences: comparisons of the economic well-being of the elderly, without taking private pensions into account, would be seriously misleading since their relative importance varies across nations. The private-public mix is also likely to affect the overall inequality among the elderly. Cross-national data presented below in this chapter seem to support such a hypothesis.

Pension policy is an arena for strategic policy making of the major interest groups in industrial societies, and private pensions can offer attractive alternatives for these actors. The relative importance of private pensions is likely to structure the interests in public policy initiatives and thus has wider implications for the political economy of the welfare state. The different paths followed by the four countries show, on the one hand, how political actors with the same basic social interests have chosen divergent strategies and, on the other hand, how similar political reforms have been backed up by different political parties.

In the comparative research on the factors that bring about cross-national variation in welfare state provisions, a variety of strategies have been applied. The results produced by the different strategies diverge; the "variable approach" gives priority to party political factors for explaining the variation, while the "policy process approach" tends to suggest that factors within the state bureaucracies have been more decisive for the policy outcome (see Palme 1988). By both describing the policy making behind the various pension reforms in the four countries, and analyzing the policy outcomes in a wider international perspective, we hope to come to a better understanding of these seemingly contradictory results.

The structure of the first part of the chapter mirrors, at least to some extent, a continuum from the most public to the most private pension programs. The presentation begins with a discussion of the basic (minimum) pensions followed by a section on the statutory supplementary (legislated and income/work-related) schemes and a section on separate programs for government employees. The relative importance of the collective and individual private programs is then examined by looking primarily at expenditure data. In the following section, another aspect of the private-public mix, the benefit structure, is analyzed. The income inequality among the elderly is also related to the relative importance of public pensions. To test a few hypotheses on the determinants of the private-public mix, a greater number of countries are considered in the comparative analysis. The next to last section of the chapter focuses on the differences in financing, and the relative importance of funding in the different programs and countries. In the last section, the major findings of the study are discussed.

It has already been noted that the structure of the private-public mix in the pension systems has wide implications. The context of the present chapter has forced us to concentrate the analysis on the ''benefit side'' of the phenomenon. Not denying that other aspects are important, too, we claim that the results in the present analysis show that the benefit structure is vital for the understanding of the development of and cross-national differences in the private-public mix.

Legislated basic pensions

''Institutional social policy'' has been regarded as the trademark of the Scandinavian welfare states (Esping-Andersen and Korpi 1987). The present Nordic pension systems are, however, products of different historical processes, which have yielded different outcomes. There were also great differences in timing: Denmark was one of the pioneering countries to legislate on pensions (in 1891). In Sweden, too, the first scheme was implemented before World War I. Norway (1936) and Finland (1937) were latecomers—of the current European Organization for Economic Cooperation and Development (OECD) countries only Switzerland lagged behind them (see, e.g., Social Security Administration 1984).

Although universal in their coverage, the early Scandinavian schemes did not provide old-age pensions for everybody, since means testing and other qualifying conditions were applied. In Norway and Sweden the pension take-up ratios (pension receivers as a percentage of the population above pension age) were nearly universal already in the late 1930s, since over 80 percent of the elderly were receiving benefits. In Denmark, the ratio was about 50 percent, whereas only 14 percent of the Finnish elderly were entitled to old-age benefits in the early 1950s. Internationally, the differences among the Scandinavian countries were the widest possible: Sweden and Norway were two leading countries regarding take-up ratio, the Danish figures equalled the European mean, and the Finnish ratio was the lowest in Europe (SSIB 1989).

After World War II, the basic pension programs were reformed in all the Scandinavian countries and full universality was established in the sense that everybody over the pension age was guaranteed a basic pension. In Denmark, Sweden, and Norway, the pension was awarded without means testing. The universal base amount in the Finnish system remained quite low, and the main part of the national basic pension was paid after an income test (see Figure 7.2 on p. 210).

Universalism—a Social Democratic achievement?

Pensions for everyone above pension age with universal coverage providing benefits without a means test has often been regarded as a result of Social Democratic efforts, especially in the Swedish and Danish cases (see, e.g., Esping-Andersen 1985, 157). The coincidence in Scandinavia of universal and generous basic pensions (see below) with comparatively strong political left representation in both parliament and government seems to support such an explanation. However, the Norwegian development has been sketched in the light of consensus (Kuhnle 1986) and the Finnish experience seems to distort the picture from both the Social Democratic and the consensual points of view (Alestalo et al. 1985). In Finland, the most distinctive spokesman for universalism has been the Agrarian/Center party, while the Social Democrats have been stubborn supporters of the income test (Kangas 1986).

A closer examination of the policy process involved in pension reforms in Denmark and Sweden provides a more in-depth picture of the making of universal pension rights, exemplified by the creation of basic pensions without a means test. The Swedish Conservative party was, after World War II, eager to guarantee full national pensions to all citizens (Elmer 1960, 85). The position of the Social Democrats was more divided. The minister of finance, Ernst Wigforss—and the prime minister, Per Albin Hansson—recommended an income-tested system, whereas the minister of social affairs, Gustav Möller, was a spokesman for universal pensions (Elmer 1960, 85–95). Finally, the Social Democrats also supported universal pensions and the Labor cabinet introduced the plan in 1948. Sweden, as the first Nordic country, implemented universal coverage and flat-rate benefits without qualifying conditions (Olsson 1986, 82).

In Denmark, the Conservatives and the Agrarian Liberals advocated pensions based on the insurance model with limited coverage and individual contributions. This was sharply opposed by the Social Democrats, who preferred a tax-financed scheme. In order to ensure better pensions for the needy, the Social Democrats accepted income testing. A compromise was found in the proposition put forward by the Radical Liberals, who suggested universal flat-rate pensions (Nørby Johansen 1986, 354–55). Negotiations resulted in a package deal that realized both the socialist demand on the financial form and the bourgeois requirement on tax credits for pension contributions. Consequently, the bill was accepted in 1956 by a great parliamentary majority (Vesterø Jensen 1985, 113–15). Since then, the bourgeois parties have been the most eager supporters of universalism; in contrast, the Social Democrats have, since the early 1970s, made attempts to reintroduce a means test. In fact, a Social Democratic cabinet reinstituted partial income testing in the beginning of the 1980s (Marklund 1988).

Similarly, the Norwegian nonsocialist parties were in favor of abolishing the means test. The Liberals and the Conservatives were eager advocates of universal old-age pensions, while the governing Labor party mainly advocated general invalidity insurance (Hatland 1987, 65). In 1957, as a result of the bourgeois parties' pressure, the Labor cabinet was obliged to implement universal old-age pension before a disability pension act.

There were also important structural preconditions common to the Scandinavian countries at the time when the first pension schemes were legislated. Compared to continental Europe, Scandinavia was poorly developed in terms of both industrialization and urbanization (Alber 1982, 231–62). Under such circumstances, a pure workers' insurance would have left the rural population without benefits. This was clearly difficult to accept, especially by the strong agrarian parties. It must also be remembered that the early Scandinavian Social Democracy had its roots in the peasantry (Alestalo and Kuhnle 1987; Esping-Andersen 1985; Kettunen 1986), which fortified the interest articulation of the small holders and landless proletariat. In addition, not only the living conditions of industrial workers, but agrarian poverty as well were dealt with as social problems. There was also pressure for a nationwide pension program from the rural municipalities restrained by the poor law duties (Kuhnle 1981, 136). As a result, the Scandinavian pension schemes were initiated universally in the sense that, in principle, the entire population was protected. This was in contrast to the schemes of continental Europe, in which only some segments were protected.

In summary, describing the Scandinavian basic pensions solely in terms of Social Democratic progress or consecutive consensual decisions is an oversimplification. The consensual emphasis on the legislation phase of the decision-making process conceals conflicting goals and strategies of the different actors in the preparation period of a bill. The Social Democratic hypothesis, for its part, tends to neglect the other actors involved in the making of the welfare state (see, e.g., Therborn 1986, 1987). Universalism in the Scandinavian basic pensions is the product of an interplay between wider and rather different political interests.

The level of the basic pensions

Despite structural differences among their programs (see Figure 7.2), the Nordic countries have become more similar when it comes to the basic pensions. Traditionally, the Danish benefit levels have been highest, but during the 1970s, the development of the basic pensions in the other countries was more rapid. Consequently, the Swedish, Finnish, and Norwegian replacement rates reached and even exceeded their Danish counterpart (SSIB 1989). In the mid-1980s the net (after tax) replacement rate of the basic pensions was about half of the average industrial wage (APW) in all four countries.

The Scandinavian basic pensions are internationally high: only in Austria, the Netherlands, and New Zealand do the replacement ratios reach the Scandinavian level. Figure 7.1 shows that the Scandinavian basic pensions are distinctive not only in terms of high compensation levels but also with respect to pension coverage. There are, however, some other countries where pensions are universal or nearly universal, too, but since the replacement rates tend to be lower in these countries, the Scandinavian countries form a cluster.[5] Therefore, in the context of basic pensions, it seems to be empirically justified to speak about an institutional Scandinavian social policy model characterized by universal coverage and high benefit levels.

During the 1980s, some shifts took place within this Scandinavian pension model. Whereas Finland has abolished the income test, previously the most rigorous of the four countries, leaving national basic pensions reduced only by other pension income, the opposite development has occurred in Denmark, where the income test was reintroduced in 1980 for pensioners below seventy years of age (Marklund 1988, 32). Thus, in terms of the Scandinavian model, basic pensions have clearly converged regarding replacement levels; the Finnish system has become more similar to the Swedish and Norwegian pensions concerning the income test, whereas Denmark seems to be moving toward a more selective pension policy.

The development of statutory supplementary pensions

While the implementation of the basic pensions in the Scandinavian countries occurred over almost half a century, the legislated occupational pensions were implemented more simultaneously: Sweden pioneered (1959), followed by Finland (1961), Denmark (1964), and Norway (1966). In spite of this, country-specific variation can be found regarding both the political affiliations and the outcome.

In Sweden, the Social Democratic strategy was aimed at a "public" solution; a fully legislated scheme with pension funds under state control. Although ideologically unanimous in their resistance against the Social Democratic proposal, the bourgeois parties were not able to forge their own uniform strategy. Instead, they put forward two alternatives. While the Agrarians proposed higher basic pensions to be supplemented by voluntary individual insurances, the Conservatives and Liberals preferred that the supplementary pensions be contracted

Figure 7.1. **Basic Pension Replacement Level and Pension Take-up Ratio in Eighteen OECD Countries, 1980**

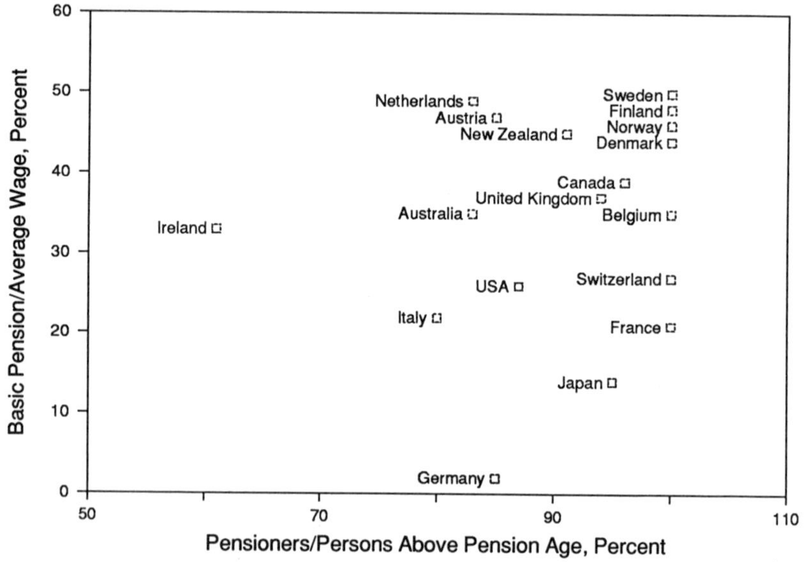

Source: SSIB (1989).
Notes: The replacement level is the net benefit as percentage of net average industrial wage; the take-up ratio is the proportion of pension recipients in the population above normal pension age.

collectively between employer and employees. The Swedish Employer Federation (SAF) favored this model since it was in accordance with its earlier proposals from the 1940s and the early 1950s. At that time, these proposals were rejected by the Federation of the Trade Unions (LO) as being insufficient (Molin 1965).

After an advisory referendum, a governmental crisis, a dissolution of parliament, new elections, and highly dramatic struggles in the Parliament, the statutory supplementary pensions (ATP) plan was finally passed with a one-vote majority (Lewin 1984; Esping-Andersen and Korpi 1987; Olsson 1986).

The Swedish ATP model figured in the Norwegian discussions on statutory supplementary pensions. The greatest enthusiasm for the model was shown among the Liberals—scared by the fate of their Swedish sister party which lost a great deal of its electoral support in the ATP struggle (Ringen 1987, 74). Surprisingly, the Norwegian Social Democrats were at first skeptical of the Swedish ATP and preferred, like the Conservatives, labor market solutions (Hatland 1986,

58). However, the Social Democrats changed their minds and made a proposal on a pension system resembling the Swedish one. Partially, this was due to purely political tactics since the bourgeois parties in the cabinet had different opinions on pension policy and the issue provided an opportunity to divide the bourgeois parties (Ringen 1987). By this action, the Swedish model was adopted as a point of departure. Due to the defeat of the Swedish bourgeois parties in the pension struggle, the Norwegian nonsocialists feared that the issue would become too politicized. The bourgeois cabinet put conflicting opinions aside and prepared a proposition for income-related pensions (Hatland 1986, 59). The act was finally passed unanimously in 1966 (Kuhnle 1986, 174).

In Denmark, the first initiatives for a supplementary pension plan (ATP) were taken in the context of income policy packages in the early 1960s. Some years later, the Social Democratic cabinet laid down a proposition on an ATP scheme that would cover all regular employees and provide pensions at the age of sixty-seven. The benefits, however, were not to be income-graduated. The amount of pension was dependent solely on the length of time the claimant had been insured (see Esping-Andersen 1985; Vesterø Jensen 1985; Nelson 1984).

In parliament, the bourgeois parties, especially the Agrarian Liberals, criticized the proposition for its nonuniversal coverage, and the Conservatives were not satisfied with the flat-rate system and demanded income-related pensions based on the Swedish model (Nelson 1984, 70).[6] The Social Democrats refuted the bourgeois arguments by arguing that the ATP scheme was a first step toward a universal occupational pension system, and in 1964, the bill was passed with a large parliamentary majority (Nelson 1984, 79).

Since the ATP reform, the Social Democrats and LO have made several propositions on a general income-related and funded pension scheme (ITP), but without success. The initiatives have failed because of the resistance from the more or less unanimous bourgeois parties and white-collar employees (Vesterø Jensen 1985, 126–42). This opposition was generated partly by the fact that a large proportion of the white-collar employees is already covered by either occupational or individual pension arrangements. Thus, although the Danish Social Democrats of 1956 were able to realize their plans, in the case of the basic pensions, the acts were in the long run more advantageous for the bourgeois strategy. The tax exemptions consented to in the context of a national pension prepared the ground for an expansion of programs outside the legislated schemes, which eventually inhibited the implementation of statutory income-graduated pensions.

In Finland, the National Pension Act of 1956 was a disappointment to the wage earners and salaried employees. Because of the strong resistance from the Agrarian party, the act did not realize income-related old-age provisions as originally planned (Alestalo and Uusitalo 1986; Salminen 1987). The employees' organizations began to prepare a separate legislated superannuation scheme. At first, the scheme was categorically rejected by the employers but, gradually, their attitudes became more favorable. Here, the experience from the Swedish ATP struggle was important. The Finnish employers consulted their Swedish colleagues and were advised to accept the legislated scheme if the result would be a decentralized scheme carried by private insurance companies (Ahtokari 1988, 240; Niemel 1988, 115–17).

The most urgent issue for the employees was to secure adequate pensions; the problem of how this would be organized was of less importance to them. If not for this, the centralized scheme probably would have been channeled through the National Pension Institute, considered to be in the hands the Agrarian party (Salminen 1987, 86–87; Ahtokari 1988, 236–38). For this reason, the employees could make a deal with the employers. The former got their statutory pensions financed by employer contributions, the price being a decentralized system, mainly organized through private insurance companies, which gave the employers control over the pension funds.

This pension package negotiated by the labor market partners was sharply criticized by the Agrarian party and the Communists, who faulted the proposal's limited coverage: only regular workers were to be insured—seasonal employees and farmers were excluded (Salminen 1987, 92–95). To win the support of the agrarian groups, the Social Democrats made a concession according to which short-term employees got their occupational pension scheme simultaneously with the private sector employees pension act in 1961.[7] Farmers and other self-employed individuals got their pension programs in 1970, and from then on the total labor force has been covered by income-related statutory schemes (Kangas and Palme 1989).

The making of the Scandinavian supplementary pensions shows country-specific variations. In Sweden, and to some extent Denmark, the Social Democrats aimed for a purely "public" scheme. In Norway, the labor movement at first favored a collective, "private" solution but later changed its mind in favor of the Swedish model. The choice of the Finnish labor movement was different: a program that was fully legislated but decentralized and organized through private insurance companies. The organization of the Finnish statutory pensions resembles that of the private occupational pensions in the other Scandinavian countries, since the control over the schemes is in the hands of the labor market partners (as is the case in Denmark). The reason for this is obvious. The Finnish Social Democrats, contrary to the Swedish party, did not control "politics" to the same extent, since the Agrarian party had such a strong position both in the Parliament and in the cabinet. Since the agrarians were stubborn supporters of flat-rate benefits, a more "market"-oriented solution seemed to be the best alternative to realize income-related pensions.

The making of the Scandinavian supplementary legislated schemes shows that the labor parties have not in every instance striven for greater public control over the programs. Much seems to have been dependent on the prevailing interests that have dominated the political arena. The Scandinavian comparisons seem to support the hypothesis that if the labor parties control the political arena (as in Sweden), the distributional conflicts will find mainly political resolution. Where left participation is weaker (as in Finland), the conflicts are more likely to be resolved in the labor market (see Korpi and Shalev 1979; Korpi 1981; Therborn 1987).

The structure and level of supplementary pensions

When it comes to the structure and level of pension benefits, and the coordination between basic and statutory supplementary pensions, the outcomes differ. The Swedish and Norwegian schemes are structurally similar. The earnings-related pensions are added to the basic pensions, but only income up to a certain ceiling is taken into consideration when calculating the income-related benefits. Those with low or no ATP pensions receive a special supplement (see Figure 7.2). In the Danish ATP program, the size of the pension is not related to income but to years of insured status. In addition, the ATP pensions have remained very low: in 1980 they corresponded to only two percent of the average wage of a production worker. The structure of the Finnish pensions deviates from the other countries in two respects. First, there is no income ceiling for benefit purposes; the full supplementary pension is

Figure 7.2. **Structure of Scandinavian Statutory Pensions**

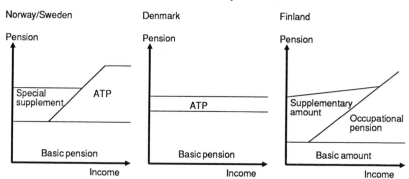

Note: ATP = Allmänn tilläggspension = Statutory supplementary pension.

60 percent of earnings irrespective of the size of the wage or salary (although the replacement level is higher in the low-income groups because of the basic pensions). Second, in Finland, only the basic pension ''base amount'' is equal for all, but statutory pensions reduce the ''supplementary amount'' as described in Figure 7.2.

The structural differences in the Scandinavian pension systems are directly mirrored in the pension expenditure (see chapter 2 in this volume). The basic pension in 1985 is clearly a more important part of old-age security in Denmark (76 percent of all expenditure in 1985) than in Finland (39 percent), Norway (50 percent), or Sweden (45 percent), whereas the legislated occupational pensions are more important in Finland and Sweden (Kangas and Palme 1989).

In order to illustrate the development of legislated pension rights in the Scandinavian countries, old-age pensions have been calculated for a worker with an average industrial wage assuming that he has worked full-time for thirty-five years, and for ten years in his latest employment. Benefits, expressed as a proportion of net income, are calculated for single persons, and taxed if subject to income taxes (see Palme 1988). To illustrate how pensions are related to previous income, benefits have also been calculated for three additional types of income earners: a low-paid employee with earnings of half the industrial average (0.5 APW), an employee with twice the average wage (2 APW), and a person whose income is three times the industrial average (3 APW).

These model calculations show that the earnings-related superannu-

Figure 7.3. **Pension Replacement Rates for Different Income Groups in the Nordic Countries, 1960–85**
(net pension as percent of net income)

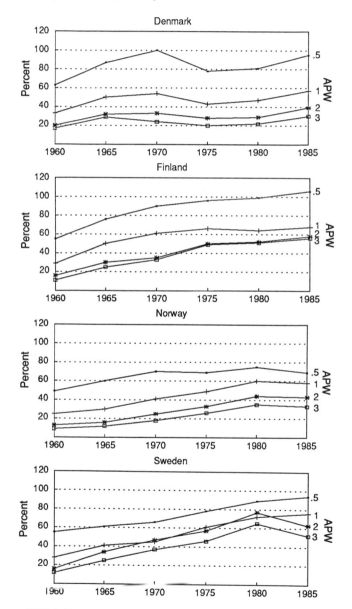

Sources: SSIB (1989); Hagen (1988).
Note: APW = average production worker.

ation schemes have increased the degree of old-age income security remarkably in the Scandinavian countries (see Figure 7.3). But differences between the countries can be found in both levels and trends. The Danish basic pensions supplemented by the meager ATP benefits have secured high compensation levels in the low (0.5 APW) and medium (APW) income groups. But during the years of high inflation in the early 1970s, the Danish pensions declined remarkably due to a poor indexation, and the replacement ratios fell behind the other Scandinavian countries. Because of the lack of income graduation the replacement rates remain quite low in the higher income groups. In Finland, the replacement rates increased rapidly until the mid-1970s. Thereafter, improvements in the medium and high income groups have been slower due to the fact that the level of the basic pension decreases proportionately as the statutory supplementary pension exceeds a certain limit. Thus, during the last ten years, the improvements in levels of compensation have been dependent on the statutory supplementary pensions coming into full effect. As this continues, the differences between medium and high income groups will gradually diminish.

Figure 7.3 represents the rapid increase in replacement rates in Sweden up to the early 1980s. Also, in Norway, the APW pension replacement has increased substantially, and during the eighties ranged around 60 percent. However, in the last few years, both the Norwegian and the Swedish replacement rates for the high income earners have declined. This is mainly due to changes in taxation (lower marginal taxes on high incomes). But because the pension ceilings have not kept pace with economic growth, more and more people have incomes above the maximum limit and gross replacement levels have fallen. It has been calculated that in the beginning of the next millennium, half of the Swedish male employees will reach the ceiling (RFV 1987).[8] Consequently, if the maximum limit is not increased, the ATP system will gradually lose its character of an income-related scheme and the private schemes will inevitably be of greater importance (see also Figure 7.7).

Figure 7.4 displays the net replacement levels for an average production worker with a thirty-five year work record, retiring in 1980, in eighteen OECD countries. We can see that the net replacement rate exceeds 70 percent in Sweden and Italy. Finland and Norway are among a group of countries where pensions replace about 65 percent of the previous wage. The Danish replacement rate for an average

Figure 7.4. **Replacement Rates of Statutory Supplementary Schemes for an Average Industrial Worker in Eighteen OECD Countries, 1980** (net benefit as percent of net wage)

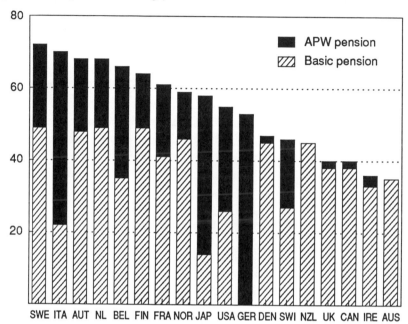

Source: SSIB (1989).
Note: APW = average production worker.

production worker, on the other hand, falls below the OECD mean. The figure also shows to what extent the pensions in these eighteen countries are related to previous work effort. The light part of the bars reflects the replacement of the basic pensions (including means-tested pensions). The dark part of the bars thus reflects the difference between what is paid to an average production worker and the basic pension.

In such countries as Australia, Canada, Ireland, New Zealand, and the United Kingdom, work-related benefits make little or no difference. In other countries, the "work-merit" makes a significant contribution to the size of pensions, thus approaching what Titmuss labelled the "industrial achievement-performance model of social policy" (Titmuss 1974). This is especially true for Germany, Italy, and Japan, where the work-related pensions amount to more than three times the basic pensions. In Belgium, France, Switzerland, and the United

States, work-related pensions are twice, or nearly twice, the size of the basic pensions. In Austria, Finland, the Netherlands, Norway, and Sweden, work-related benefits also contribute; however, these countries provide both high basic and work-related pensions. While in regard to basic pensions the Scandinavian countries seemed to form a cluster, there is less uniformity with the statutory supplementary pensions. Although coverage is nearly universal, as in the national pensions, the replacement rates indicate a weaker Scandinavian model. But it must be noted that the Finnish and Norwegian schemes—unlike their many Continental counterparts—are not yet mature (see Social Security Administration 1984). When the pension programs in these two countries are fully effective, the legislated supplementary pensions will be at nearly the same internationally high level as those in Sweden.

Government pensions—occupational and legislated

The Scandinavian countries were the first to legislate earnings-related pension schemes for civil servants. A common feature in these programs was that the benefits were expressed as a certain proportion of the previous salary. The implementation of the general supplementary programs, however, led to some changes in the government schemes. In Sweden and Norway, the public sector pensions were integrated with the ATP systems and the National Insurance (NI). The amount of the state pension was to be calculated as a difference between the target replacement level and what was paid from the NI and ATP (Hatland 1986, 151–53; O'Higgins 1986, 116). In Denmark, a similar procedure has been applied since the introduction of the full basic pension in 1970 (Henriksen et al. 1987, 34–37). Thus, in Denmark, Norway, and Sweden, the basic pensions and ATP benefits are supplemented by the government schemes in order to guarantee adequate replacement levels. Although the maturing ATP systems have decreased the relative importance of the public employees' pensions, they are still financially the most extensive programs outside statutory supplementary pension schemes (Kangas and Palme 1989). They are an especially important source of income for the higher paid employees due to the falling compensation grade in the ATP schemes. The public sector schemes in Finland developed differently from the other Scandinavian countries. When private sector pensions were implemented, the existing state and municipal systems remained independent and the private sector programs were built up separately. Therefore, the Finnish public sector schemes have the primary function of guaranteeing "basic occupational" pensions in the same way as the private sector programs, not providing extra benefits for public employees like in the other Scandinavian countries.[9] In this respect, the Finnish public employees' pensions have more in common with the continental European schemes than with the Scandinavian programs.

The different status of the Scandinavian government pensions can be seen in Table 7.1. Although the coverage and take-up ratios of the public sector schemes in Finland are at about the same level as those in Norway and Sweden, the expenditure share is markedly higher. The opposite is true for the Swedish public employee pensions: their coverage is larger than in the other countries, but on the other hand, their share of the total pension expenditure is lowest, indicating that the ATP system has crowded out the public sector schemes. As regards coverage, Denmark's low rates are exceptional. In terms of replacement rates, public employees in Denmark and Norway seem to be more privileged than their Finnish and Swedish colleagues as far as medium income groups are concerned, but the higher one's salary, the more advantageous the Finnish and Swedish systems appear to be.

From the private-public point of view, the central and local government schemes described above are problematic. They are usually legislated, obligatory, and administered by public organizations and, therefore, should be classified as "public." On the other hand, in some aspects they are "private," that is, they aim to give extra benefits to some exclusive groups in the same way as the purely private occupational pensions. Moreover, since in some instances it is impossible to make a clear distinction between certain local government pension arrangements (particularly in Norway and Denmark) and collective "private" funds, government employee pensions can be viewed as borderline cases between the public and private spheres.

Private pensions—collective and individual

The government superannuation schemes also came to play an influential role for the development of other occupational pensions. In order to recruit employees and to maintain intersectoral labor force mobility, private enterprises began to introduce old-age security for their salaried

Table 7.1

Public Employees' Pensions in Four Scandinavian Countries, 1985

	Coverage of Employees		Recipients	Expenditure	Replacement Rates		
	All	Public	Percent of Pensioners	Share of Total Expenditure	APW	2APW	3APW
Denmark	9	35	14	10	80	57	45
Finland	33	100	27	25	66	66	66
Norway	31	90–100	22	7	75	62	52
Sweden	36	100	24	7	73	70	67

Sources: Elmer (1986), 132; Finansministeriet (1988); Henriksen et al. (1987), 44, 54; OECD (1987), 38; Statens Pensjonskasse (1988); NCM (1987), 321.

employees, following the public sector example. Employees also established their own collective and individual pension systems. The extension of these early superannuation schemes, and the way they were integrated with the legislated pensions, were important factors in the development of the private-public mix.

The political deal in Denmark in 1956 that resulted in basic pensions without an income test also introduced large tax credits and a state guarantee of the real value of private pension insurance. As a consequence, the popularity of the insurance skyrocketed and in the early 1970s there were already over two million insurance policies. These private programs—mainly provided by insurance companies and banks on the basis of collective or individual contracts—are of more importance in Denmark than in the other Scandinavian countries. In addition, their proportional significance has rapidly increased during the last five years (Figure 7.5). Also, the number of members in mutual pension funds has increased steadily in Denmark, while the opposite development is true for the other Scandinavian countries (Kangas and Palme 1989).

The private pensions have been viewed as problematic since the benefit level varies greatly between different schemes. Furthermore, the coverage tends to be strongly skewed in favor of the upper white-collar workers (Henriksen et al. 1987). These aspects have been regarded as an indicator of the dual character of the Danish pension system (Vesterø Jensen 1985). The rapid expansion of the nonstatutory pensions points out that this duality will continue in the future, and private pensions will become a more essential part of the Danish pension security.

The pattern in Finland is the opposite. Although the voluntary pension schemes expanded in the late fifties, their coverage remained low (Ahtokari 1988, 231), and they did not constitute a serious alternative to statutory supplementary pensions. The implementation of the Employees' Pension Act (EPA) then strongly conditioned subsequent developments in the private pension area. The main part of the funds and foundations, previously providing voluntary benefits, was integrated into the statutory system to guarantee EPA pensions. Nevertheless, some of them continued to provide non-legislated extra benefits, but their proportional relevance has been eroding over the last twenty years (Figure 7.5). This tendency will continue since even the absolute number of the employees covered by the non-legislated schemes has begun to decrease—contrary to the pattern in the other Scandinavian countries (Kangas and Palme 1989).

In the early sixties, the question of the Norwegian earnings-graduated pensions seemed to have been resolved via the labor market when LO and the employer federation subscribed to a contractual agreement on a superannuation scheme. However, when the political parties decided in favor of legislated pensions, the National Insurance took over the duties of the contractual scheme which was abolished. Such a comprehensive plan has never been reestablished. Instead, the private collective pension programs are negotiated at the company level and organized through insurance companies. In addition, the individual firms can choose to build up separate funds, but that option is not widely used and the importance of these funds has remained quite low (Kangas and Palme 1989). Some companies pay their occupational pensions directly from their running budget, but unfortunately, data on such arrangements is sparse. However, estimates (presented in Figure 7.5) indicate that they correspond to about 2–3 percent of the expenditure on pensions from the National Insurance (Hippe and Pedersen 1986, 31–32). Although it is difficult to get reliable data on the Norwegian collective pensions, it is evident that since the mid-seventies, the private arrangements have increased in terms of both coverage and expenditure share.

In Sweden, the first pension fund for private sector employees was

Figure 7.5. **Private Pension Expenditure as a Percent of Total Pension Expenditure in the Nordic Countries, 1960–85**

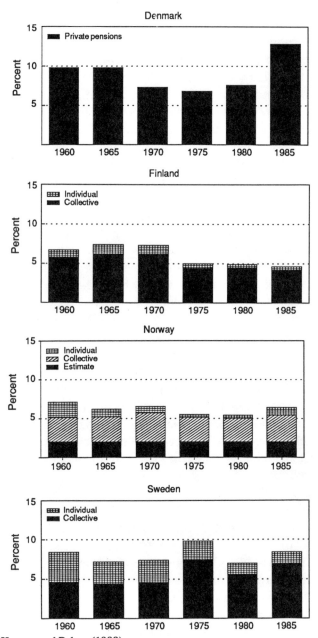

Source: Kangas and Palme (1988).

founded as early as 1916, and as a consequence of the expansion of these funds, many white-collar employees already had their superannuation organized when the discussion of the legislated occupational pensions began in the 1950s (Molin 1965, 134). Therefore, the representatives of the salaried employees had ambivalent opinions of the ATP plan.[10] One of the most crucial questions was the coordination of the existing private pensions and the ATP scheme. These discussions resulted in an agreement between SAF and the salaried employees in the private sector and in an extra pension scheme, ITP (Molin 1965, 115–18).

The same option had also been open for LO. Since the 1940s SAF, expressed its readiness to endorse contractual pensions. Such propositions were continuously rejected by LO, which preferred legislated arrangements (Molin 1965, 129–32). However, after the ATP reform, attitudes in the LO sector gradually changed. To achieve similar benefits as those obtained by the white-collar workers, LO and SAF founded a special supplementary pension scheme (STP) for the blue-collar workers in the private sector (Edebalk and Wadensjö 1988, 4).[11]

Because of the centralized labor market institutions, the Swedish occupational pensions, contrary to those of the other Scandinavian countries, came to cover all the private sector employees. As a consequence, the proportion of the private collective pensions increased during the early 1970s up to 6 percent of the total expenditure, but during the seventies their share decreased. Since the beginning of the 1980s, both collective and individual private expenditures have increased and this tendency will probably persist due to the maturation of the collective schemes (see Figure 7.5). Compared to those of the other Scandinavian countries, the Swedish private collective pension coverage is clearly the most comprehensive: if the public sector occupational schemes are included, the coverage of the employees is almost complete (Sweden1 and Sweden2 in Figure 7.6). Despite this, the expenditure level is low, indicating that the economic importance of the private schemes is only marginal for the majority of the recipients. If the individual pension policies are added (Sweden3), the expenditure proportion increases somewhat. More recently these private individual insurance policies have expanded very quickly. In 1985, there were 120,000 new subscriptions (Hort 1986; see also Figure 7.5). But the reasons for the growth of the individual contracts are not likely to be found in the increased demand for old-age security. Probably more important is the fact that private individual pensions are treated favorably in terms of taxation, and thus offer an advantageous form of saving.

The Danish pattern is quite different. The expenditure share of the private collective pensions does not deviate as strongly from the other countries, and the coverage is low (Denmark1 and Denmark2). But when the individual policies are added Denmark3 becomes a clear outlier, which manifests heavier reliance on individually contracted insurances.[12]

In Norway, the collective schemes in the private sector (Norway1) include every fourth employee, and together with the governmental schemes, the coverage increases to 54 percent (Hippe and Pedersen 1988, 75). The situation does not change essentially if the individual pensions are included (Norway3). Although the number of individual pension policies and their expenditure share have also increased recently, their importance is lower than in Denmark and Sweden. Since the companies can design their pension schemes freely, there is more diversity here than in Sweden. But compared to Denmark, the company-centered Norwegian[13] model provides more uniform benefits.

Finland occupies a bottom ranking as to the importance of the private schemes. In addition, the gap between the other Scandinavian countries will grow since both the coverage and expenditure shares of the private schemes are shrinking, while the opposite is true for the other countries (Figure 7.5; Kangas and Palme 1989). The only private pension form in Finland that has increased in popularity is individual pension insurance. However, the number of annual subscriptions—two thousand in 1985—is, by Scandinavian standards, very low (Kangas 1988, 47–48). In a wider, OECD perspective, Finland has, together with Italy, New Zealand, and Austria, a very small share of private pensions (Esping-Andersen 1987, 78; Eurostat 1977, 148–65). Norway and Sweden, too, are among the countries with minor private pensions, whereas Denmark seems to be moving toward the private dominance that characterizes Switzerland, the United States, France, and Japan.

The stratification effects of the private-public mix

So far, we have examined the relative importance of the different pension schemes by examining expenditure levels and coverage rates. An alternative way of looking at the relative weight of public and

Figure 7.6. **Coverage and Share of Expenditure of Private Pensions in the Nordic Countries, 1985**

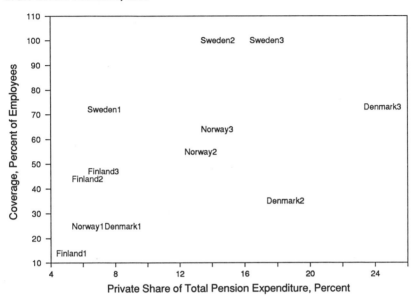

Sources: Vesterø Jensen (1985), 172; Kangas and Palme (1988).
Note: Numbers after the country names indicate; 1: *Only* private collective schemes; 2: Both private collective *and* public employees' schemes; 3: Private collective, *and* public sector schemes, *and* private individual.

private pensions is to examine the benefit structure across different income groups. Figure 7.7 displays the relative replacement of earnings of different income groups by different pension schemes.[14] The figures reveal substantial variation among the four countries.

In Denmark, the falling replacement rate of the basic pension (NP) and ATP is compensated by collective and individual insurance, although the level of compensation varies greatly among employment categories and different schemes (illustrated by the zigzag lines in Figure 7.7). On the upper end of the income ladder, the private pensions are clearly the most important source of income, and in many cases the legislated benefits provide only a nominal supplement to the private pensions.

A move upward on the income ladder decreases the relative importance of public pensions in Norway and Sweden, too, and the negotiated benefits turn out to be of more importance. In the Norwegian case this is exemplified by the Norsk Hydro plan (the largest single com-

222   KANGAS AND PALME

Figure 7.7. **Compensation Profile of the Public Pensions and Additional Occupational Pensions across Different Income Groups in the Nordic Countries, 1985** (percent of gross income)

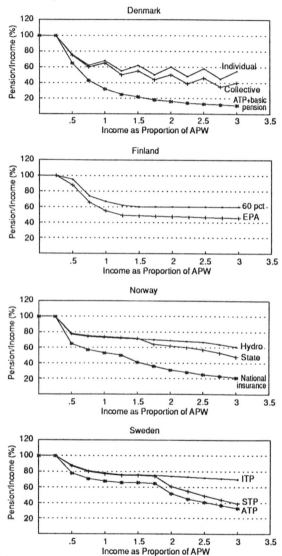

Source: Kangas and Palme (1988).
Notes: APW = average production worker; ATP = allmänn tilläggspension (Statutory Supplementary Pension); ITP = industrins tiläggspension (Occupational Pension Scheme for White-Collar Workers in the Private Sector); STP = särskild tiläggspension (Occupational Pension Scheme for Blue-Collar Workers in the Private Sector); EPA = Employee's Pension Act, the legislated supplementary Pension Scheme for the private sector employees; Hydro = Norsk Hydro (The Biggest Company Based Pension Scheme); 60% = the Target Level in the Legislated Supplementary Pension Scheme for the Private Sector Employees.

pany pension program) and by the civil servants' pensions, the latter having often served as a model for the private sector occupational plans which, however, tend to lag behind (Øverbye 1988b). The Swedish case is exemplified by the white-collar ITP scheme and the blue-collar STP pensions. Together with the legislated pensions, these schemes guarantee gross replacement rates exceeding 70 percent of previous earnings. In the Norwegian government scheme and the Swedish STP pensions, replacement levels begin to fall if income exceeds a certain limit, whereas the Norsk Hydro and the ITP continually guarantee high income replacements, for high income earners also.

Compared to the Danish system, the Norwegian National Insurance and the Swedish ATP maintain high replacement rates in higher income levels also. Consequently, the public pensions persist in being the most important source of income for an overwhelming majority of the employees. This is also reflected in the differences in the private pension spending levels among Denmark and the two other countries.

Finland is the only Scandinavian country where there is no income ceiling in the legislated pensions. Since the legislated occupational pensions in the private sector (EPA) have not yet matured, there is still a gap between the target level (60 percent) and the replacement rates of those who will retire in the near future. To fill the gap, some of those in the interim phase have obtained additional EPA pensions, which, though contracted voluntarily, are fully regulated by the EPA laws. The pension funds and foundations usually provide the same kind of benefits (Ylieläketyöryhmän muistio 1985). Therefore, the main part of the Finnish private pensions has a different function than, for example, STP pensions in Sweden. STP is paid in addition to the legislated pensions, whereas the Finnish private pensions are paid to make up for the difference between the target and actual levels (in this respect, the Norwegian state employees' pensions resemble the additional EPA benefits). The closer the actual replacement level of the legislated pensions gets to the target level in Finland, the less the scope will be for additional pensions. In the other Scandinavian countries, the private occupational pensions do not have this temporary character.

It is evident that the private collective pensions can increase the level of the retirement income considerably (Kohl 1988). This is true in the Scandinavian context, as illustrated in Figure 7.7 and the differences are even more pronounced in a wider international perspective (see, e.g., Horlick 1987). But does it make a difference what kind of

Figure 7.8. **Social Security Transfers as a Percent of Total Household Income of the Elderly, and Income Inequality among the Elderly in Eight OECD Countries, 1980**

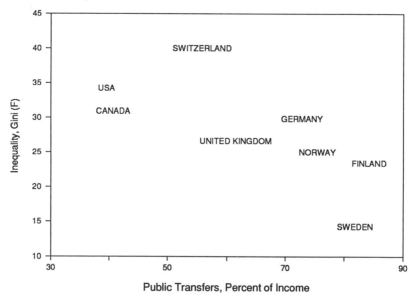

Sources: Esping-Andersen (1987), 79; Hedström and Ringen (1987), 236; Kohl (1988), 11, 35; Uusitalo (1988).

mix exists in pension provisions? Since private pensions tend to be socioeconomically unevenly distributed and have a limited coverage (Vesterø Jensen 1985), the relative size of the private component in the private-public mix can be expected to enlarge the overall inequality among the elderly. Such a hypothesis is at least supported by the data in Figure 7.8, where the bivariate relationship between relative size of the public social transfers and the degree of inequality (as measured by the gini-coefficient) among the elderly (sixty-five to seventy-four years of age) is plotted for eight OECD countries.

The figure indicates that the greater the importance of the public transfers in the income package of the elderly is, the more even is the income distribution. The public share is largest and the income distribution most equal in the Scandinavian countries, whereas the social transfers play a smaller role in Germany and the United Kingdom, not to mention Switzerland, Canada, and the United States, which are paralleled by higher income differences. The relative size of the public pensions is of course not the only factor behind the greater equality among the elderly in Scandinavia; the overall income distribution is also more equal. However, the income differences in the Scandinavian countries, not least in Sweden, seem to be lower for those above normal pension age. In other countries, the opposite tends to be true (see Kohl 1988, 11; chapter 3 in this volume).

Determinants of the private-public mix

In the Scandinavian context we have seen how the cross-national differences in the private share of the total pension expenditure have been patterned to a large extent by the development of statutory supplementary pensions. Does this apply in a wider international perspective? Earlier studies in this field have shown, on the one hand, that the ranking of countries does not change if private expenditure is added to the public pension expenditure (Rein and Rainwater 1986, 16–17), but on the other hand, previous research has also proved that there is a fairly strong negative association between the private expenditure level and the public one (expenditure as a percentage of gross domestic product (GDP) (Esping-Andersen 1987).

But how can the cross-national differences in public pension provisions, obviously important for the private development, be explained? Results reported elsewhere show a positive association between the relative strength of the political left and the size of minimum pensions, as well as for high coverage and take-up rates. Economic and demographic factors seem to be of less importance. Standard worker replacement rates, however, could not be explained by differences in working-class mobilization, at least not if analyzed separately (Palme 1988).

We will try to develop some features of the previous analysis (e.g., Esping-Andersen 1987) to illustrate the relationship between different aspects of the public and private pensions. Table 7.2 presents the coefficients of correlation between private pensions and different aspects of the public pension provisions and the size of GDP per capita.

The data on private pensions used for the computations in Tables 7.2 and 7.3 refer to 1980, and three different indicators have been used: first, the relative size of private individual pension expenditure; second, the relative size of private collective pension expenditure; and third, the total, collective, and individual private expenditure. Since the focus in this chapter is on the private-public mix, all three

Table 7.2

Coefficients of Correlation between Private Pension Expenditure and Public Pension Provisions in Eighteen OECD Countries

	Quality of Public Pensions					
Private Pensions	Coverage	Take-up	Minimum	Standard	Maximum	GDP/ Worker Capita
Individual	.30	.07	−.20	−.48	−.37	.20
Collective	−.07	−.07	−.32	−.46	−.54	.54
Total	.14	.14	−.32	−.58	−.56	.47

Sources: Esping-Andersen (1987); SSIB (1989).

indicators are expressed as percentages of total pension expenditure (both public and private). An alternative would be to measure the private expenditure as a percentage of GDP, with or without weighing for the relative size of the elderly population. This has also been done and the result was a consistent pattern of association, even though the correlations were a little weaker on the whole. The public pension variables are expressed as averages for four time-points; 1965, 1970, 1975, and 1980, to account for lagged effects. GDP per capita is also measured as an average for these four time-points and is expressed in U.S. dollars.

What we expect from previous research (Esping-Andersen 1987) is that public pensions should be negatively related to private pension expenditure, following the hypothesis that public pensions ''crowd out'' the private. The association between private pensions and GDP per capita can, on the other hand, be expected to be positive. The latter variable has been included in the analysis as an indicator of the productivity within an economy; the higher the productivity, the higher the pressure will be for retiring older workers, and thus the higher the pressure to develop retirement programs (Esping-Andersen 1987; Graebner 1980).

The correlations of private pensions with coverage and take-up are weak and exhibit much variation. The correlations with minimum pensions are negative but not as strong as for the standard worker and maximum replacement rates. The correlations with GDP per capita are positive and fairly strong for both collective and individual private

Table 7.3

The Determinants of the Relative Share of Private Pension Expenditure in Eighteen OECD Countries, 1980
(standardized regression-coefficients)

Variables	Model 1	Model 2
Institutional index[a]	−.61**	—
Income security index[b]	—	−.53**
GDP per capita[c]	.43**	.39*
Degrees of freedom	15	15
R-square	.59	.50

Sources: Esping-Andersen (1987); SSIB (1989).

Note: Private individual and collective expenditure as+ percentage of total pension expenditure. For description and definition of the statistical concepts: standardized regression coefficients, degrees of freedom and R-square, see Koutsoyannis 1986.

[a]Additive index of all the public pension indicators in Table 7.2.

[b]Additive index of "standard worker" and "maximum" replacements (see Table 7.2).

[c]GDP per capita as an average for four time-points 1965–80 (U.S. dollars).

* level of significance <.05.

** level of significance <.01.

pensions. These relationships confirm the "income-loss compensation" aspect of the factors behind cross-national variations in private pension provisions.

The simultaneous effects of the size of public pension provisions and GDP per capita on the relative size of private pensions have been tested with the regression technique. The results are presented in Table 7.3. It goes without saying that the results should be interpreted with caution since the analysis is based on only eighteen cases.[15] The results suggest that the variables in the two models both have unique and strong effects in the expected directions, and that a substantial part of the variance in private spending can be explained. The table displays the effects from two different indices on the quality of public pension provision. The "institutional index" is an additive measure including all the public pension variables in Table 7.2. The "income security index" is also additive but only includes "standard worker" and "maximum" replacements. It appears that the inclusion of coverage, takeup rate, and minimum benefits improves the model somewhat.

The political economy of the private-public mix

We have so far discussed pensions mainly as social rights, and the emphasis has been on the benefit side. However, pension programs have far-reaching economic implications, and, in the sphere of the political economy of pensions, interests other than those of providing social security are obvious (see von Nordheim Nielsen 1987a, 1987b). Here, the financing of the schemes and the control over the pension funds have been of crucial importance. These issues, interestingly enough, show considerable inter-Scandinavian variation.

Financing via tax revenue has sometimes been regarded as one of the characteristics of Scandinavian social policy (Esping-Andersen and Korpi 1987, 54). On the other hand, as stated in the introductory section, the source of financing has also been used as an indicator of whether a program is predominantly public or private. Taxes have been connected with the public schemes, whereas contributions from the insured person have been associated with the private systems. It turns out, however, that tax financing cannot be considered a trademark of the Scandinavian pensions, and public schemes cannot be distinguished from the private ones on these grounds. The only scheme that in this respect qualifies as "Scandinavian" or "public" is the Danish basic pension scheme which is wholly (99.8 percent) financed from the public purse. The financial responsibility of the state and municipalities is remarkably smaller in Finland (21 percent of revenues), Norway (25 percent), and Sweden (30 percent). When it comes to the total pension expenditure, other sources become even more dominant. In Finland and Sweden, the employer contributions make up about 80 percent of total costs, while in Denmark, a corresponding proportion comes from tax revenue. In Norway, the financial burden is more evenly distributed among the state, the insured person, and the employer (see NSS 1986, 133–49).

Regarding the most private schemes, individual insurance policies, it is debatable to what extent it is just the individual insurance holder who finally pays for benefits. By providing tax reliefs, the state makes an indirect contribution to the financing of these benefits (see e.g., Hort 1986; Papadakis and Taylor-Gooby 1987).

The pension funds provide a remarkable source for investment capital. In Sweden, the ATP scheme substantially increased the public control of the credit markets and the ATP assets were used mainly to

PENSION PROVISION 229

finance public housing (Esping-Andersen and Korpi 1987, 67–68). The financial form of the ATP pensions and the use of the assets did not satisfy the employers who had offered LO since World War II a mandated pension program based on employer financing and control (Molin 1965). After being defeated in the ATP struggle, SAF went along quite easily with contractual pension agreements, first with white-collar organizations and then with LO. The explanation for this might be that from SAF's point of view, it was more advantageous to pay insurance premiums for job-related benefits than the corresponding sum in wages, provided that the employers could use the funded assets (von Nordheim Nielsen 1987a, 1987b; Edebalk and Wadensjö 1988). Such an arrangement is especially attractive—from both the employer's and the employees' point of view—if it is scarcely possible to secure real wage increases due to inflation and high marginal tax rates (Esping-Andersen et al., 1988, 344). In addition, through collective insurance programs with practically universal coverage, SAF can coordinate occupational pensions and facilitate labor mobility. As a consequence of the expansion of the private pension schemes, their macroeconomic importance has increased rapidly. In 1978, the private pension funds corresponded to 24 percent of the ATP funds, and by 1984, this proportion rose to 40 percent (NSS 1986, 197).

In Finland the funded basic pension system was abandoned by the 1956 law, after which the financial importance of the publicly controlled National Pension Institution declined and has been totally superseded by the legislated occupational pensions in the private sector (see Kangas 1988, 29). This shift has reduced public control of the credit markets since the Finnish legislated occupational pensions are mainly organized through private insurance companies, and the funded assets are partially and directly reloaned by the employers. In Finland, contrary to Sweden, the employers' need for and control of investment capital was satisfied via the legislated scheme. In the same way, the insurance companies profited from the legislated occupational pensions, which diminished their need to propagate for additional insurances (Ahtokari 1988, 380). For the insurance companies, it appeared to be important to secure a position in the campaign of legislated pension assets. It was not until recently that the companies adopted a more active role in marketing individual pension insurances.

During the 1950s, the Danish Social Democrats rejected an insurance-based pension scheme by referring to the premium funds that they regarded as detrimental for the nation's economy (Vesterø Jensen 1985, 104). But since the debates on income-related pensions began, they have strongly advocated funded schemes. They have been more successful in implementing funded schemes than income-related pensions. The ATP scheme, controlled by the labor market partners, is heavily funded. In relation to expenditure, the Danish funds are the largest among the Nordic countries. In 1984, the assets corresponded to 71 times the yearly annual disbursements. The respective ratio was 7 in Sweden, 3 in Finland, and only 0.8 in Norway (NSS 1986, 182–83). Although the ATP rules allow employers to reloan pension assets, this activity has remained limited. The capital is mainly invested in bonds and stocks (ATP Beretning og regnskab 1986, 14–15; von Nordheim Nielsen 1987a, 17–19). In a situation where employers' access to the public pension funds is marginal, and employees' need for better pensions is obvious—as was the case in Denmark—ample occupational schemes are likely to emerge (von Nordheim Nielsen 1987a, 1987b). Yet, the Danish occupational programs are less ample than, for example, the Swedish ones. Three factors have been important for this. First, the influence of the employers on the occupational pension funds has been limited by state regulation since the 1930s (von Nordheim Nielsen 1987a, 23). Second, large companies are the most prone to use occupational pensions as fringe benefits, but in Denmark very important small and medium-size industries have counteracted the expansion of the occupational schemes. Third, due to the divided Danish labor market, employers and trade unions have not been able to build up comprehensive occupational pension systems like in Sweden, although the need for extra pensions has been greater in Denmark (Esping-Andersen 1985, 205–15).

There were in Norway, too, political differences regarding the proper size of the pension fund, but the question of control over the funds never became as polarized as in Sweden. In Norway, there always existed a higher degree of consensus on the active role of the state in economic policy making (Esping-Andersen 1985, 217; Kuhnle 1986, 121–25; Kosonen 1987, 181). Here, however, fund accumulation has been very modest (Hatland 1986, 177).

In Norway, government control of investments is based both on the statutory pension funds and to some extent on the private insurance sector. The private pension funds and insurance companies (which administer larger funds than the National Insurance scheme) tend to place a part of their investments in the public sector (see Kreditt-markedstatistikk 1984–85, 23–26). Thus private insurance is partly directed to promote public investment. The situation mirrors the Norwegian tradition of strong public control over the credit market (Esping-Andersen 1985; 217–23). Due to the investment credits provided by the state, Norwegian employers have been in the same situation as their Finnish colleagues. Their need for occupational pension funds has been limited.

The political economy of the Scandinavian pension schemes clearly demonstrates that social policy is not made in a vacuum, in a ''pure'' realm of social policy. Social reforms have economic consequences but are also adjusted to the economic circumstances. The relationship between private economy and public social policy has been patterned in different ways in the Scandinavian countries, reflecting inter-Nordic differences in political parties, interest group formation, and priorities in economic policy making.

Conclusions

The purpose of this has been to describe the development of the private-public pension mix in the Scandinavian countries. While we have found both commonality and variation among the four countries, there clearly are good reasons to refer to a Scandinavian model regarding the basic pensions. In an international perspective, the Nordic countries constitute a separate cluster if both the take-up and replacement rates of the basic pensions are taken into consideration. But if the trademark of the Scandinavian model is a maximum degree of public responsibility in welfare provisions, the model is weaker beyond the basic pensions; a complete commonality does not exist.

The differences between the Scandinavian countries cut across several dimensions. The variation is substantial in terms of the relative importance of the private pensions. But differences between the private programs in the Scandinavian countries are not only a matter of their relative size. Private pensions also differ in terms of coverage, administration, coordination with the public schemes, distribution of benefits, and the importance of collective and individual arrangements.

How can the inter-Scandinavian similarities and differences in the private-public mix be explained? The review of the historical process behind the making of the Scandinavian pension systems revealed

country-specific differences in political orientations. Results from earlier studies have shown that the relative strength of the political left
was important for interpreting cross-national differences in minimum
pensions. This does not imply, however, that the political right, or the
center parties, have been against the basic pension reforms in the Scandinavian countries. Quite the contrary, the major reforms in this area
gained unanimous support, and in some cases the bourgeois parties
were the most eager reformers, not least to get rid of the means testing.
This needs to be explained, since these reforms violate the liberal and
conservative ideals of a minimalist state. It might be fruitful to see it as
a form of strategic policy making in a situation where mobilized labor
movements would legislate pensions in any case, and where means-
tested pensions had excluded higher income earners from benefits.

The history of the statutory supplementary pensions was distinguished by sharper political controversies. The strength of the political
left and the strategies chosen by the labor parties came to be of crucial
importance for the organization of the occupational pensions. But the
strategies chosen by the left and other actors vary across nations and
over time—remarkable shifts took place even during short time periods—depending on the power resources, the need for social security,
and the options which appeared to be most advantageous either from
the viewpoint of social policy or from more strategic political considerations.

The political power constellations cannot directly explain the prominence of the private pensions. It may be more fruitful to look at the
level and structure of the public pensions. Our analysis shows that in
countries where the income graduation in the public programs is frag-
mentary (e.g., where pensions are flat-rate) earnings-related pensions
have been provided through the private sector. However, due to their
skewed socioeconomic distribution, the private arrangements are problematic regarding the effects on income inequality among the elderly.
Paradoxically, the most egalitarian public pensions do not necessarily
secure the most equal income distribution among the elderly.

The level and structure of the legislated pensions are not the only
factors affecting the expansion of the private pensions. The formation
of the labor market organizations, trade unions, and employers' confederations apparently have conditioned the development of the private
schemes.

The relationship between the public and private institutions is, however, not uni-directional in the sense that only the public pensions affect the extent of private programs. The early occupational arrangements and their integration with the legislated systems are important for understanding the development of the private-public mix. In the process of social policy development, the previous systems, both public and private, have prepared the ground for different social actors to operate on. The existing institutions have patterned the different strategies that have later been applied (see, e.g., Heclo 1974; Kuhnle 1981; Weir and Skocpol 1985). The fact that actors representing the same class interests in the four countries have, from time to time, chosen different strategies must be understood in this institutional perspective. To associate very specific social policy models with certain social classes and their ideologies seems to be an oversimplification.

We would further claim that the analysis of the development of the different pension programs in Scandinavia exemplifies that there are good reasons for maintaining a flexible approach to definitions of *public* and *private* in welfare provisions. The issue has several dimensions that can and should be taken into consideration. ''Public'' and ''private,'' ''politics'' and ''markets,'' are interwoven and interdependent in a number of ways, and it apparently is not fruitful to draw sharp lines of distinction between them.

Notes

1. ITP=Industrins Tiläggspension (Occupational Pension Scheme for White-Collar Workers in the Private Sector).

2. KPA=Kommunernas Pensionsanstalt (Occupational Pension Scheme for the Employees of Local Government).

3. SPV=Statens Pensionsverk (Occupational Pension Scheme for State Employees).

4. STP=Särskild Tiläggspension (Occupational Pension Scheme for Blue-Collar Workers in the Private Sector).

5. The pension take-up ratio is now universal in the Netherlands also, since married women got the right to an individual pension in 1985.

6. This attitude is interesting in the sense that three years later the Conservatives rejected the Social Democratic proposal on an ITP reform aiming for income graduated benefits (Vesterø Jensen 1985, 127). ITP=Industrins Tiläggspension (Occupational Pension Scheme for White-Collar Workers in the Private Sector).

7. Here the different rules for parliamentary decision making in Finland and in Sweden played a certain role. The Swedish ATP was accepted by a one-vote majority whereas in Finland, one-third of the members of Parliament can in certain cases suspend a vote on legislation until a new election has been held (see

Nousiainen 1971, 200). This inevitably obliges the parties to cooperate and make deals.

8. In the Norwegian case the problem is not so urgent since the maximum limit is higher than in Sweden.

9. The public sector pensions are, however, more generous than the private sector schemes; pension is 66 percent of final salary after thirty years in office compared to 60 percent after working forty years in the private sector.

10. In fact, 46 percent of the members of the white-collar union TCO were against the obligatory scheme while 31 percent accepted it, and 23 percent had no definitive opinion on the issue (Molin 1965, 65).

11. In principle, both STP and ITP provide a pension corresponding to 10 percent of pensionable income, but there are some differences in favor of ITP dealing with the calculation of the size of the pension amount and the pension age (Elmer 1986, 132).

12. For Denmark it is not possible to make a sharp distinction between the private collective and private individual schemes. Here the total expenditure has been decomposed according to Esping-Andersen (1987).

13. Most of the schemes provide pensions that, together with the NI benefits, correspond to about 65 percent of the previous earnings (Øverbye 1988a, 330).

14. Here, gross benefits have been related to the gross earnings of the respective income group; the pensions are calculated with the assumption of a thirty-five-year, full-time working career.

15. However, the standard techniques for regression diagnostics (Bollen and Jackman 1985) have been applied to test for outliers and "influential cases." The exclusion of such cases from the analysis has not yielded significantly different results, and all countries were therefore kept in the final analysis.

References

Ahtokari, R. 1988. *Tuntematon vaikuttaja*. Porvoo, Helsinki, and Juva: WSOY.

Alber, J. 1982. *Vom Armenhaus zum Wohlfahrtsstaat*. Frankfurt and New York: Campus.

Alestalo, M., Flora, P., and Uusitalo, H. 1985. "Structure and Politics in the Making of the Welfare State." In R. Alapuro et al. eds., *Small States in Comparative Perspective*. Oslo: Norwegian University Press, 188–210.

Alestalo, M., and Kuhnle, S. 1987. "The Scandinavian Route." In R. Erikson et al., eds., *The Scandinavian Model. Welfare States and Welfare Research*. London and Armonk, NY: M. E. Sharpe, 3–38.

Alestalo, M., and Uusitalo, H. 1986. "Finland." In P. Flora, ed., *Growth to Limits*. Vol. 1. Berlin and New York: de Gruyter, 293–381.

ATP Beretning og regnskab 1986. Hillerød: ATP-huset.

Bollen, K. A., and Jackman, R. W. 1985. "Regression Diagnostics." *Sociological Methods and Research 13, no. 4 (May):510–42*.

Edebalk, P. G. and Wadensjö, E. 1988. *Contractually Determined Insurance Schemes for Manual Workers*. Stockholm: Institute for Social Research, Meddelande 5.

Elmer, Å. 1960. *Folkpensioneringen i Sverige med särskild hänsyn till ålderspensioneringen*. Lund: CWK Gleerup.

————. 1986. *Svensk socialpolitik*. Stockholm: Liber.
Esping-Andersen, G. 1985. *Politics Against Markets*. Princeton: Princeton University Press.
————. 1987. *State and Market in the Formation of Social Security Regimes*. Working Papers No. 87/281. Florence: EUI.
Esping-Andersen, G., and Korpi, W. 1987. "From Poor Relief towards Institutional Welfare States." In R. Erikson et al., eds., *The Scandinavian Model*. London and Armonk, NY: M. E. Sharpe, 39–74.
Esping-Andersen, G., Rainwater, L., and Rein, M. 1988. "Institutional and Political Factors Affecting the Well-Being of the Elderly." In J. L. Palmer et al., eds., *The Vulnerable*. Washington, DC: The Urban Institute Press, 333–49.
Eurostat. 1977. *Accounts of Social Protection in the EC 1970–1975*. Brussels: Statistical Office of the European Communities.
Finansministeriet. 1988. Unpublished data on the Danish state pension scheme from Administrations og Persondepartmentet.
Graebner, W. 1980. *A History of Retirement*. New Haven: Yale University Press.
Hagen, K. 1988. "Calculations on pension replacement rate for different income groups in Norway." Stencil. Oslo: FAFO.
Hatland, A. 1986. *The Future of Norwegian Social Insurance*. Oslo: Institute of Applied Social Research.
————. 1987. *Oslotrygden*. Rapport 87:10. Oslo: Institute for Applied Social Research.
Heclo, H. 1974. *Modern Social Politics in Britain and Sweden*. New Haven: Yale University Press.
Hedström, P., and Ringen, S. 1987. "Age and Income in Contemporary Society." *Journal of Social Policy* 16, pt. 2:227–39.
Henriksen, J. P., Kampmann, P., and Rasmussen, J. 1987. "Fordelingen af private pensioner. Rapport til Socialministeriet fra forskningsprojektet Private pensioner frem till mod år 2000." Stencil. Copenhagen: Sociologisk Institut.
Hippe, J., and Pedersen, A. 1986. *Velferd til salgs*. Rapport no. 065. Oslo: FAFO.
————. 1988. *For lang og tro tjeneste?* Rapport no. 084. Oslo: FAFO.
Horlick, M. 1987. "The Relationship Between Public and Private Pension Schemes." In *Studies and Research* no. 24. Geneva: ISSA, 11–27.
Hort, K. 1986. "Välfärdsstat och marknadsekonomi." *Zenit 1986*. 4:25–35.
Kangas, O. 1986. *Luokkaintressit ja hyvinvointivaltio*. Serie D–84. Helsinki: Helsinki School of Economics.
————. 1988. *Politik och ekonomi i pensionsförsäkringen*. Working Paper no. 5/1988. Stockholm: Institute for Social Research.
Kangas, O., and Palme, J. 1989. *Public and private pensions. The Nordic countries in a comparative perspective*. Working Paper no. 3/1989. Stockholm: Institute for Social Research.
Kettunen, P. 1986. *Poliittinen liike ja sosiaalinen kollektiivisuus*. Helsinki: Suomen Historiallinen Seura.
Kohl, J. 1988. "Inequality and Poverty in Old Age." Paper presented at the workshop on Comparative Research in Social Policy, Labour Markets, Inequality, and Distributional Conflict (ISA Research Committee 19) at Hässelby Slott. Stockholm. August 25–28.

Korpi, W. 1981. *Den demokratiska klasskampen.* Stockholm: Tiden.
Korpi, W., and Shalev, M. 1979. "Strikes, Industrial Relations and Class Conflict in Capitalist Societies." *The British Journal of Sociology* 30, no. 2:164–87.
Kosonen, P. 1987. *Hyvinvointivaltion haasteet ja pohjoismaiset mallit.* Tampere: Vastapaino.
Koutsoyannis, A. 1986. *Theory of Econometrics. An Introductory Exposition of Econometric Methods.* London: Macmillan.
Kredittmarkedsstatistikk. 1984–85. *Norges offisielle statistikk B 648.* Oslo: Statistisk Sentralbyrå.
Kuhnle, S. 1983. *Velferdsstaten.* Bergen: Tiden Norsk Forlag.
———. 1986. "Norway." In P. Flora, ed., *Growth to Limits.* Vol. 1. Berlin and New York: de Gruyter, 117–96.
Lewin, L. 1984. *Ideologi och strategi.* Stockholm: Norstedts.
Marklund, S. 1988. *Paradise Lost? The Nordic Welfare States and the Recession 1975–1985.* Lund: Arkiv.
Molin, B. 1965. *Tjänstepensionsfrågan.* Lund: Akademiförlaget.
Nelson, G. 1984. *ATP's historie 1964–83 i hovedtræk.* Hillerrød: ATP-huset.
Niemelä, H. 1988. *Suomen kokonaiseläkejärjestelmän muotoutuminen.* Helsinki: Kansaneläkelaitos.
Nørby Johansen, L. 1986. "Denmark." In P. Flora, ed., *Growth to Limits.* Vol. 1. Berlin and New York: de Gruyter, 293–381.
Nordic Council of Ministers (NCM). *Yearbook of Nordic Statistics.* 1987. Stockholm: Nordic Council of Ministers.
Nordisk Statistisk Skriftserie (NSS). 1986. *Social Tryghed i de nordiske lande. Omfang, udgifter og finansiering 1984.* Copenhagen: Nordisk Statistisk Sekretariat, no. 47.
Nousiainen, J. 1971. *The Finnish Political System.* Cambridge, MA: Harvard University Press.
O'Higgins, M. 1986. "Public/Private Interaction and Pension Provision." In M. Rein and L. Rainwater, eds., *Public/Private Interplay in Social Protection.* Armonk, NY: M. E. Sharpe, 99–148.
Olsson, S. E. 1986. "Sweden." In P. Flora, ed., *Growth to Limits.* Vol. 1. Berlin and New York: de Gruyter, 7–116.
Organization for Economic Cooperation and Development. 1987. *Economic Outlook. Historical Statistics 1960–1985.* Paris: OECD.
Øverbye, E. 1988a. "Jakten på det private." In H. Bogen and O. Langeland, eds., *Offentlig eller privat?* Rapport 078. Oslo: FAFO, 311–43.
———. 1988b. "Fordelingsvirkninger av tjenstepensjonsordninger." *Trygd og Pensjon* 3:14–15.
Palme, J. 1988. "The Determinants of old Age Pensions in 18 OECD Countries 1930 to 1980." Paper presented at the workshop on Comparative Research in Social Policy, Labor Markets, Inequality, and Distributional Conflict (ISA Research Committee 19) at Hässelby Slott. Stockholm. August 25–28.
Papadakis, E., and Taylor-Gooby, P. 1987. *The Private Provision of Public Welfare.* Sussex and New York: Wheatsheaf Books and St. Martin's Press.
Rein, M., and Rainwater, L. 1986, eds., *Public/Private Interplay in Social Protection.* Armonk, NY: M. E. Sharpe.

———. 1987. "From Welfare State to Welfare Society." In M. Rein et al. eds., *Stagnation and Renewal in Social Policy*. London and New York: M. E. Sharpe, 143–59.

RFV. 1987. *Riksförsäkringsverket anser 9*. Stockholm: Riksförsäkringsverket.

Ringen, S. 1987. "Mål og motiv i velferdspolitikken." *Norsk statsvitenskaplig tidsskrift* 7:63–76.

Salminen, K. 1987. *Yhteiskunnan rakenne, politiikka ja eläketurva*. Helsinki: Eläketurvakeskus, tutkimuksia 2.

Social Security Administration. 1984. *Social Security Systems Throughout the World 1983*. Washington, DC: US Department of Health and Human Services. Social Security Administration. Research reports 59.

SSIB. 1989. Data bank compiled within the research project "Svensk socialpolitik i internationell belysning." Stockholm: University of Stockholm, Institutet för Social Forskning. Unpublished.

Statens Pensjonskasse. 1988. Unpublished data on the Norwegian state employees' pensions. Oslo: Statens Pensjonskasse, Utredningsgruppen.

Tamburi, G., and Mouton, P. 1987. "The uncertain frontier between private and public pension schemes." In *Studies and Research* no. 24. Geneva: ISSA, 29–43.

Therborn, G. 1986. "The Working Class and The Welfare State." In P. Kettunen, ed., *Det nordiska i den nordiska arbetarrörelsen*. Tammerfors: Finnish Society for Labor History and Cultural Tradition, 1–75.

———. 1987. "Welfare States and Capitalist Markets." *Acta Sociologica*. 30, nos. 3 and 4:237–54.

Titmuss, R. 1974. *Social Policy*. London: Allen and Unwin.

Uusitalo, H. 1988. Unpublished data file on household income distribution in Finland 1966–1985.

Vesterø Jensen, C. 1985. *Det tvedelte pensionssystem*. Roskilde: Forlaget Samfundsøkonomi og Planlægning.

von Nordheim Nielsen, F. 1987a. "Pensionssystemer og pensionspolitiske dilemmaer i Norden." Stencil. Florence: European University Institute.

———. 1987b. "Markeder og statslige politikker i Erhvervspensionernes vækst." Stencil. Florence: European University Institute.

Ylieläketyöryhmän muistio. 1985. Helsinki: Sosiaali- ja terveysministeriö.

Weir, M., and Skocpol, T. 1985. "State Structures and the Possibilities for Keynesian Responses to the Great Depression in Sweden, Britain, and the United States." In P. R. Evans, D. Rueschemeyer, and T. Skocpol (eds.), *Bringing the State Back In*. Cambridge: Cambridge University Press.

Index

Contributors

Matti Alestalo, Research Fellow, Group for Comparative Sociology, University of Helsinki, Finland.

Sven Bislev, Associate Professor, Copenhagen Business School, Denmark.

Gøsta Esping-Andersen, Professor of Political and Social Sciences, European University Institute, Florence, Italy.

Kåre Hagen, Research Fellow, Department of Political Science, University of Oslo, Norway.

Olli Kangas, Research Fellow, Helsinki School of Economics, Finland; and Institute for Social Research, University of Stockholm, Sweden.

Jon Eivind Kolberg, Professor of Sociology, Department of Sociology, University of Bergen, Norway.

Rafael Lindqvist, Research Associate, Department of Sociology, University of Umeå, Sweden.

Joakim Palme, Research Fellow, Institute for Social Research, University of Stockholm, Sweden.

Stein Ringen, Professor of Sociology and Social Policy, University of Oxford, Great Britain.

Hannu Uusitalo, Deputy Director, Department of Research and Information Services, National Agency for Welfare and Health, Helsinki, Finland.